THE SAINT MAKER SERIES

DAILY ADVENT MEDITATIONS FROM THE WORKS OF
ST. ALPHONSUS

SENSUS FIDELIUM PRESS
Gastonia, North Carolina

Copyright © 2023 Sensus Fidelium Press

All rights reserved.

Originally published by R. Washbourne, London and M. H. Gill & Son, Dublin, Ireland. The Sensus Fidelium Press edition has been retypeset, updated spelling & language. No portion of this book may be reproduced in any form without written permission from the publisher.

ISBN: 978-1-962639-18-7

For more information, please visit sensusfideliumpress.com

Contents

Daily Prayers	V
1. First Sunday of Advent	1
2. Monday--First Week of Advent	7
3. Tuesday--First Week of Advent	13
4. Wednesday--First Week of Advent	19
5. Thursday--First Week of Advent	25
6. Friday--First Week of Advent	33
7. Saturday--First Week of Advent	41
8. Second Sunday of Advent	47
9. Monday--Second Week of Advent	54
10. Feast of the Immaculate Conception (8 December)	61
11. Tuesday--Second Week of Advent	70
12. Wednesday--Second Week of Advent	77
13. Thursday--Second Week of Advent	84
14. Friday--Second Week of Advent	90
15. Saturday--Second Week of Advent	97
16. Third Sunday of Advent	103
17. Monday--Third Week of Advent	111
18. Tuesday--Third Week of Advent	118
19. Wednesday--Third Week of Advent	125
20. Thursday--Third Week of Advent	132

21.	Friday--Third Week of Advent	139
22.	Saturday--Third Week of Advent	145
23.	Fourth Sunday of Advent	152
24.	Monday--Fourth Week of Advent	159
25.	Tuesday--Fourth Week of Advent	166
26.	Wednesday–Fourth Week of Advent	173
27.	Thursday--Fourth Week of Advent	179
28.	Friday--Fourth Week of Advent	185

Daily Prayers

Morning and Evening Prayers

LATIN RITE PRAYERS

Morning Offering

O JESUS, through the Immaculate Heart of Mary, I offer Thee my prayers, works, joys and sufferings of this day for all the intentions of Thy Sacred Heart, in union with the Holy Sacrifice of the Mass throughout the world, in reparation for my sins, for the intentions of all our Associates and in particular for the intention of the Apostleship of Prayer.

Act of Faith

O MY God, I firmly believe that Thou art one God in Three Divine Persons, Father, Son and Holy Ghost. I believe that Thy Divine Son became man, and died for our sins, and that He will come to judge the living and the dead. I believe these and all the truths which the Holy Catholic Church teaches, because Thou hast revealed them, Who canst neither deceive nor be deceived.

Act of Hope

O MY God, relying on Thy almighty power and infinite mercy and promises, I hope to obtain pardon of my sins, the help of Thy grace, and life everlasting, through the merits of Jesus Christ, my Lord and Redeemer.

Act of Charity

O MY God, I love Thee above all things, with my whole heart and soul, because Thou art all-good and worthy of all love. I love my neighbour as myself for the love of Thee. I forgive all who have injured me, and ask pardon of all whom I have injured.

Prayers for the Day Ahead

Grace at Meals

Before:
BLESS us, O Lord, and these Thy gifts, which we are about to receive from Thy bounty. Through Christ our Lord. Amen.

After:
WE give Thee thanks, O almighty God, for all Thy mercies. Who livest and reignest forever and ever. Amen.

Act of Spiritual Communion

My Jesus, I believe that Thou art present in the Most Holy Sacrament. I love Thee above all things, and I desire to receive Thee into my soul. Since I cannot at this moment receive Thee sacramentally, come at least spiritually into my heart. I embrace Thee as if Thou wert already there and unite myself wholly to Thee. Never permit me to be separated from Thee. Amen.

BYZANTINE PRAYERS

OPENING PRAYERS

In the Name of the Father, + and of the Son, and of the Holy Spirit. Glory be to You, O God; glory be to You.

O Heavenly King, Comforter, Spirit of Truth, You are everywhere present and fill all things. Treasury of Blessings and Giver of Life, come and dwell within us, cleanse us of all stain, and save our souls, O gracious Lord.

Holy God, + Holy and Mighty, Holy and Immortal, have mercy on us. (3 times)

Glory be to the Father, + and of the Son, and of the Holy Spirit, now and ever, and forever. Amen.

O Most Holy Trinity, have mercy on us; O Lord, cleanse us of our sins; O Master, forgive our transgressions; O Holy One, come to us and heal our infirmities for Your Name's sake.

Lord, have mercy. (3 times)

Glory be to the Father, + and of the Son, and of the Holy Spirit, now and ever and forever. Amen.

Our Father, Who art in Heaven, hallowed be Thy name; Thy Kingdom come, Thy will be done on earth as it is in Heaven. Give us this day our daily bread; and forgive us our trespasses as we forgive those who trespass against us And lead us not into temptation, but deliver us from evil.

For Thine is the kingdom and the power and the glory, Father, + Son, and Holy Spirit, now and ever and, forever. Amen.

MORNING PRAYERS

Awakening from sleep, I worship You, O blessed God; and offer the Angelic Hymn to You, O powerful Lord: Holy, holy, holy are You, O God! Through the intercession of Your Heavenly Hosts, have mercy on me.

Glory be to the Father, + and of the Son, and of the Holy Spirit:

O Lord, You have lifted me up from my bed and from sleep; now enlighten my mind, open my heart and my lips that I may sing to You, O Holy Trinity: Holy, holy, holy are You, O God! Through the prayers of all Your Saints, have mercy on me.

Now and ever, and forever. Amen.

The Judge shall come suddenly, and the deeds of all shall be brought to light. In fear, I cry out at the break of day: Holy, holy, holy are You, O God! Through the prayers of the Mother of God, have mercy on me. Lord, have mercy. (12 times)

I give thanks to You, O Holy Trinity. Because of Your great goodness and endless patience, You did not become angry with me, a slothful and sinful being; nor did You destroy me because of my transgressions. But, as always, You have shown Your love for us; and have raised me up as I lay in despair, that I might recite these prayers and sing the praises of Your power. Enlighten the eyes of my understanding, that I may meditate upon Your Words, understand Your Commandments, and accomplish Your Will. Open my mouth that I may sing to You in sincere praise; and that I may proclaim Your Most Holy Name, Father, + Son, and Holy Spirit, now and ever and, forever. Amen.

Come, let us adore the King, our God.
Come, let us adore Christ, the King and our God.
Come, let us adore and bow down to the only Lord Jesus Christ, the King and our God.

The Psalm of Repentance (Psalm 50) or another appropriate Psalm is now recited.

PSALM 50:

O God, have mercy on me in the greatness of Your love; in the abundance of Your tender mercies wipe out my offense. Wash me thoroughly from malice and cleanse me from sin; for I am well aware of my malice, and my sins are before me always. It is You alone I have offended, I have done what is evil in Your sight; wherefore, You are just in Your deeds and triumphant in Your judgment. Behold, I was born in iniquities, and in sins my mother conceived me. But You are the Lover of Truth; You have shown me the depths and secrets of Your wisdom. Wash me with hyssop, and I shall be pure; cleanse me, and I shall be whiter than snow. Let me hear sounds of joy and feasting; the bones that were afflicted shall rejoice. Turn Your face away from my offenses, and wipe off all my sins. A spotless heart create in me, O God; renew a steadfast spirit in my breast. Cast me not afar from Your face; take not Your blessed Spirit out of me. Restore to me the joy of Your salvation, and let Your guiding Spirit dwell in me. I will teach Your ways to the sinners, and the wicked shall return to You. Deliver me from blood-guilt, O God, my saving God, and my tongue will joyfully sing Your justice. O Lord, You shall open my lips, and my mouth will declare Your praise. Had You desired sacrifice, I would have offered it, but You will not be satisfied with whole-burnt offerings. Sacrifice to God is a contrite spirit; a crushed and humbled heart God will not spurn. In Your kindness, O Lord be bountiful to Sion; may the walls of Jerusalem be restored. Then will You delight in just oblation, in sacrifice and whole-burnt offerings. Then shall they offer calves upon Your altar.

NICENE CREED:
I believe in one God, the Father Almighty, Creator of heaven and earth, and of all things visible and invisible. And in one Lord Jesus Christ, Son of God, the only-begotten, born of the Father before all ages. Light of Light, true God of true God; begotten, not made; of one substance with the Father, through Whom all things were made. Who for us men and for our salvation, came down from heaven, and was incarnate from the Holy Spirit and Mary the Virgin, and became man. He was also crucified for us under Pontius Pilate, and suffered, and was buried. And He rose again on the third day, according to the Scriptures. And He ascended into heaven, and sits at the right hand of the Father. And He will come again with glory, to judge the living and the dead; and of His kingdom there will be no end. And in the Holy Spirit, the Lord, and Giver of Life, Who proceeds from the Father; Who together with the Father and the Son is worshipped and glorified; Who spoke through the prophets. In one, holy, catholic, and apostolic Church. I profess one baptism for the remission of sins. I expect the resurrection of the dead, and the life of the world to come. Amen.

PRAYER OF PENANCE:
Remit, pardon, and forgive, O God, our sins committed voluntarily and involuntarily, by word and deed, knowingly and in ignorance, by thought and purpose, by day and night. Forgive all these, for You are gracious and love us all.

ANGELIC SALUTATION:

Hail Mary, Full of Grace, the Lord is with thee. Blessed art thou amongst women, and blessed is the Fruit of thy womb; for thou hast borne Christ, the Savior and Deliverer of our souls.

PRAYERS FOR INTERCESSION:

We fly to your patronage, O Virgin Mother of God. Despise not our prayers in our necessities, but who are alone pure and blessed, deliver us from all danger.

O most glorious ever Virgin Mary, Mother of Christ our God, receive our prayers and offer them to your Son, our God, that He, for your sake, enlighten and save our souls.

PRAYERS TO THE ANGELS AND SAINTS:

All you heavenly powers, holy Angels and Archangels, beseech God for us sinners.
O holy and glorious Apostles, Prophets, Martyrs, and Saints, beseech God for us sinners.

PRAYER OF THE PUBLICAN:

O God, + be merciful to me, a sinner.
O God, + cleanse me of my sins and have mercy on me.
O Lord, + forgive me, for I have sinned without number.

EVENING PRAYERS

Take the opening prayers up to "For Thine is the kingdom... Amen."

Have mercy on us, O God, have mercy on us. Since we have no defense, we sinners offer this supplication to You, our Master; have mercy on us.

Glory be to the Father, + and of the Son, and of the Holy Spirit:

Lord, have mercy on us; for in You we place our hope. Be not exceedingly angry with us, nor mindful of our transgressions; but look upon us even now with mercy, and deliver us from our enemies. For You are our God, and we are Your people; we are all the work of Your Hands, and we call upon Your Name.

Now and ever, and forever. Amen.

Open unto us the doors of mercy, O blessed Mother of God; that we, who place our trust in you, may not perish; but that through you we be delivered from misfortune. For you are the salvation of all Christians.

Lord, have mercy. (12 times)

O eternal God, and Ruler of all creation, You have allowed me to reach this hour. Forgive the sins I have this day committed by word, deed, or thought. Purify me from every spiritual and physical stain. Grant me to rise from this sleep to glorify You by my deeds throughout the remainder of my life, and that I be victorious over every spiritual and physical enemy which fights against me. Deliver me, O Lord, from all vain thoughts and evil desires. For Thine is the Kingdom, and the Power, and the Glory, Father, + Son, and Holy Spirit, now and ever, and forever. Amen.

O loving mother of our most gracious King, O pure and blessed Virgin Mary, pour forth into my restless soul the grace of your Son, our God. Lead me by your prayers to salutary deeds, that I might spend the remainder of my life without fault, and attain paradise through you, O Virgin Mother of God. For you are pure and blessed forever.

O Guardian Angel, protector of my soul and body, to your care I have been entrusted by Christ. Obtain for me the forgiveness of the sins committed by me this day. Pray for me, your sinful and unworthy servant, that I may become worthy of the grace and mercy of the Most Holy Trinity and the Mother of our Lord God, Jesus Christ. Amen.

We are yours, O Mother of God. Since you have delivered us from all tribulation, we give thanks to you by dedicating our songs of victory to you, O Saving Champion. In your invincible might, deliver us from all dangers that we may exclaim to you: "Hail, Full of Grace!"

O most glorious, ever-virgin Mother of Christ our God, offer up our prayers to your Son and our God, so that through you, O Mother of God, He may save our souls. I place all my hope in you, Mother of God. Do not turn away from me, a sinner, for I need your help and intercession. Have mercy on me, for my soul hopes in you.

The Father + is my hope! The Son + is my refuge! And the Holy Spirit + is my protection! O Most Holy Trinity +, glory be to You!

It is truly proper to glorify you, who have borne God; the ever-blessed, immaculate, and the Mother of our God. More honorable than the Cherubim, and beyond compare, more glorious than the Seraphim; who, a virgin, gave birth to God, the Word. You, truly the Mother of God, we magnify.

HYMN OF THE EVENING:
O Joyful Light! Light and Holy Glory of the Father immortal; the heavenly, holy, the blessed One, O Jesus Christ. Now that we have reached the setting of the sun, and see the evening light, we sing to God, Father, + Son, and Holy Spirit. It is fitting at all times to raise a song of praise in measured melody to You, O Son of God, the Giver of Life. Behold, the universe sings Your glory

First Sunday of Advent

Morning Meditation

THE DAY OF THE LAST JUDGMENT

That day is a day of wrath ... a day of calamity and misery. -- Soph: i. 15.

On the Last Day will be verified the prediction of St. John: And they say to the mountains and to the rocks: Fall upon us and hide us from the face of him that sitteth upon the throne and from the wrath of the Lamb. (Apoc. vi., 16).

Send forth O Lord, the Lamb, the Ruler of the earth Who by sacrificing Himself shall satisfy Thy justice for us, and so reign in the hearts of men. O Lamb of God, pardon me before the arrival of that day on which Thou shalt judge me.

I.

The Last Day is called in Scripture a day of wrath and misery; and such it will be for all those unhappy beings who have died in mortal sin; for on that day their most secret crimes will be made manifest to the whole world, and themselves separated from the company of the Saints, and condemned to the eternal prison of hell, where they will suffer all the agonies of ever dying yet always remaining alive. St. Jerome, in the Cave at Bethlehem, devoted to continual prayer and penance, trembled at the bare thought of the General Judgement. The Ven. Father Juvenal Ancina, hearing that Sequence for the Dead sung, Dies ire, dies illa, was so struck with the anticipation of Judgment that he left the world and embraced the Religious life.

O Jesus! What will become of me on that day? Shall I be placed on Thy right hand with the Elect, or on Thy left with the reprobate? I know that I have deserved to be placed on

Thy left, but I know also that Thou wilt still pardon me if I repent of my sins: therefore, do I repent of them with my whole heart, and am resolved rather to die than offend Thee anymore.

II.

As this will be a day of calamity and terror for the reprobate, so will it be a day of joy and triumph for the Elect; for then, in the sight of all mankind, will the blessed souls of the Elect be proclaimed queens of Paradise and spouses of the Immaculate Lamb.

O Jesus! Thy precious Blood is my hope. Remember not the offences that I have committed against Thee and inflame my whole soul with Thy love. I love Thee, my sovereign Good, and I trust that in that day I shall be associated with those loving souls who will praise and love Thee for all eternity.

Choose, my soul; choose now either an eternal crown in that blessed kingdom, where God will be seen and loved face to face in the company of the Saints, of the Angels, and of Mary, the Mother of Jesus; or the prison of hell, where you must weep and lament forever, abandoned by God and by all.

"O Lamb of God that takes away the sins of the world, have mercy on us!" O divine Lamb, Who, to deliver us from the pains of hell, was pleased to sacrifice Thy divine life by a bitter death upon the Cross, have compassion on us; but more particularly upon me who have more than others offended Thee. I am sorry above every evil for having dishonored Thee by my sins, but I hope on that day to honor Thee before men and Angels, by proclaiming Thy mercies towards me. O Jesus! help me to love Thee; I desire Thee alone. O Mary, holy Queen! protect me on that day.

Spiritual Reading

THE NATIONS IN THE VALLEY OF JOSAPHAT

St. Jerome spent his days in the Cave of Bethlehem in prayer and penance and trembled at the thought of Jesus coming at the Last Day to judge the world.

At present God is not known and, therefore He is as much despised by sinners as if He could not avenge, whenever He pleases, the injuries offered to Him. The wicked looked upon the Almighty as if he could do nothing. (Job, xxii., 17). But the Lord has fixed a day, called in the Scriptures, the day of the Lord, Dies Domini, on which the Eternal Judge will make known His power and majesty. The Lord, says the Psalmist, shall be known when he exercises judgment. (Ps. ix., 17). On this text St. Bernard writes: "The Lord, who is now unknown while He seeks mercy, shall be known when He executes justice." The Prophet Sophonias calls the Day of the Lord a day of wrath -- a day of tribulation and distress, a day of calamity and misery. (Soph. i., 15).

This day shall commence with fire from the heavens which will burn the earth, all men then living, and all things upon the earth. And the earth and the works which are in it shall be burnt up. (2 Pet. iii., 10). All shall become one heap of ashes.

After the death of all men, the trumpet shall sound, and the dead shall rise again. (1 Cor. xv., 52). St. Jerome used to say: "As often as I consider the Day of Judgment, I tremble. Whether I eat or drink, or whatever else I do, that terrible trumpet appears to sound in my ears, 'Arise ye dead, and come to judgment'"; and St. Augustine declared, that nothing banished earthly thoughts from him so effectually as the fear of the Judgment.

At the sound of that trumpet the souls of the Blessed shall descend from Heaven to be united to the bodies with which they served God on earth; and the unhappy souls of the damned shall come up from hell to take possession again of those same bodies with which they offended God. Oh! how different the appearance of the former, compared with that of the latter! The damned will appear deformed and black, like so many firebrands of hell; but the just shall shine as the sun. (Matt. xiii., 43). Oh! how great will then be the happiness of those who have mortified their bodies by works of penance! We may estimate their felicity from the words addressed by St. Peter of Alcantara, after death, to St. Teresa: "O happy penance! which merited for me such glory!"

After the Resurrection they shall be summoned by the Angels to appear in the Valley of Josaphat. Nations, nations in the valley of destruction, for the day of the Lord is near. (Joel, iii.,14). Then the Angels shall come and separate the reprobate from the Elect, placing the latter on the right, and the former on the left. The Angels shall go out and shall separate the wicked from among the just. (Matt. xiii. 40). Oh! how great will then be the confusion which the unhappy damned shall suffer! This punishment alone, says St. Chrysostom, would be sufficient to constitute a hell for the wicked. Brother shall be separated from brother, husband from wife, son from father.

But behold! the heavens are opened -- the Angels come to assist at the General Judgment, carrying, as St. Thomas says, the Standard of the Cross and the other instruments of the Passion of the Redeemer. The same may be inferred from the Twenty-fourth Chapter of St. Matthew: And then shall appear the sign of the Son of Man in heaven; and then shall all the tribes of the earth mourn. (xxiv. 30). Sinners shall weep at the sight of the Cross; for, as St. Chrysostom says, the nails will complain of them -- the Wounds and the Cross of Jesus Christ will speak against them.

Most holy Mary, the Queen of Saints and Angels, shall come to assist at the Last Judgment; and lastly, the Eternal Judge shall appear in the clouds, full of splendor and majesty. And they shall see the Son of Man coming in the clouds of heaven with much power and majesty. (Ib). Oh, how great shall be the agony of the reprobate at the sight of the Judge! At their presence, says the Prophet Joel, the people shall be in grievous pains. (Joel, ii). According to St. Jerome the presence of Jesus Christ will give the reprobate more pain than hell itself. "It would," he says, "be easier for the damned to bear the torments of hell than the presence of the Lord." Hence on that day, the wicked shall, according to St. John, call on the mountains to fall on them and to hide them from the sight of the Judge. And they shall say to the mountains and the rocks: Fall upon us and hide us from the face of him that sits on the throne, and from the wrath of the Lamb. (Apoc. vi., 16).

Evening Meditation

THE GOODNESS OF GOD IN THE WORK OF THE REDEMPTION

I.

And He was incarnate by the Holy Ghost ... and was made man. -- Nicene Creed.

Consider that God, having created the first man to serve Him and love Him in this life, and to be afterwards taken by Him to reign eternally with Him in Paradise, enriched him for this end with many lights and graces. But ungrateful man rebelled against God, refusing Him the obedience which he owed Him both in justice and gratitude; and thus, he unhappily remained as a rebel, deprived, with all his posterity, of Divine grace, and forever excluded from Paradise. Behold then, in consequence of this ruin caused by sin, all mankind lost! All were spiritually blind, living in the midst of darkness and the shadow of death.

But God, seeing men reduced to this so miserable a condition, was moved to pity and resolved to save them. And how did He save them? He did not send an Angel, or a Seraph; but to show to the world the immense love that He bore to these ungrateful worms, He sent his own Son in the likeness of sinful flesh. (Rom. viii., 3). Yes, He sent His own Son to become Man, and to clothe Himself with the same flesh as that of sinful men, in order that He, by His sufferings and death, might satisfy Divine justice for their crimes, and thus deliver them from eternal death, and reconciling them to His Divine Father, obtain for them Divine grace, and render them worthy to enter the eternal kingdom of Heaven.

But how is it, my Jesus, that after Thou hadst repaired this ruin of sin by Thy death, I have so often willfully renewed it again by the many offences I have committed against Thee? Thou didst save me at so great a cost, and I have so often chosen to lose myself by losing Thee, O infinite Good! But Thy words give me confidence, for Thou hast said that when the sinner who has turned his back upon Thee is afterwards converted to Thee, thou dost not refuse to embrace him: Turn ye to me and I will turn to you. (Zach. i., 3). And Thou hast likewise said: If any man ... open to me the door, I will come into him. (Apoc. iii., 20). Behold, O Lord, I am one of these rebels, an ungrateful traitor, who have often turned my back upon Thee, and driven Thee from my soul; but now I repent with all my heart for having thus ill-treated Thee and despised Thy grace; I repent of it, and I love Thee above everything. Behold, the door of my heart is now open, enter Thou in, but enter never to leave it again. I well know that Thou wilt never leave me, if I do not again drive Thee away; but this is my fear, and this is the grace which I ask of Thee, and which I hope always to ask: let me die rather than be guilty of this fresh and greater ingratitude.

II.

Here pause to consider, on the one hand, the immense ruin that sin brings upon souls, since it deprives them of the friendship of God, and of Paradise, and condemns them to an eternity of torments. And consider, on the other hand, the infinite love which God showed in this great work of the Incarnation of the Word, causing this His only begotten Son to come and sacrifice His Divine life by the hands of executioners, in a sea of pain and infamy, to obtain for us pardon and eternal salvation. Oh, when we contemplate this great mystery and this excess of Divine love, each one of us should do nothing but exclaim: O infinite Goodness! O infinite Mercy! O infinite love! That a God should become Man and die for me!

My dearest Redeemer, I do not deserve to love Thee, after all the offences I have committed against Thee; but I ask of Thee through Thy merits, the gift of Thy holy love. Therefore, make me know the great good Thou art, the love Thou hast borne me, and how much Thou hast done to oblige me to love Thee. Ah, my God and my Savior, let me no longer live ungrateful to Thy great goodness. My Jesus, I will never leave Thee again; I have offended Thee enough already. It is but right that I should spend the remaining years of my life loving Thee and pleasing Thee. My Jesus, my Jesus, help me; help a sinner who desires to love Thee. O Mary my Mother, thou hast all power with Jesus, for thou art His Mother. Tell Him to pardon me; tell Him to enchain me with His holy love. Thou art my hope, in thee do I trust.

Monday--First Week of Advent

Morning Meditation

GOD DISHONOURED BY SIN

Before the coming of our Redeemer, the whole unhappy race of mankind groaned in misery upon this earth: all were children of wrath, nor was there one who could appease God, justly indignant at their sins. O God of Mercy, lest Thy Divine Wisdom might reproach us with our offences against Thee, thou hast hidden under an infant's form! Thou hast concealed Thy Justice under the most profound abasement that it might not condemn us!

I.

Consider how sin dishonors God. *By transgression of the law thou dishonors God* (Rom. ii., 23), says St. Paul. When the sinner deliberates whether he shall give or refuse his consent to sin, he takes the balance into his hands to decide which is of greater value -- the favor of God, or some passion, some worldly interest or pleasure. When he yields to temptation, what does he do? He decides that some wretched gratification is more desirable than the favor of God. Thus, it is that he dishonors God, declaring, by his consent, that a miserable pleasure is preferable to the Divine friendship. Thus, then, O God, have I so many times dishonored Thee, by esteeming Thee less than my miserable passions!

Of this the Almighty complains by the Prophet Ezechiel, when He says: *They violated me among my people for a handful of barley and a piece of bread.* (Ezech. xiii., 19). If the sinner should exchange God for a treasure of jewels, or for a kingdom, it would indeed be doing a great evil, because God is of infinitely more value than all the treasures and kingdoms of the earth. But for what do so many exchange Him. For a vapor, for a little dirt, for a poisoned pleasure, which is no sooner tasted than it is fled. O God, how could I have had the heart, for such vile things, so often to despise Thee, who hast shown so much love for me! But behold, my Redeemer, how I now love Thee above all things; and because I love Thee, I feel more regret for having lost Thee, my God, than if I had lost all my other goods, and even my life. Have pity on me, and forgive me, I will never more incur Thy displeasure. Grant that I may rather die than offend Thee anymore.

II.

Lord, who is like to thee? (Ps. xxxiv., 10).

And what good things, O God, can be comparable to Thee, O infinite Goodness? And how could I have turned my back upon Thee, to give myself to those vile things which sin held out to me? Thou hast forsaken me, saith the Lord, thou hast gone backward. (Jer. xv., 6). God complains and says: Ungrateful soul, thou hast forsaken Me! I would never have forsaken thee hadst not thou first turned thy back upon Me! Thou hast gone backward. O God, with what consternation will these words fill the soul of the sinner when he shall stand to be judged before the divine tribunal! O Jesus, Thy precious Blood is my hope. Thou hast promised to hear him who prays to Thee. I ask Thee not for the goods of this world; I ask Thee for the pardon of the sins I have committed against Thee, and for which I am sorry above every other evil. I ask Thee for perseverance in Thy grace until the end of my life. I ask Thee for the gift of Thy holy love; my soul is enamored of Thy goodness: hear me, O Lord. Only grant that I may love Thee both here and hereafter, and as to all things else, do with me as Thou pleases. My Lord and my only Good, suffer me not to be any more separated from Thee! Mary, Mother of God, do thou also listen to me, and obtain for me that I may ever belong to God, and that God may be my inheritance forever.

Spiritual Reading

THE JUDGMENT AND THE SENTENCE

The judgment sat and the books were opened. (Dan. vii., 10). The books of conscience are opened, and the Judgment commences. The Apostle says that the Lord will bring to light the hidden things of darkness. (1 Cor. iv., 5). And, by the mouth of His Prophet,

Jesus Christ has said: I will search Jerusalem with lamps. (Soph. i., 12). The light of the lamp reveals all that is hidden.

"A judgment," says St. Chrysostom, "terrible to sinners, but desirable and sweet to the just." The Last Judgment will fill sinners with terror but will be a source of joy and sweetness to the elect; for God will then give praise to each one according to his works. The Apostle tells us that on that day the just will be raised above the clouds to be united to the Angels, and to increase the number of those who pay homage to the Lord. We shall be taken up together with them in the clouds to meet Christ, into the air. (1 Thess. iv., 16).

Worldlings now regard as fools the Saints who led mortified and humble lives; but then they shall confess their own folly, and say: We fools esteemed their life madness, and their end without honor. Behold how they are numbered among the children of God, and their lot is among the saints. (Wis. v., 4). In this world, the rich and the noble are called happy; but true happiness consists in a life of sanctity. Rejoice, ye souls who live in tribulation; your sorrow shall be turned into joy. (Jo. xvi., 20). In the valley of Josaphat you shall be seated on thrones of glory.

But the reprobate, like goats destined for slaughter, shall be placed on the left to await their last condemnation. On the Day of Judgment there is no hope of mercy for poor sinners. The greatest punishment of sin for those who live in enmity with God is to lose the fear and remembrance of the divine judgment. Continue, continue, says the Apostle, to live obstinately in sin; but in proportion to your obstinacy, you shall have accumulated for the Day of Judgment a treasure of the wrath of God. But according to thy hardness and impenitent heart, thou treasure up to thyself wrath against the day of wrath. (Rom. ii., 5).

Then sinners will not be able to hide themselves; but, with insufferable pain, they will be compelled to appear in judgment. "To lie hid," says St. Anselm, "will be impossible -- to appear will be intolerable." The devils will perform their office as accusers, and, as St. Augustine says, will say to the Judge: Most just God, declare him to be ours, who was unwilling to be yours. The witnesses against the wicked shall be: first, their own conscience -- Their conscience bearing witness to them (Ib. ii., 15); secondly, the very walls of the house in which they sinned shall cry out against them -- The stone shall cry out of the wall (Hab. ii., 11); thirdly, the Judge Himself will say -- I am the judge and the witness

(Jer. xxix., 23). Hence, according to Saint Augustine, "He who is now the witness of your life shall be the judge of your cause." To Christians particularly He will say: Woe to thee, Corozain, woe to thee, Bethsaida; for if in Tyre and Sidon had been wrought the miracles that have been wrought in you, they had long ago done penance in sackcloth and ashes. (Matt. xi., 21). Christians, He will say, if the graces which I have bestowed on you had been given to the Turks or to the Pagans, they would have done penance for their sins; but you have ceased to sin only with your death. He shall then manifest to all men their most hidden crimes. I will discover thy shame to thy face. (Nah. iii., 5). He shall expose to view all their secret impurities, injustices, and cruelties. I will set all thy abominations against thee. (Ezech. vii., 3). Each of the damned shall carry his sins written on his forehead.

What excuses can save the wicked on that day? Ah! They can offer no excuses. All iniquity shall stop her mouth. (Ps. cvi., 42). Their very sins will close the mouth of the reprobate, so that they will not have courage to excuse themselves. They shall pronounce their own condemnation.

The Sentence of the Judge

Jesus Christ, then, will first turn to the Elect, and with a serene countenance will say: Come, ye blessed of my Father, possess the kingdom prepared for you from the foundation of the world. (Matt. xxv., 34). He will then bless all the tears shed through sorrow for their sins, and all their good works, their prayers, mortifications, and communions; above all, He will bless for them the pains of His Passion and the Blood shed for their salvation. And, after these benedictions, the Elect, singing Alleluias, shall enter Paradise to praise and love God for all eternity.

The Judge shall then turn to the reprobate and pronounce their condemnation in these words: Depart from me, ye cursed, into everlasting fire. (Ib. 41). They shall then be forever accursed, separated from God, and sent to burn forever in the fire of hell. And these shall go into everlasting punishment: but the just into life everlasting. (Ib. 46).

After this Sentence, the wicked shall, according to St. Ephrem, be compelled to take leave forever of their relatives, of Paradise, of the Saints, and of Mary the divine Mother. "Farewell, ye just! Farewell, O Cross! Farewell, O Paradise! Farewell, fathers, and brothers: we shall never see you again! Farewell, O Mary, Mother of God!" Then a great pit shall open in the middle of the valley: the unhappy damned shall be cast into it and shall see those gates shut which shall never again be opened. O accursed sin! to what a miserable end will you one day conduct so many souls redeemed by the Blood of Jesus Christ. O unhappy souls! for whom is prepared such a melancholy end. But let us have confidence, for Jesus Christ is now a Father, and not a Judge. He is ready to pardon all who repent. For us men and for our salvation, He came down from Heaven and was made man.

Evening Meditation

JESUS CHARGED WITH THE SINS OF THE WHOLE WORLD.

I.

He shall bear their iniquities. (Is., liii., 11).

Consider that the Divine Word, in becoming Man, chose not only to take the form of a sinner, but also to bear all the sins of men, and to satisfy for them as if they were His own: *He shall bear their iniquities.* Cornelius a Lapide adds: "as if He had committed them Himself." Let us here reflect what an oppression and anguish the Heart of the Infant Jesus must have felt, who had already charged Himself with the sins of the whole world, in finding that Divine Justice insisted on His making a full satisfaction for them.

Well did Our Lord know the malice of every sin, for, through the divine light which accompanied Him, He knew immeasurably more than all men and Angels the infinite goodness of His Father, and how infinitely deserving He is of being revered and loved. And then He saw drawn up in array before Him a countless number of transgressions which would be committed by men and for which He was to suffer and die.

My beloved Jesus, I, who have offended Thee, am not worthy of Thy favors, but through the merit of that pain which Thou didst suffer, and which Thou didst offer up to God at the sight of my sins, and to satisfy divine justice for them, give me a share in that light by which Thou didst see their malice, and in that hatred with which Thou didst then abominate them. O Lord! Thou hast indeed died to save me; but Thy death will not save me if I do not, on my part, detest every evil, and have true sorrow for the sins I have committed against Thee. But even this sorrow must be given to me by Thee. Thou give it to him that asks it of Thee. I ask it of Thee through the merits of all the sufferings Thou didst endure on this earth; give me sorrow for my sins, but a sorrow that will correspond to my transgressions.

II.

Our Lord once showed St. Catherine of Siena the hideousness of one single venial sin; and such was the dread and sorrow of the Saint that she fell senseless to the ground. What, then, must have been the sufferings of the Infant Jesus when, on His entrance into the world, He saw before Him the immense array of all the crimes of men for which He was to make satisfaction!

And then He knew in particular every sin of each one of us: "He had regard to every particular sin," says St. Bernardine of Siena. And Cardinal Hugo says that the executioners "caused Him exterior pain by crucifying Him, but we interior pain by sinning against Him." He means that each one of our sins afflicted the soul of Jesus Christ more than crucifixion and death afflicted His body. Such is the beautiful recompense which has been rendered to our Divine Savior for His love by everyone who remembers to have offended Him by mortal sin!

O Eternal God, supreme and infinite Good! I, a miserable worm, have dared to lose respect for Thee, and to despise Thy grace; I detest above every evil and abhor the injustice I have committed against Thee; I repent of all with my whole heart, not so much on account of hell, which I have deserved, as because I have offended Thy infinite Goodness. I hope for pardon from Thee through the merits of Jesus Christ; and I hope also to obtain, together with Thy pardon, the grace of loving Thee. I love Thee, O God, who art worthy of infinite love, and I will always repeat to Thee, I love Thee, I love Thee, I love Thee! And as Thy beloved St. Catherine of Genoa said to Thee, while she stood in spirit at the foot of Thy crucified Image, so will I also say to Thee now that I am standing at Thy feet: "My Lord, no more sins, no more sins!" No, for Thou indeed dost not deserve to be offended, O my Jesus, but Thou only deserve to be loved. My Blessed Redeemer, help me. My Mother Mary, assist me, I pray thee; I only ask of thee to obtain for me that I may love God during the time that is left me in this life.

Tuesday--First Week of Advent

Morning Meditation

THE GREAT AFFAIR OF SALVATION

Consider that our most important affair is that of our eternal salvation. Our eternity depends our happiness or misery forever. Whether we shall live forever happily or forever miserable.

Before man is life and death ... that which he shall choose shall be given him. (Ecclus. xv., 18).

Oh, let us make such a choice now as we shall not have to regret in eternity.

I.

The affair of our eternal salvation is of all affairs the most important. But how comes it that men use all diligence to succeed in the affairs of this world, leave no means untried to obtain a desirable situation, to gain a lawsuit, or to bring about a marriage; reject no counsels, neglect no measures by which to secure their object; neither eat nor sleep, and yet do nothing to gain eternal salvation -- nothing to gain it, but everything to forfeit it, as though Hell, Heaven, and Eternity were not Articles of Faith, but only fables and lies?

O God! assist me by Thy divine light; suffer me not to be any longer blinded, as I hitherto have been.

If an accident happens to a house, what is not immediately done to repair it? If a jewel is lost, what is not done to recover it? The soul is lost, the grace of God is lost, and men sleep and laugh! We attend most carefully to our temporal welfare, and almost entirely neglect our eternal salvation! We call those happy who have renounced all things for God; why then are we so much attached to earthly things?

O Jesus! Thou hast so much desired my salvation as to shed Thy Blood and lay down Thy life to secure it; and I have been so indifferent to the preservation of Thy grace as to renounce and forfeit it for a mere nothing! I am sorry, O Lord, for having thus dishonored Thee. I will renounce all things to attend only to Thy love, my God, Who art most worthy of all love.

II.

The Son of God gives His life to save our souls; the devil is most diligent in his endeavors to bring them to eternal ruin: and what care do we take of them? St. Philip Neri convicts that man of the height of folly who is inattentive to the salvation of his soul. Let us rouse our Faith: it is certain that, after this short life, another life awaits us, which will be either eternally happy or eternally miserable. God has given us to choose which we will. Before man is life and death ... that which he shall choose shall be given him. Ah! let us make such a choice now as we shall not have to repent of for all eternity.

O God, make me sensible of the great wrong I have done Thee in offending Thee and renouncing Thee for the love of creatures. I am sorry with my whole heart for having despised Thee, my sovereign Good; do not reject me now that I return to Thee. I love Thee above all things, and for the future I will renounce all things rather than lose Thy grace. Through the love which Thou hast shown me in dying for me, succor me with Thy help, and do not abandon me. O Mary, Mother of God, be thou my advocate.

Spiritual Reading

MENTAL PRAYER

I. ITS IMPORTANCE

In the first place, Mental Prayer is necessary in order that we may have light on the journey we are making towards eternity. The Eternal Truths are spiritual things which are not seen with the eyes of the body, but only in the mind by consideration. He that does not meditate does not see them; therefore, he walks with difficulty on the way of Salvation. And further, he who does not meditate does not know his defects, and therefore, says St.

Bernard, does not detest them. So also, he does not see the danger to Salvation in which he is, and therefore does not think of avoiding it. God enlightens us in Meditation. Come ye to him and be enlightened. (Ps. xxxiii., 6). In Meditation God speaks to us and makes us know what we are to avoid and what we are to do. I will lead her into solitude, and I will speak to her heart. (Osee, ii., 14). St. Bernard says that Meditation regulates our affections, directs our actions, and corrects our defects.

In the second place, without Mental Prayer we have no strength to resist temptation and practice virtue. St. Teresa used to say that when a man leaves off Mental Prayer, the devil has no need of carrying him to hell, for he throws himself into it of his own accord. And the reason is, that without Meditation there is no prayer. God is most willing to give us His graces; but St. Gregory says that before giving them He desires to be asked, and, as it were, compelled to give them through our prayers. But without Meditation there is no light: we walk in darkness, and walking in darkness, we do not see the danger we are in, we do not make use of the means to avoid it, or pray to God to help us, and so we are lost. Cardinal Bellarmine declared it to be morally impossible for a Christian who does not meditate to persevere in the grace of God: whereas he who makes his Meditation every day can scarcely fall into sin -- and if unhappily he should fall occasionally, by continuing his prayer he will return immediately to God. It was said by a servant of God that "Mental Prayer and mortal sin cannot exist together."

And further, Meditation is the blessed furnace in which souls are inflamed with divine love. In my meditation, says the Psalmist, a fire shall flame out (Ps. xxviii., 4). St. Catherine of Bologna said: "Meditation is that bond which binds the soul to God." In Meditation the soul, retiring to converse alone with God, is raised above itself. He shall sit solitary and hold his peace (Lam. ii., 28), says the Prophet Jeremias. When the soul sits solitary, that is, remains alone in Meditation to consider how worthy God is of love, and how great is the love He bears to it, it will then relish the sweetness of God and fill its mind with holy thoughts. There it will detach itself from earthly affections; there it will conceive great desires to become holy, and finally resolve to give itself wholly to God. And where have the Saints made those generous resolutions which have lifted them up to a sublime degree of perfection, if not in Mental Prayer? St. Aloysius Gonzaga used to say that no one will ever attain a high degree of perfection who is not given to much Mental Prayer.

Let us, then, devote ourselves to it, and not neglect it on account of any weariness that we may experience: the weariness which we endure for God will be abundantly recompensed by Him.

Resolve, then, to make every day, either in the morning or in the evening -- but it is better in the morning -- half an hour's Meditation. In tomorrow's "Spiritual Reading" you will see briefly explained an easy method of making this Prayer. For the rest it is sufficient that during the time you should recollect yourself by reading some book of Meditation -- either this one or one of the many others -- and from time to time excite some good affection or some aspiration as will be explained in the Method. Above all I beg you never to leave Mental Prayer, which you should practice at least once a day, although you may be in great aridity and feel great weariness in performing it. If you do not discontinue it you will certainly be saved.

Evening Meditation

THE LOVE OF GOD FOR MEN

I.

God so loved the world as to give his only-begotten Son. (St. John iii., 16).

Consider that the Eternal Father, in giving us His Son for a Redeemer, the victim and price of our ransom, could not give us stronger motives for hope and love, to inspire us with confidence, and to oblige us to love Him. "In giving us His Son," says St. Augustine, "He could give us nothing more." He desires that we should avail ourselves of this immense Gift in order to gain for ourselves eternal Salvation, and every grace that we want; for in Jesus, we find all that we can desire; we find light, strength, peace, confidence, love, and eternal glory; for Jesus Christ is a Gift which contains all the gifts that we can seek for or desire. How hath he not also, with him, given us all things? (Rom. vii., 32). God having given us His beloved only begotten Son, who is the fountain and treasure of all good, who could fear that He would deny us any favor that we ask of Him?

O Eternal God! who could ever have given us this treasure of infinite value, but Thou, Who art a God of infinite love? O my Creator, what more could Thou have done to give us confidence in Thy mercy, and to put us under an obligation of loving Thee? O Lord, I have repaid Thee with ingratitude; but Thou hast said: To them that love God all things work together unto good (Rom. viii., 28). Therefore, notwithstanding the great number and the enormity of my sins, I will not despair of Thy bounty; rather let my transgressions serve to humble me the more whenever I meet with any insult; insults and humiliations does he indeed deserve who has had the temerity to offend Thy divine Majesty. I wish that my sins may serve to reconcile me more to the crosses which Thou shalt send me, that I may be more diligent in serving and honoring Thee in order to compensate for the injuries I have committed against Thee. O my God, I will always remember the displeasure I have caused Thee in order that I may the more exalt Thy mercy and be inflamed with love for Thee.

II.

Christ Jesus is of God made unto us wisdom, and justice, and sanctification, and redemption. (1 Cor. i., 30). God hath given Jesus to us in order that He might be to us ignorant and blind creatures light and wisdom, wherewith to walk in the way of salvation; in order that to us who are deserving of hell He might be justice, enabling us to aspire to Paradise; that to us sinners He might be sanctification, to obtain for us holiness; that finally, to us slaves of the devil He might be a ransom to purchase for us the liberty of the sons of God. In short, the Apostle says that with Jesus Christ we have been enriched with every good gift and every grace, if we ask it through His merits: In all things you are made rich in him … so that nothing is wanting to you in any grace. (1 Cor. i., 5).

And this gift which God has made us of His Son is a gift to each one of us; for He hath given Him entirely to each of us, as if He had given Him to each one alone, so that every one of us may say: Jesus is all mine; His body is mine; His blood is mine; His life is mine; His sorrows, His death, His merits, are all mine. Wherefore St. Paul said: He loved me and delivered himself for me. (Gal. ii., 20). And everyone may say the same thing: "My Redeemer has loved me; and for the love that He bore me He has given Himself entirely to me."

My God, my God, how can I ever leave off loving Thee and separate myself again from Thy love! I repent and will always repent of the outrages I have committed against Thee; I depend upon Thee to help me. O my God, for Thy Glory's sake, vouchsafe to grant that, as I have offended Thee much, I may also love Thee much!

O Mary, my Queen, do thou assist me. Thou knows my weakness. Grant that I may have recourse to thee whenever the devil tries to separate me from God. My Mother, my hope, do thou help me. Amen.

WEDNESDAY--FIRST WEEK OF ADVENT

Morning Meditation

THE GREAT THOUGHT OF ETERNITY

Man shall go into the house of his eternity. (Eccles. xii, 5).

He who builds a house for himself takes great pains to make it commodious, airy and handsome, and says: "I labor and give myself a great deal of trouble about this house, because I shall have to live in it all my life." And yet how little is the House of Eternity thought of!

I.

Thus did St. Augustine designate the thought of eternity: "The Great Thought" -- Magna Cogitatio. It was this thought that induced so many solitaries to retire into deserts; so many Religious, even kings and queens, to shut themselves up in cloisters; and so many Martyrs to sacrifice their lives in the midst of torments, in order to acquire a happy eternity in Heaven, and to avoid a miserable eternity in hell. The Blessed John of Avila converted a certain lady with these two words: "Reflect," said he to her, "on these two words: Ever and Never." A certain monk went down into a grave that he might meditate continually on Eternity, and constantly repeated, "O Eternity! Eternity!"

How frequently, my God, have I deserved the eternity of hell! Oh, that I had never offended Thee! Grant me sorrow for my sins; have compassion for me.

The same Blessed John of Avila says that he who believes in eternity and becomes not a Saint should be confined as one deranged. When we arrive at eternity there will be no question of our residing in a house more or less commodious, or more or less airy: the question will be of our dwelling in a palace over-flowing with delights, or in a gulf of endless torments. And for how long a time? Not for forty or fifty years, but forever, as long as God shall be God. The Saints, to obtain salvation, thought it little to give their whole life to prayer, penance, and the practice of good works. And what do we do for the same end?

O my God! many years of my life are already past; already death is near at hand, and what have I hitherto done for Thee? Give me light, and strength, to devote the remainder of my days to Thy service. Too much, alas! have I offended Thee; I desire henceforth to love Thee.

II.

With fear and trembling work out thy salvation (Phil. ii, 12).

To obtain salvation we must tremble at the thought of being lost, and tremble not so much at the thought of hell, as of sin, which alone can send us thither. He who dreads sin avoids dangerous occasions, frequently recommends himself to God, and has recourse to the means of keeping himself in the state of grace. He who acts thus will be saved; but for him who lives not in this manner it is morally impossible to be saved. Let us attend to that saying of St. Bernard: "We cannot be too secure where Eternity is at stake."

Thy Blood, O Jesus, my Redeemer, is my security. I should have already been lost on account of my sins, hadst Thou not offered me Thy pardon, on condition of my repentance for having offended Thee. I am sorry therefore, with my whole heart, for having offended Thee, Who art infinite Goodness. I love Thee, O sovereign Good, above every other good. I know that Thou wills my salvation, and I will endeavor to secure it by loving Thee forever. O Mary, Mother of God, pray to Jesus for me.

Spiritual Reading

MENTAL PRAYER

II. ITS END AND OBJECT

In order to practice Mental Prayer, or Meditation, well, and to make it truly profitable to the soul, we must clearly ascertain the ends for which we make it.

1. We must meditate to unite ourselves more completely to God. It is not so much good thoughts in the intelligence, as good acts of the will, or holy desires, that unite us to God; and such are the acts that we perform in Meditation, acts of humility, of confidence, self-sacrifice, resignation, and especially of love and of repentance for our sins. "Acts of love," says St. Teresa, "are those that keep the soul inflamed with holy love."

2. We must meditate in order to obtain from God, by prayer, the graces that are necessary in order to enable us to advance on the way of salvation, to avoid sin, and to take the means that will lead us to perfection. The best fruit, then, that comes from Meditation is the exercise of prayer. Almighty God, ordinarily speaking, does not give grace to any but to those who pray. St. Gregory writes: "God desires to be entreated, He desires to be constrained, He desires to be, as it were, conquered by importunity." At times, to obtain graces of special value, it is not enough simply to pray; we must pray urgently, and, as it were, compel God, by our prayers, to give them. It is always true that the Lord is ready to hear us; but at the time of Meditation, when we are most truly in converse with God, He is most bountiful in giving us His aid.

Above all, we must apply ourselves to Meditation, to obtain perseverance and the holy love of God. Final perseverance is not a single grace, but a chain of graces, to which must correspond the chain of our prayers; if we cease to pray, God will cease to give us His help, and we shall perish. He who does not practice Meditation will find the greatest difficulty in persevering in grace till death. Palafox, in his Notes on St. Teresa's Letters writes thus: "How will the Lord give us perseverance if we do not ask it? And how shall we ask for it without Meditation? Without Meditation there is no communion with God."

Thus, must we be urgent in prayer to obtain from God His holy love. St. Francis de Sales said that all virtues come in union with holy love. *All good things came to me together with her.* (Wis. vii, 7). Let our prayer for perseverance and love, therefore, be continual; and, to pray with greater confidence, let us ever bear in mind the promise made us by Jesus Christ, that whatever we seek from God through the merits of His Son, He will give us. Let us, then, pray, and pray always, if we would that God make us abound in every blessing. Let us pray for ourselves, and, if we have zeal for the glory of God, let us pray for others. God is most pleased to be entreated for unbelievers and heretics and all sinners. *Let the people confess to thee, O God! let all the people confess to thee.* (Ps. lxvi, 6). Let us say: O Lord! make them know thee, make them love Thee. We read in the Lives of St.

Teresa and St. Mary Magdalen de Pazzi how God inspired these holy women to pray for sinners. And to prayers for sinners let us also add prayers for the Holy Souls in Purgatory.

3. We must apply ourselves to Meditation, not for the sake of spiritual consolations, but chiefly to learn what is the will of God concerning us. Speak, Lord, said Samuel to God, for thy servant heareth. (1 Kings iii, 9). Lord, make me know what Thou wilt, that I may do it. Some persons continue Meditation if consolations continue; but when these cease, they leave off Meditation. It is true that God is accustomed to comfort His beloved souls at the time of Meditation, and to give them some foretaste of the delights He prepares in Heaven for those who love Him. These are things which lovers of the world do not comprehend; they who have no taste except for earthly delights despise those that are celestial. Oh, if they were wise, how surely would they leave such pleasures to recollect themselves and speak alone with God! Meditation is nothing more than converse between the soul and God; the soul pours forth to Him its affections, its desires, its fears, its requests; and God speaks to the heart, causing it to know His goodness, and the love which He bears it, and what it must do to please Him. I will lead her into solitude and speak to her heart. (Osee, ii, 14).

But these delights are not constant, and, for the most part, holy souls experience much dryness of spirit in Meditation. "With dryness and temptations," says St. Teresa, "the Lord makes proof of those who love Him." And she adds: "Even if this dryness lasts through life, let not the soul leave off Meditation; the time will come when all will be well rewarded." The time of dryness is the time for gaining the greatest rewards; and when we find ourselves apparently without fervor, without good desires, and, as it were, unable to do a good act, let us humble ourselves and resign ourselves, for this very Meditation will be more fruitful than others. It is enough then to say, if we can say nothing more: "O Lord! help me, have mercy on me, abandon me not!" Happy he, who does not leave off Meditation in the hour of desolation. God will make him abound in graces.

Evening Meditation

THE WORD WAS MADE MAN IN THE FULNESS OF TIME.

I.

When the fulness of time was come God sent his Son. (Gal. iv, 4).

Consider that God allowed four thousand years to pass, after the transgression of Adam, before He sent His Son upon earth to redeem the world. And in the meantime, oh, what fatal darkness reigned upon the earth! The true God was not known or adored, except in one small corner of the world. Idolatry reigned everywhere; so that devils and stones and beasts were adored as gods.

But let us admire in this the Divine Wisdom: He deferred the coming of the Redeemer to render His advent more welcome to man, in order that the malice of sin might be better known, as well as the necessity of a remedy and the grace of the Savior. If Jesus Christ had come into the world immediately after the fall of Adam, the greatness of this favor would have been but slightly appreciated. Let us therefore thank the goodness of God for having sent us into the world after the great work of Redemption had been accomplished. Behold, the happy time is come which was called the fulness of time: When the fulness of time was come, God sent his Son... that he might redeem them that were under the law. (Gal. iv, 4).

O Divine Word, become Man for me, though I behold Thee thus humbled and become a little Infant in the womb of Mary, yet I confess and acknowledge Thee for my Lord and King, but a King of Love. My dearest Savior, since Thou hast come down upon earth and clothed Thyself with our miserable flesh, in order to reign over our hearts, I beseech Thee come and establish Thy reign in my heart also, which was once, alas, ruled over by Thine enemies, but is now, I hope, Thine, as I desire that it may be always Thine, and that from this day forth Thou mayst be its only Lord: Rule thou in the midst of thy enemies. (Ps. cix, 2). Other kings reign by the strength of arms, but Thou comes to reign by the power of Thy love; and therefore, Thou dost not come with regal pomp, or clothed in purple and gold, or adorned with scepter and crown, or surrounded by armies of soldiers. Thou came into the world to be born in a stable -- poor, forsaken, placed in a manger on a little straw, because thus Thou wouldst begin to reign in our hearts.

II.

It is called fulness, on account of the fulness of grace which the Son of God came to communicate to men by the Redemption of the world. Behold the Angel who is sent as ambassador into the town of Nazareth to announce to the Virgin Mary the coming of the Word, who desires to become incarnate in her womb. The Angel salutes her, calls her full of grace and blessed among women. (Luke, i, 28). The humble Virgin, chosen to be the

Mother of the Son of God, is troubled at these praises on account of her great humility: but the Angel encourages her, and tells her that she has found grace with God; that is to say, that grace which brought peace between God and man, and the reparation of the ruin caused by sin. He then tells her that she must give her Son the Name of Savior: Thou shalt call his name Jesus (Ib. 31), and that this her Son is the very Son of God, Wwhois to redeem the world, and thus to reign over the hearts of men. Behold, at last Mary consents to be the Mother of such a Son: Be it done unto me according to thy word. (Ib. 38). And the Eternal Word takes flesh and becomes Man: And the Word was made flesh. (Jo. i, 14).

Let us thank this Son, and let us also thank His Mother, who, in consenting to be the Mother of such a Son, consented also to be the Mother of our salvation, and the Mother of sorrows, accepting at that time the martyrdom of sorrow that it would cost her to be the Mother of a Son Who was to come into the world to suffer and die for man.

Ah, my Infant King, how could I have so often rebelled against Thee, and lived so long Thy enemy, deprived of Thy grace, when, to oblige me to love Thee, Thou hast put off Thy divine majesty, and hast humbled Thyself even to appearing, first, as a Babe in a cave; then as a servant in a shop, and as a criminal on the Cross? Oh, happy me, if, now that I have been freed, as I hope, from the slavery of Satan, I allow myself forever to be governed by Thee and by Thy love! O Jesus, my King, Who art so amiable and so loving to our souls, take possession, I pray Thee, of mine; I give it entirely to Thee; accept it, that it may serve Thee forever, but serve Thee only for love. Thy majesty deserves to be feared, but Thy goodness still more deserves to be loved. Thou art my King, and shalt be always the only object of my love; and the only fear I have is the fear of displeasing Thee. That is what I hope. Do Thou help me with Thy grace. O Mary, my dear Lady! It is for thee to obtain for me that I may be faithful to this beloved King of my soul.

Thursday--First Week of Advent

Morning Meditation

PORTRAIT OF A MAN WHO IS BUT A SHORT TIME GONE INTO THE HOUSE OF HIS ETERNITY.

Under thee shall the moth be strewed, and worms shall be thy covering. (Is. xiv, 11).

The moment the soul leaves the body it shall go into eternity and the body shall return to dust. The same lot awaits all, nobleman and peasant, prince, and vassal. Thou shalt take away their breath, and they shall return to their dust. (Ps. ciii, 29).

O my God, I will no longer resist Thy calls.

I.

Consider that thou art dust and that thou shalt return to dust. A day will come when thou shalt die and rot in a grave where worms shall be thy covering.

Imagine that thou beholds a person who has just died. Look at that body lying on the bed, the head fallen on the chest, the hair in disorder and still bathed in the sweat of death, the eyes sunk, the cheeks hollow, the face the color of ashes, the lips and tongue like iron, the body cold and heavy. The beholders grow pale and tremble. How many at the sight of a deceased relative or friend have changed their lives and retired from the world!

Still greater horror will be excited when the body begins to putrefy. Twenty-four hours have not elapsed since the death of that young man, and his body already sends forth an offensive smell. The windows must be opened, and to prevent the communication of disease to the entire family, he must soon be transferred to the church and buried in the earth. "If he has been one of the rich and noble of the world, his body shall send forth a more intolerable stench," says St. Ambrose.

Behold the end of that proud, that lewd, voluptuous man! Before his death, desired and sought after in conversation, and now become an object of horror and disgust to all who behold him! His relatives are in haste to remove him from the house. They hire men to shut him up in a coffin and carry him to the churchyard and throw him into a grave!

O Jesus, my Redeemer, I thank Thee for not having taken me out of life when I was Thy enemy. For how many years have I deserved to be in hell! Had I died on such a day or such a night, what would be my lot for all eternity? Lord, I thank Thee! I accept my death in satisfaction for my sins and I accept it in the way Thou wilt be pleased to send it. But since Thou hast borne with me till now, wait for me a little longer. Suffer me, therefore, that I may lament my sorrow a little. (Job x, 20). Give me time to bewail my offences before Thou dost judge me. I will no longer resist Thy calls. Who knows but the words I have just read may be the last call for me! Behold the penitent traitor who has recourse to Thee. A contrite and humble heart, O God, thou wilt not despise. (Ps. l, 19).

II.

Consider that as thou hast acted on the occasion of the death of friends and relatives so others will act on the occasion of thy death. During life, the fame of his wit, of his politeness, of the elegance of his manners and his facetiousness, was spread far and wide, but after death the dead man is soon forgotten. On hearing the news of his death some say: "He was an honor to his family;" "He has provided well for his children." Some regret his death because he had done them some service during life; others rejoice at it because it is an advantage to them. But in a little time, no one speaks of him. In the beginning the relatives are afflicted for a short time, but soon they feel unwilling to hear his name through fear of renewing their grief. In visits of condolence all are careful to make no mention of the deceased, and should anyone happen to speak of him the relatives exclaim: "For God's sake do not mention his name!"

They occupy the possessions and offices of the deceased, and they are consoled by the share of the property which falls to them. But the dead are no longer remembered. Their memory hath perished with a noise. (Ps. ix, 7). Thus, in a short time your death will be rather a source of joy; and in the very room in which you have breathed forth your soul, and in which you have been judged by Jesus Christ, others will dance and eat, and play and laugh as before! And where will your soul be then?

O God cast me not away from Thy face! For Thy mercy's sake cast me not away! Thou hast said: Him that cometh to me I will not cast out. (Jo. vi, 37). It is true that I have outraged Thee more than others because I have been more favored with Thy lights and graces. But the Blood which Thou hast shed for me gives me courage and pardon if I repent. My Sovereign Good, I am sorry with my whole heart for having offended Thee. Pardon me and give me grace to love Thee for the future. I have offended Thee enough! The rest of my life I wish to spend in weeping unceasingly over the insults I have offered Thee and in loving with my whole heart a God worthy of infinite love. O Mary, my hope, pray to Jesus for me.

Spiritual Reading

MENTAL PRAYER

III. ITS PLACE AND TIME

We can meditate in every place, at home or elsewhere, even when walking or working. How many are there who, not being able to do otherwise, raise their hearts to God and apply their minds to Mental Prayer without for this purpose leaving their occupations, their work, or meditate even when travelling. He who seeks God will always find Him everywhere and at all times.

The essential condition of converse with God is solitude of the heart, without which prayer would be worthless, and, as St. Gregory says: "it would profit us little or nothing to be with the body in a solitary place, while the heart is full of worldly thoughts and affections." But to enjoy the solitude of the heart, which consists in being disengaged from worldly thoughts and affections, deserts and caves are not, of course, necessary. Those who from necessity are obliged to converse with the world, whenever their hearts are free from worldly attachments, even in the public streets, in places of resort, and public assemblies, can possess a solitude of heart and continue united with God. All occupations we undertake to fulfil the Divine Will have no power to disturb the solitude of the heart. St. Catherine of Siena truly found God amid the household labors in which her parents kept her employed in order to draw her from devotional exercises; for in the midst of these affairs she preserved a place of retirement in her heart, which she called her cell, and there ceased not to converse with God alone.

However, when we can, we should retire to a solitary place to do our Meditation. Our Lord has said: When thou shalt pray, enter thy chamber, and having shut the door, pray to thy Father in secret. St. Bernard says that silence and the absence of all noise almost force the soul to think of the goods of Heaven.

But the best place for making Mental Prayer is the church; for Jesus Christ especially delights in the Meditation that is made before the Blessed Sacrament, since there it appears that He bestows light and grace most abundantly upon those who visit Him. He has left Himself in this Sacrament, not only to be the food of souls that receive Him in Holy Communion, but also to be always found by everyone who seeks Him. Devout pilgrims go to the Holy House of Loreto, where Jesus Christ dwelt during His life; and to Jerusalem, where He died on the Cross; but how much greater ought our devotion to be when we find Him before us in the Tabernacle, in which this Lord Himself dwells in person, who lived on earth, and died for us on Calvary! It is not permitted in the world for persons of all ranks to speak alone with kings; but with Jesus Christ, the King of kings, both nobles and plebeians, rich and poor, can converse at their will, setting before Him their wants, and seeking His grace; and in the Tabernacle Jesus gives audience to all, hears all, and comforts all.

THE TIME

We have to consider two things, namely:
(1) The time of day most suitable for Mental Prayer; and
(2) The time to be spent in making it.

(1) According to St. Bonaventure, the morning and the evening are the two parts of the day which, ordinarily speaking, are the fittest for Meditation. But, according to St. Gregory of Nyssa, the morning is the most seasonable time for prayer, because, says the Saint, when prayer precedes business, sin will not find entrance into the soul. And the Venerable Father Charles Carafa, Founder of the Congregation of the Pious Workers, used to say that a fervent act of love, made in the morning during Meditation, is sufficient to maintain the soul in fervor during the entire day. Prayer, as St. Jerome has written, is also necessary in the evening. Let the body not go to rest before the soul is refreshed by

Mental Prayer, which is the food of the soul. But always and in all places, we can pray; it is enough for us to raise the mind to God, and to make good acts, for in this consists Mental Prayer.

(2) With regard to the time to be spent in Mental Prayer, the rule of the Saints was, to devote to it all the hours that were not necessary for the occupations of human life. St. Francis Borgia employed in Meditation eight hours in the day, because his Superiors would not allow him a longer time; and when the eight hours had expired, he earnestly asked permission to remain a little longer at prayer, saying: "Ah! give me another little quarter of an hour." St. Philip Neri was accustomed to spend the entire night in prayer. St. Anthony the Abbot remained the whole night in prayer; and when the sun appeared, which was the time assigned for terminating his prayer, he complained of its having risen too soon.

Father Balthassar Alvarez used to say that a soul that loves God, when not in prayer, is like a stone out of its center, in a violent state; for in this life we should, as much as possible, imitate the lives of the Saints in bliss, who are constantly employed in the contemplation of God.

But what time should Religious who seek perfection devote to Mental Prayer? Father Torres prescribed an hour's Meditation in the morning, another during the day, and a half hour's Meditation in the evening, when they should not be hindered by sickness or by any duty of obedience. If to you this appears too much, I counsel you to give at least two hours to Mental Prayer. It is certain that a half hour's Meditation would not be sufficient to attain a high degree of perfection; for beginners, however, this would be sufficient.

Sometimes the Lord wishes you to omit prayer in order to perform some work of fraternal charity; but it is necessary to attend to what St. Laurence Justinian says: "When charity requires it, the spouse of Jesus goes to serve her neighbor; but during that time, she continually sighs to return to converse with her Spouse in the solitude of her cell. Father Vincent Carafa, General of the Society of Jesus, stole as many little moments of time as he could, and employed them in prayer.

Mental Prayer is tedious to those who are attached to the world, but not to those who love God only. Ah! conversation with God is not painful or tedious to those who truly love Him. His conversation has no bitterness, His company produces not tediousness, but joy and gladness (Wis. viii, 16). "Mental Prayer," says St. John Climacus, "is nothing else than a familiar conversation and union with God." "In prayer," as St. Chrysostom says, "the soul converses with God, and God with the soul." No, the life of holy people who love prayer, and fly from earthly amusements, is not a life of bitterness. If you do not believe me, Taste, and see that the Lord is sweet. Try it, and you shall see how sweet the Lord is to those who leave all things to converse with Him alone. But the end which we ought to propose to ourselves in going to Meditation should be, as has been said several times, not spiritual consolation, but to learn from Our Lord what He wishes from us, and to divest ourselves of all self-love. "To prepare yourself for prayer," says St. John Climacus, "put off your own will." To prepare ourselves well for Meditation, we must renounce self-will, and say to God: Speak, Lord, for thy servant heareth. Lord, tell me what Thou wishes me to do; I am willing to do it. And it is necessary to say this with a resolute will, for without this disposition the Lord will not speak to us.

Evening Meditation

THE ABASEMENT OF JESUS

I.

Taking the form of a servant. (Phil. ii, 7).

The Eternal Word descends on earth to save man; and whence does He descend? His going out is from the end of heaven. (Ps. xviii, 7). He descends from the bosom of His Divine Father, where from eternity He was begotten in the brightness of the Saints. And whither does He descend? He descends into the womb of a Virgin, a child of Adam, which in comparison with the bosom of God is an object of horror; wherefore the Church sings: "Thou didst not abhor the Virgin's womb." Yes, because the Word in the bosom of the Father is God like the Father -- is immense, omnipotent, most blessed, and supreme Lord, and equal in everything to the Father. But in the womb of Mary, He is a creature, small, weak, afflicted, a servant inferior to the Father, taking the form of a servant. (Phil. ii, 7).

It is related as a great prodigy of humility in St. Alexis that, although he was the son of a Roman gentleman, he chose to live as a servant in his father's house. But how is the humility of this Saint to be compared to the humility of Jesus Christ? Between the son and the servant of the father of St. Alexis there was, it is true, some difference; but between God and the servant of God there is an infinite difference.

My beloved Jesus, thou art the Sovereign Lord of Heaven and earth; but for the love of me Thou hast made Thyself a servant even of the executioners who tore Thy flesh, pierced Thy head, and finally left Thee nailed on the Cross to die of sorrow. I adore Thee as my God and Lord, and I am ashamed to appear before Thee, when I remember how often for the sake of some miserable pleasure, I have broken Thy holy bonds, and have told Thee to Thy face that I would not serve Thee. Ah, thou mayst justly reproach me: Thou hast burst my hands, and thou said: I will not serve. (Jer. ii, 20). But still, O my Savior, thy merits, and Thy goodness which cannot despise a heart that repents and humbles itself, give me courage to hope for pardon: A contrite and humble heart, O God, thou wilt not despise. (Ps. 1, 19).

II.

Besides, this Son of God having become the servant of His Father, in obedience to Him, made Himself also the servant of His creatures of Mary and Joseph: And he was subject to them. (Luke ii, 51). Moreover, He made Himself even a servant of Pilate, who condemned Him to death, and He was obedient to him and accepted it; He became a servant of the executioners, who scourged Him, crowned Him with thorns, and crucified Him; and He humbly obeyed them all, and yielded Himself into their hands.

O God! And shall we, after this, refuse to submit ourselves to the service of so loving a Savior, Who, to save us, has subjected Himself to such painful and degrading slavery? And rather than be the servants of this great and so loving a Lord, shall we be content to remain the slaves of the devil, who does not love his servants, but hates them and treats them like a tyrant, making them miserable and wretched in this world and in the next? But if we have been guilty of this great folly, why do we not quickly give up this unhappy servitude? Courage, then, since we have been delivered by Jesus Christ from the slavery of hell; let us now embrace and bind around us with love those sweet chains, which will render us servants and lovers of Jesus Christ, and hereafter obtain for us the crown of the eternal kingdom amongst the Blessed in Paradise.

I confess, my Jesus, that I have offended Thee greatly; I confess that I deserve a thousand hells for the sins I have committed against Thee; chastise me as Thou see fit, but do not deprive me of Thy grace and love. I repent above every other evil of having despised Thee. I love Thee with my whole heart. I propose from this day forth to desire to serve Thee and love Thee alone. I pray Thee bind me by Thy merits with chains of Thy holy love, and never suffer me to break those blessed chains again. I love Thee above everything, O my Deliverer; and I would prefer being Thy servant to being master of the whole world. And of what avail would all the world be to him who lives deprived of Thy grace? "My sweetest Jesus, permit me not to separate myself from Thee." This grace I ask of Thee, and I intend always to ask it, and I beg of Thee to grant me this day the grace to repeat continually to the end of my life the prayer: My Jesus, grant that I may never again separate myself from Thy love. I ask this favor of thee also, O Mary, my Mother, help me by thy intercession that I may never separate myself again from my God.

Friday--First Week of Advent

Morning Meditation

THE UNHAPPY LIFE OF THE SINNER

There is no peace to the wicked, saith the Lord. (Is. xlviii. 22).

No, the world with all its goods cannot content the heart of man. He was created, not for them, but for God alone. Hence God alone can make man content and happy and give that peace which the world cannot give.

I.

In this life all men seek after peace. The merchant, the soldier, the man who goes to law -- all labor with the hope of making a fortune and of thus finding peace by worldly lucre, by a more exalted post, by gaining the law-suit. But poor worldlings seek from the world the peace that the world cannot give. God alone can give peace, as the Holy Church proclaims in the following words: "Give to Thy servants that peace which the world cannot give." No; the world, with all its goods, cannot content the heart of man; for he was created, not for them, but for God alone: hence God alone can make him happy and content. Brute animals, that have been made for sensual delights, find peace in earthly goods: give to an ox a bundle of hay, and to a dog a piece of flesh, and they are content, they desire nothing more. But the soul, which has been created for no other end than to love God, and to live in union with Him, shall never be able to find peace or happiness in sensual enjoyments; God alone can make her perfectly content.

The Son of God gave the appellation of fool to the rich man who, after having reaped a rich harvest from his fields, said to himself: Soul, thou hast many goods laid up for many years; take thy rest, eat, drink, and make good cheer. (Luke xii. 19). "Miserable fool!" says St. Basil, "have you the soul of a swine, of a brute, that you expect to make it happy by eating, drinking, or by sensual delights?" A man may be puffed up, but he cannot be satisfied, by the goods of this world. On the words of the Gospel, behold we have left all things (Matt. xix. 27), St. Bernard writes, that he saw different classes of fools laboring under different species of folly. All had a great thirst for happiness: some were satiated with the goods of the earth, which is a figure of the avaricious; others with wind, the figure of the ambitious, who seek after empty honors: others seated round a furnace, swallowing the sparks that were thrown from it; these were the passionate and vindictive: others, in fine, drank putrid waters from a fetid lake: and these were the voluptuous and unchaste. Hence, turning to them, the Saint exclaims: "O fools! do you not see that these things increase, rather than diminish, your thirst!"

Ah, my God, what now remains of all the offences I have offered to Thee, but pains, bitterness, and merits for hell? I am not sorry for the pain and remorse which I now feel; on the contrary they console me, because they are the gift of Thy grace, and make me hope that, since Thou inspires these sentiments, thou wishes to pardon me. What displeases me is the pain I have given Thee, my Redeemer, who has loved me so tenderly. I deserved, O my Lord, to be abandoned by Thee, but instead of abandoning me, I see that Thou dost offer me pardon, and that Thou art the first to ask for a reconciliation. O my Jesus, I wish to make peace with Thee, and I desire Thy grace more than any earthly good.

II.

The goods of the world are but goods in appearance, and therefore they cannot satisfy the heart of man. You have eaten, says the Prophet Aggeus, but have not been filled. (Agg. i. 6). Hence, the more the avaricious man possesses, the more he seeks to acquire. "The possession of great wealth," says St. Augustine, "does not close, but rather extends, the jaws of avarice." The more the unchaste man wallows in the mire of impurity, the greater is his disgust, and, at the same time, his desire for such beastly pleasures; and how can dung and carnal filthiness content the heart? The same happens to the ambitious man, who wishes to satisfy his desires by smoke; for he always attends more to what he wants than to what he possesses. After having acquired many kingdoms, Alexander the Great wept, because he had no more kingdoms to conquer. If worldly goods could content the human heart, the rich and the monarchs of the earth would enjoy complete happiness; but experience shows the contrary. Solomon tells us that he refused no indulgence to his senses. Whatsoever my eyes desired, I refused them not. (Eccles. ii. 10). But after all his sensual enjoyments what did he say? Vanity of vanities, and all is vanity. (Ib. i. 2). -- That is, everything in this world is mere vanity, a pure lie, pure folly.

I am sorry, O infinite Goodness! for having offended Thee; I would wish to die of sorrow for my offences. Ah! through the love which Thou didst entertain for me when Thou didst expire on the Cross, pardon me, receive me into Thy Heart, and change my heart, so that henceforth I may please Thee as much as I have hitherto offended Thee. I now renounce, for Thy sake, all the pleasures that the world can give me, and I resolve to forfeit my life rather than lose Thy grace. Tell me what I must do to please Thee; I wish to do it. What pleasures, what honors, what riches, can I seek? I wish only for Thee, my God, my joy, my glory, my treasure, my life, my love, my All! Give me the grace to love Thee, and then do with me what Thou pleases. Mary, my Mother and my hope, take me under thy protection and obtain for me the grace to belong entirely to God. Amen.

Spiritual Reading

MENTAL PRAYER

IV. METHOD OF MAKING IT

Mental Prayer consists of three parts:

1. The Preparation;
2. The Meditation proper;
3. The Conclusion.

The Preparation

Begin by disposing your mind and your body to enter pious recollection.

Leave outside the door of the place where you are going to converse with God all extraneous or distracting thoughts, saying with St. Bernard: "O my thoughts, wait here! After prayer we shall treat other matters." Be careful not to allow the mind to wander where it wishes.

The posture of the body most suitable for prayer is kneeling, but if this posture becomes so irksome as to cause distractions, we may, as St. John of the Cross tells us, make our Meditation modestly sitting down.

In the Preparation there should be three Acts:

1. An Act of Faith in the presence of God;
2. An Act of Humility and Contrition for sin;
3. An Act of Petition for light.

Be careful to make the Act of Faith in the presence of God well, for a lively remembrance of the Divine Presence contributes greatly to remove distractions. When a person is distracted in Meditation there is reason to think that he has not made a lively Act of Faith at the beginning. The three Acts should be made with fervor and should be short that we may pass immediately to the Meditation.

The Meditation Proper

When Mental Prayer is made in common, as in a Community of Religious, one person reads for the rest the subject of the Meditation and divides it into two parts. The first point is read at the beginning after the Prayers are said and the Preparatory Acts are made. The second point is read towards the middle of the half hour. One should read in a loud tone of voice, and slowly, to be well understood.

When you do Meditation in private you may always use a book and stop when you find yourself most touched. St. Francis de Sales says that in this we should be as the bees that stop on a flower if they find any honey in it, and then pass to another. We should stop at those passages in which the soul finds nourishment. St. Teresa used a book for seventeen years in this way. She would first read a little, then meditate for a short while on what she had read, in imitation of the dove that first drinks and then raises its eyes to heaven.

It should be remembered that the fruit of Mental Prayer does not consist so much in meditating, as in making affections, petitions, and resolutions.

1. Affections -- When you reflect on the point of the Meditation just read, and feel any pious sentiment, raise your heart to God and offer Him an Act of humility, of confidence, love, sorrow, gratitude, resignation, thanksgiving, and so on. The Acts of Love and

Contrition are the golden chain that binds the soul to God. An Act of perfect Charity is sufficient for the remission of all our sins. And among the Acts of Love towards God there is none more perfect than the taking delight in the infinite joy of God.

2. Petitions -- It is very profitable in Mental Prayer, and perhaps more useful than any other Act, to repeat petitions to God, asking with humility and confidence His graces -- His light, the strength we need to do His holy Will and to pray always, and especially the grace of Perseverance and His Holy Love.

The Ven. Paul Segneri says that until he studied Theology, he used to employ himself during the time of Mental Prayer making Reflections and Affections, but "God afterwards opened my eyes," he says, "and thenceforward I endeavored to employ myself in Petitions; and if there is any good in me I ascribe it all to this exercise of recommending myself to God." Do you likewise. Ask of God His graces in the Name of Jesus Christ and you will obtain whatever you desire.

3. Resolutions -- It is necessary to make a particular resolution in the Meditation. As, for example, to avoid some sin, or some defect into which you have more frequently fallen; to practice some virtue, such as to suffer the annoyance you receive from another person, to obey more exactly a certain superior, to perform some particular act of mortification. The same resolutions must be made several times until we find we have got rid of the defect or acquired the virtue. Afterwards do not fail to reduce to practice the resolutions you have made as soon as the occasion is presented.

You would also do well to renew your Vows, or any engagement you have made with God. This renewal is most pleasing to God, and it multiplies the merit of the good work and draws down upon us new help to persevere and grow in grace.

The Conclusion

The Conclusion consists of three acts:

1. Thanking God for the lights received, etc.;
2. Making a firm purpose to keep our resolutions;
3. Asking God, for the sake of Jesus and Mary, to give us the grace to be faithful to our resolutions.

Be careful never to omit, at the end of Meditation, to recommend to God the souls in Purgatory, and all poor sinners. St. John Chrysostom says nothing more clearly shows our love for Jesus Christ than our zeal in recommending our neighbors to Him.

A WORD ABOUT DISTRACTIONS AND DRYNESS IN PRAYER.

1. Distractions. Of these we must not take much account. It is enough to drive them away when they come. And besides, even the Saints suffered involuntary distractions. But they did not, on this account, leave off Meditation; and so also must we act. St. Francis of Sales says that if in Meditation we did nothing but drive away, or seek to drive away, distractions, our Meditation would be of great profit.

2. As for Dryness of Spirit, the greatest pain of souls in Meditation is to find themselves sometimes without a feeling of devotion, weary of Prayer, and without any sensible desire of loving God. And with this is often joined the fear of being in the wrath of God through their sins, on account of which the Lord has abandoned them; and being in this gloomy darkness they know not any way of escaping from it, for it seems to them that every way is closed against them. Let the devout soul, then, continue steadfast in Meditation, and not leave off as the devil will suggest. At such a time let it unite its desolation to that which Jesus Christ suffered on the Cross. Let it repeat: My Jesus, mercy! Lord, have mercy on me! Have pity on me! Leave me not, O Jesus! Pray, and doubt not that God will hear you and grant your petitions.

Evening Meditation

JESUS ENLIGHTENS THE WORLD AND GLORIFIES GOD

I.

The Lord hath created a new thing upon the earth. (Jer. xxxi. 22).

Before the coming of the Messias the world was buried in a dark night of ignorance and sin. The true God was hardly known, save in one single corner of the earth in Judea alone: In Judea God is known. (Ps. lxxv. 2). But everywhere else men adored as gods devils, beasts, and stones. Everywhere there reigned the night of sin, which blinds souls, and fills them with vices, and hides from them the sight of the miserable state in which they are living, as enemies of God, and worthy only of hell: Thou hast appointed darkness and it is night; in it shall all the beasts of the wood go about. (Ps. ciii. 20).

From this darkness Jesus came to deliver the world: To them that dwelt in the region of the shadow of death, light is risen. (Is. ix. 2). He delivered it from idolatry by making known the light of the true God; and He delivered the world from sin by the light of His doctrine and of His divine example: For this purpose, the Son of God appeared that he might destroy the work of the devil. (I Jo. iii. 8).

My eternal God, I have dishonored Thee by so often preferring my will to Thine, and my vile and miserable pleasures to Thy holy grace. What hope of pardon would there be for me, if Thou hadst not given me Jesus Christ, our Savior, that He might be the Hope of us miserable sinners? He is a propitiation for our sins (I Jo. ii. 2). Yes, for Jesus Christ, in sacrificing His life in satisfaction for the injuries we have done Thee, has given more honor to Thee than we have dishonor by our sins. Receive me, therefore, O my Father, for the love of Jesus Christ. I repent, O infinite Goodness, of having outraged Thee: Father, I have sinned against heaven, and before thee, I am not now worthy to be called thy son. (Luke xv. 21). I am not worthy of forgiveness; but Jesus Christ is worthy to be heard favorably by Thee. He prayed once for me on the Cross: Father, forgive; and even now in Heaven He is constantly begging Thee to receive me as a son: We have an advocate, Jesus Christ, whoever intercedes for us. (Rom. vii. 34). Receive an ungrateful son, who once forsook Thee, but now returns resolved to desire to love Thee.

II.

The Prophet Jeremias foretold that God would create a new Child to be the Redeemer of men: The Lord hath created a new thing upon the earth. (Jer. xxxi. 22). This new Child is Jesus Christ. He is the Son of God, who is the object of the love of all the Saints in Paradise, and is the Love of the Father Himself, Who thus speaks of Him: This is my beloved Son, in whom I am well pleased. (Matt. xvii. 5). And this Son is He Who made Himself man. A new Child, because He gave more glory and honor to God in the first moment of His creation than all the Angels and Saints together have given Him or shall give Him for all eternity. And therefore, did the Angels at the birth of Jesus sing: Glory to God in the highest. (Luke ii. 14). The Child Jesus has rendered more glory to God than men have deprived Him of by all their sins.

Let us therefore, poor sinners, take courage; let us offer to the eternal Father this Infant; let us present to Him the tears, the obedience, the humility, the death, and the merits of Jesus Christ, and we shall make reparation to God for all the dishonor we have caused Him by our offences.

Yes, my Father, I love Thee, and I will always love Thee. O my Father, now that I know well the love, thou hast borne me, and the patience which Thou hast shown me for so many years, I resolve no longer to live without loving Thee. Give me a great love so that I may constantly lament the displeasure I have given Thee, who art so good a Father; cause me ever to burn with love towards Thee, who art so loving a Father towards me. My Father, I love Thee, I love Thee, I love Thee! O Mary! God is my Father, and thou art my Mother. Thou canst do all things with God; help me; obtain for me holy perseverance and His holy love.

Saturday--First Week of Advent

Morning Meditation

THE POWER OF MARY'S INTERCESSION

With me are riches ... that I may enrich them that love me. (Prov. viii. 18).

If the prayers of the Saints are very powerful with God, how great must be the power of Mary's prayers! The former are the prayers of servants, the latter the prayers of a Mother! Blessed is that person, then, for whom Mary prays. Holy Mother of God, pray for us!

I.

St. Bernard tells us that Mary has received a twofold fulness of grace. The first was in the Incarnation of the Word Who was made Man in her most holy womb; the second in that fulness of grace which we receive from God by means of her prayers. So that whatever good we have from God is received through the intercession of Mary! If the prayers of the Saints are so powerful with God, how great must be the power of those of His Mother. The former are the prayers of servants, the latter the prayers of a Mother! The prayers of Mary have the force of a command with Jesus Christ. Hence it is impossible for the Son not to grant grace for which the Mother asks. "Rejoice, rejoice, O Mary," says St. Methodius, "thou hast thy Son for a debtor. We are all debtors to Him, but He is a debtor to thee alone." Blessed, then, is the person for whom Mary prays!

O great Mother of God, pray to Jesus for me! Behold the miseries of my soul and pity me. Pray and never cease to pray until thou sees me safe in Paradise. O Mary, thou art my hope; abandon me not. Holy Mother of God, pray for me.

II.

Jesus rejoices when His most beloved Mother prays to Him, that He may have the pleasure of granting her all she asks. One day St. Bridget heard Jesus speak to Mary and say "O Mother, thou well knows that I cannot do otherwise than grant thy prayers; therefore, ask of Me what thou wilt. Since thou, when on earth, didst deny me nothing, it is becoming, now that I am in Heaven, that I should deny thee nothing that thou asks of Me." Mary has only to speak and her Divine Son grants her all she asks. Let us, therefore, pray to His Divine Mother without ceasing, if we wish to secure our eternal salvation, and let us address her in the words of St. Andrew of Crete: "We beseech thee, therefore, O holy Virgin, to grant us the help of thy prayers with God; prayers that are more precious than all the treasures of the world; prayers that obtain for us a very great abundance of graces; prayers that confound all enemies, and triumph over their strength."

Ah, my Lady, had I always invoked thee in temptation I should never have fallen. In the future I will never cease to invoke thee, saying: Mary, help me! Mary, succor me! Amen.

Spiritual Reading

THE VALUE OF SPIRITUAL READING

To a spiritual life the Reading of Holy Books is, perhaps, not less useful than Mental Prayer. St. Bernard says that reading instructs at once both in prayer and in the practice of virtue. Hence, he concluded that Spiritual Reading and Prayer are the weapons by which hell is conquered and Heaven is won.

We cannot always have access to a Spiritual Father for counsel in our actions, and particularly in our doubts; but reading will abundantly supply his place by giving us light and direction to escape the illusions of the devil and of our own self-love, and at the same time to submit to the Divine Will. St. Athanasius used to say that no one is found devoted to the service of God who does not practice Spiritual Reading. Hence all the Founders of Religious Orders have strongly recommended this holy exercise to their Religious. But above all the Apostle, St. Paul, prescribed Spiritual Reading to Timothy. Attend unto reading. (Tim. iv. 3). Mark the word attend, which signifies that although Timothy, being a Bishop, was greatly occupied with the care of his flock, still the Apostle wished him to attend to the reading of holy books, not in a passing way and for a short time, but regularly and for a considerable time.

The reading of spiritual books is as profitable as the reading of bad books is noxious. The first author of pious books is the Spirit of God, as the author of pernicious writings is the devil. Consider some of the great blessings the reading of spiritual books brings to the soul.

As the reading of bad books fills the mind with worldly and poisonous sentiments, pious reading fills the soul with holy thoughts and good desires. He that keeps the mind filled with devout thoughts, such as spiritual maxims, examples of the virtuous actions of the Saints, will, not only during prayer, but at other times also, be accompanied by these thoughts, and by them be kept almost continually united to God. St. Bernard explains this by a beautiful similitude in his exposition of the words seek and you shall find (Matt. vii. 7), when he says: "Seek by reading books of devotion, and you shall find in Meditation; for reading, as it were, puts the food in the mouth, which is afterwards masticated by Meditation.

The soul that is imbued with holy thoughts in Reading is ever and always prepared to banish its internal temptations. St. Jerome advised his disciple, Salvina: "Endeavour to have ever in your hands a pious book that with this shield you may repel all the arrows of bad thoughts."

Spiritual Reading serves to make us see the stains that infect the soul and helps us to remove them. The same St. Jerome recommends Demetriade to avail herself of Spiritual Reading as of a mirror. As a mirror exhibits the stains of the countenance, holy books show us the defects of the soul. St. Gregory, speaking of Spiritual Reading says: "There we perceive the losses we have sustained and the good things we have acquired; our falling back or our progress in virtue."

In the reading of holy books, we receive many lights and divine calls. St. Jerome says that when we pray, we speak to God; but when we read, God speaks to us. St. Ambrose says the same: "We address Him when we pray; we hear Him when we read." In prayer God hears our petitions, but in reading we listen to His voice. We cannot, as I have already said, always have at hand a Spiritual Father, nor often hear the sermons of sacred orators, to direct us and give us light to walk well in the way of God. Good books supply the place of sermons. St. Augustine writes that good books are, as it were, so many "love-letters" the Lord sends us. In them He warns us of our dangers, teaches us the way of salvation, animates us to suffer adversity, enlightens us and inflames us with Divine love. Whoever, then, desires to acquire divine love and to be holy, should often read those letters of Paradise. Oh, how many Saints have, by the reading of a spiritual book, been induced to forsake the world and to give themselves to God! St. Augustine, St. Ignatius, St. John Colombino, and many more. "My God," exclaims St. Augustine, "the examples of Thy servants, when I meditated on them, consumed my tepidity and inflamed me with Thy holy love."

But to draw great fruit from Spiritual Reading:

(1) You should recommend yourself beforehand to God that He may enlighten the mind while you read. It has already been said that in Spiritual Reading the Lord condescends to speak to us; and therefore, in taking up the book, we should pray to God in the words of Samuel: Speak, Lord, for thy servant heareth (1 Kings, iii. 9). Speak, O my God, for I wish to obey Thee in all Thou shalt make known to me to be Thy will.

(2) You should read, not to acquire learning, or to indulge curiosity, but for the sole purpose of advancing in divine love. To read for the sake of mere knowledge is not Spiritual Reading, but rather, at that time, a study unprofitable to the soul. It is still worse to read through curiosity, as certain people do, who devour books, seeking only to finish them in a short time to gratify curiosity. All the time devoted to such reading is time lost. St. Gregory says that many read, and read a great deal, but because they read from curiosity they rise from the reading as hungry as if they had not been reading.

(3) You should therefore read pious books slowly and with attention. "Nourish your soul with divine reading," says St. Augustine. Now, to receive nourishment from food it must not be devoured, but well masticated. Masticate and ponder well what you read, applying to yourself what is inculcated there. And when what you read makes a lively impression on you, St. Ephrem counsels you to read it a second time. Imitate the bees that will not pass to another flower until they have gathered all the honey to be found in the first.

(4) When you receive any special light in your reading, or any instruction that penetrates the heart, it will be very useful to stop, and to raise the mind to God by making a good resolution, or a good act, or a fervent prayer. And at the end of your reading select some sentiment of devotion excited by what you have read and carry it away with you as a flower from a Garden of Delights.

Evening Meditation

THE SON OF GOD WAS LADEN WITH ALL OUR INIQUITIES.

I.

God, sending his own Son, in the likeness of sinful flesh and of sin, hath condemned sin in the flesh. (Rom. viii. 3).

Consider the humble state to which the Son of God chose to abase Himself. He vouchsafed to take upon Himself the form, not only of a servant, but of a sinful servant, appearing in the likeness of sinful flesh. Therefore, St. Bernard writes: "He assumed not merely the form of a servant, that He might be under subjection, but even that of a wicked servant, that He might be beaten." He would assume not only the condition of a servant-He Who was Lord of all; but even the appearance of a guilty servant-He who was the Saint of Saints. For this end He clothed Himself with that same flesh of Adam which had been infected with sin. Our Redeemer, to obtain salvation for us, offered Himself voluntarily to His Father to make satisfaction for all our sins: *He was offered because it was his own will.* (Is. liii. 7). And His Father loaded Him with all our crimes: *He hath laid on him the iniquities of us all.* (Ib. 6). And thus, behold the Divine Word, innocent, most pure and holy-behold Him, even as an Infant, charged with all the blasphemies, with all the impurities, with all the sacrileges, and all the other crimes of men; and in this way become, for the love of us, the object of Divine malediction, on account of the sins for which He had bound Himself to satisfy the Divine Justice.

O my innocent Lord, Mirror without spot, Love of the Eternal Father! Ah, no, chastisements and maledictions were not due to Thee; but they were due to me, a miserable sinner. Nevertheless, thou wouldst show to the world this excess of love, by sacrificing Thy life to obtain pardon and salvation for us, paying by Thy sufferings the penalties which we had deserved. May all creatures praise and bless Thy infinite mercy and goodness! I thank Thee on behalf of all men, but especially for myself; because as I have offended Thee more than others, so Thou hast suffered the pains which Thou didst endure, more for me than for others. I curse a thousand times those sinful pleasures of mine, which have cost Thee so much suffering. But since Thou hast paid the price of my ransom, oh, let not the Blood which Thou hast shed for me be lost to me. I am sorry that I have despised Thee, O my Love; but, oh, give me more sorrow.

II.

Jesus loaded Himself with as many maledictions as there ever have been, or ever will be mortal sins committed by all mankind. And in this state, He presented Himself to His Father when He came into the world. Yes, even from the commencement of His life, he presented Himself as a criminal and a debtor for all our misdeeds, and as such was condemned by His Father to die upon a Cross as a malefactor, and accursed. God hath condemned sin in the flesh. (Rom. viii. 3). Oh, if the Eternal Father had been capable of feeling grief, what anguish would He not have endured, at seeing Himself obliged to treat as a criminal, and the most, monstrous criminal in the world, this innocent Son, His beloved One, who was so worthy of all His love! Behold the Man! said Pilate, when he showed Jesus to the Jews, in order to move them to pity for this innocent One so cruelly treated. Behold the Man! the Eternal Father seems to say to us all, showing Him to us in the stable of Bethlehem: -- "This poor Infant, whom you behold, O men, laid in a manger for beasts, and lying upon straw, is My beloved Son, Who has come to take upon Himself your sins and your sorrows! Love Him, then, because He is most worthy of your love, and you are under the greatest obligations to love Him."

Make me know the evil I have committed in offending Thee, my Redeemer and my God, Who hast suffered so much to oblige me to love Thee! I love Thee, O infinite Goodness, but I desire to love Thee more; I desire to love Thee as much as Thou deserves to be loved. Make Thyself loved, O my Jesus, make Thyself loved by me and by all men; for well dost Thou deserve to be loved. Enlighten, I pray Thee, the minds of those sinners who will not know Thee or will not love Thee; make them comprehend how much Thou hast done for love of them, and the desire Thou hast for their salvation. Most holy Mary, pray for me and for all sinners; obtain for us light and grace to love thy Son, who has loved us so much.

Second Sunday of Advent

Morning Meditation

THE ADVANTAGES OF TRIBULATIONS

What things soever were written were written for our learning, that through patience and the comfort of the scriptures we might have hope. (Epistle of Sunday. Rom. xv. 4-13).

In tribulations God enriches His beloved souls with the greatest graces. It is in his chains that St. John comes to the knowledge of the works of Jesus Christ. Let us believe that these scourges of the Lord, with which we are chastised have happened for our amendment and not for our destruction (Judith, viii. 27).

I.

By tribulation we atone for the sins we have committed much better than by voluntary works of penance. "Be assured," says St. Augustine, "that God is a physician, and that tribulation is a salutary medicine." Oh, how great is the efficacy of tribulation in healing the wounds caused by our sins! Hence the same Saint rebukes the sinner who complains of God for sending him tribulations. "Why," he says, "do you complain? What you suffer is a remedy, not a punishment." Job called those men happy whom God corrects by tribulation; because He heals them with the very hands by which He strikes and wounds them. *Blessed is the man whom God corrects... For He wounds and cures. He strikes, and His hand shall heal* (Job v. 17). Hence, St. Paul gloried in his tribulations: *We glory also in tribulations* (Rom. v. 3).

Tribulations enable us to acquire great merits before God, by giving us opportunities of exercising the virtues of humility, of patience, and of resignation to the divine will. The

Blessed John of Avila used to say that one Blessed be God in adversity is worth more than a thousand in prosperity. "Take away," says St. Ambrose, "the contests of the Martyrs, and you have taken away their crowns." Oh, what a treasure of merit is acquired by patiently bearing insults, poverty, and sickness! Insults from men were the great object of the desires of the Saints, who sought to be despised for the love of Jesus Christ, and thus to be made like unto Him.

My Jesus, I have hitherto offended Thee grievously by resisting Thy holy Will. This gives me greater pain than if I had suffered every other evil. I repent of it and I am sorry for it with my whole heart. I deserve chastisement: I do not refuse it: I accept it. Preserve me only from the chastisement of being deprived of Thy love, and then do with me what Thou pleases. I love Thee, my dear Redeemer! I love Thee, my God! And because I love Thee, I wish to do whatever Thou wishes. Amen.

II.

St. Francis de Sales used to say: "To suffer constantly for Jesus is the science of the Saints; we shall thus soon become Saints." It is by sufferings that God proves His servants and finds them worthy of Himself. God hath tried them and found them worthy of himself (Wis. iii. 5). Whom, says St. Paul, the Lord loveth he chastises; and he scourges every son whom he receives (Heb. xii. 6). Hence, Jesus Christ once said to St. Teresa: "Be assured that the souls dearest to My Father are those who suffer the greatest afflictions." Hence Job said: If we have received good things at the hand of God, why should we not receive evil? (Job ii. 10). If we have gladly received from God the goods of this earth, why should we not receive more cheerfully tribulations, which are far more useful to us than worldly prosperity? St. Gregory informs us that, as a flame fanned by the wind increases, so the soul is made perfect when she is oppressed by tribulations.

In fine, the scourges of Heaven are sent, not for our injury, but for our good. Let us believe that these scourges of the Lord, with which, like servants, we are chastised, have happened for our amendment and not for our destruction (Judith, viii. 27). "God," says St. Augustine, "is angry when He does not scourge the sinner." When we see a sinner in tribulation in this life, we may infer that God wishes to have mercy on him in the next, and that he exchanges eternal for temporal chastisement. But miserable the sinner whom the Lord does not punish in this life! For those whom He does not chastise here, He treasures up His wrath, and for them He reserves eternal chastisement.

O Will of God, Thou art my love! O Blood of Jesus, Thou art my hope! I hope to be from this day forward always united to Thy Divine Will. It shall be my guide, my desire, my love, my hope. Thy Will be done! My Jesus, through Thy merits grant me the grace always to repeat: Thy Will be done! Thy Will be done!

Ah, my blessed Mother Mary, thou hast been pleased to suffer so much for me, obtain for me, by thy merits, sorrow for my sins, and patience under the trials of life which will always be light in comparison with my demerits for I have often deserved hell. Immaculate Virgin, from thee do I hope for help to bear all crosses with patience. Amen.

Spiritual Reading

THE POVERTY OF THE INFANT JESUS

What went ye out to see? A man clothed in soft garments? Behold they that are clothed in soft garments are in the houses of kings. (Gospel of Sunday. Matt. xi. 2-10).

Instead of soft garments the Infant Jesus has but a few poor, rough, cold, damp rags. "The Creator of the Angels," says St. Peter Damian, "is not said to be clothed in purple but to have been wrapped in rags." Everything that is in Heaven and on earth is God's: *The world is mine, and the fulness thereof* (Ps. xlix. 12). But even this is little. Heaven and earth are but the least portions of the riches of God. The riches of God are infinite, and can never fail, because His riches do not depend on others, but He, who is the Infinite Good, possesses them Himself. For this reason, it was that David said: *Thou art my God, for thou hast no need of my goods* (Ps. xv. 2). Now this God, who is so rich, made Himself poor by becoming Man, that He might thereby make us poor sinners rich: *Being rich, he became poor for your sakes; that through his poverty you might be rich* (2 Cor. viii. 9).

What! a God become poor? And why? Let us understand the reason. The riches of this world can be nothing but dust and mire; but it is mire that so completely blinds men that they can no longer see which are the true riches. Before the coming of Jesus Christ, the world was full of darkness because it was full of sin: *All flesh had corrupted its way upon the earth* (Gen. vi. 12). Mankind had corrupted the law and reason, so that, living like brutes, intent only on acquiring the riches and pleasures of this world, men cared no more for the riches of eternity. But the divine mercy ordained that the very Son of God

Himself should come down to enlighten these blind creatures: *To them that dwelt in the region of the shadow of death light is risen* (Is. ix. 2).

Jesus was called the Light of the Gentiles: *A light for the revelation of the Gentiles* (Luke ii. 32); *The light shineth in darkness* (Jo. i. 5). Thus did the Lord from the first promise to be Himself our Master, and a Master Who should be seen by us; Who should teach us the way of salvation, which consists in the practice of all the virtues, and especially that of holy poverty: *And thy eyes shall see thy Teacher*. Moreover, this Master was not only to teach us by His words, but still more by the example of His life.

St. Bernard says that poverty was not to be found in Heaven, it existed only on earth; but that man, not knowing its value, did not seek after it. Therefore, the Son of God came down from Heaven to this earth and chose it for His companion throughout His whole life, that by His example He might also render it precious and desirable to us: "Poverty was not found in Heaven, but she was well known on earth, and men knew not her excellence. So, the Son of God loved her and came down from Heaven to take her to Himself, that we might learn to value her when we see how He regards her." And behold our Redeemer as an Infant, who at the very beginning of His life made Himself a Teacher of poverty in the Cave of Bethlehem; which is expressly called by the same St. Bernard the School of Christ, and by St. Augustine the Grotto of Doctrine.

For this end was it decreed by God that the Edict of Caesar should come forth; namely, that His Son should not only be born poor, but the poorest of men, causing Him to be born away from His own house, in a cave which was inhabited by animals. Other poor people, who are born in their own houses, have certainly more comforts in the way of clothes, of fire, and the assistance of persons who lend their aid, even if it is out of compassion. What son of a poor mother was ever born in a stable? In a stable beasts only are born. St. Luke relates how it happened. The time comes that Mary was to be delivered, Joseph goes to seek some lodging for her in Bethlehem. He goes about and enquires at every house, and he finds none. He tries to find one in an inn, but neither there does he find any: *There was no room for them in the inn* (Luke ii. 7). So that Mary is obliged to take shelter and bring forth her Son in that cave.

When the sons of princes are born, they have warm rooms prepared for them, adorned with hangings, silver cradles, the finest clothes, and they are waited on by the highest nobles and ladies in the kingdom. The King of Heaven, instead of a warm and beautiful room, has nothing but a cold grotto, whose only ornament is the grass that grows there; instead of a bed of feathers, He has nothing but a little hard, sharp straw; instead of fine garments He has but a few poor, rough, cold and damp rags: "The Creator of Angels," writes St. Peter Damien, "is not said to have been clad in purple, but to have been wrapped in rags. Let worldly pride blush at the resplendent humility of the Savior." Instead of a fire, and of the attendance of great people, He has but the warm breath and the company of two animals; finally, in place of the silver cradle, He must lie in a vile manger. "What is this," said St. Gregory of Nyssa, "the King of kings, who fills Heaven and earth with His presence finds no better place in which to be born than a stable for beasts! He Who encompasses all things in His embrace is laid in the manger of brute cattle." Yes, this King of kings for our sake wished to be poor and the poorest of all. Even the children of the poor have milk enough provided for them, but Jesus Christ wished to be poor even in this; for the milk of Mary was miraculous, and she received it not naturally, but from Heaven, as the Holy Church teaches us: "The Virgin gave Him milk from a breast filled from Heaven." And God, in order to comply with the desire of His Son, who wished to be poor in everything, did not provide Mary with milk in abundance, but only with as much as would barely suffice to sustain the life of her Son; whence the same Holy Church says: "He was fed on a little milk."

And Jesus Christ, as He was born poor, continued in poverty all His life long.

Evening Meditation

GOD SENDS HIS SON TO DIE IN ORDER TO RESTORE US TO LIFE.

I.

But God, who is rich in mercy, for his exceeding charity wherewith he loved us, even when we were dead in sins, hath quickened us together in Christ (Eph. ii. 4, 5).

Consider that sin is the death of the soul because this enemy of God deprives us of Divine grace, which is the life of the soul. We, therefore, miserable sinners, were already by our sins dead and condemned to hell. God, through the immense love which He bears to our souls, determined to restore us to life; and how did He do so? He sent His only begotten Son into the world to die, in order that by His death He might restore us to life.

With reason therefore does the Apostle call this work of love exceeding charity; too much love; yes, indeed, for man could never have had hope to receive life in such a loving manner if God had not found this means of redeeming him: Having obtained eternal redemption (Heb. ix. 12). All men were therefore dead -- there was no remedy for them. But the Son of God, through the bowels of His mercy has come down from Heaven, the Orient from on High, and has given us life. Justly, therefore, does the Apostle call Jesus Christ our Life: When Christ shall appear, who is your life (Col. iii. 4).

O my Jesus! If Thou hadst not accepted and suffered death for me, I should have remained dead in my sins, without hope of salvation and without the power of ever loving Thee. But though Thou hast obtained life for me by Thy death, I have again many times voluntarily forfeited it by returning to sin. Thou didst die to gain my heart to Thyself, and I by my rebellion have made it a slave of the devil. I lost all reverence for Thee, and I said that I would no longer have Thee for my Master. All this is true; but it is also true that Thou desires not the death of the sinner, but that he should be converted and live; and therefore, didst Thou die to give us life. I repent of having offended Thee, my dearest Redeemer; and do Thou pardon me through the merits of Thy Passion; give me Thy grace.

II.

Behold, our Redeemer clothed with flesh and become an Infant, says: I have come that they may have life, and may have it more abundantly (Jo. x. 10). For this end He accepted death, that He might give us life. It is but reasonable, therefore, that we should live only to God, Who has condescended to die for us: Christ died, that they who live may not live to themselves, but unto him who died for them (2 Cor. V. 15). It is reasonable that Jesus Christ should be the only Sovereign of our hearts since He has spent His blood and His life to gain them to Himself: To this end Christ died and rose again, that he might be Lord of both the dead and of the living (Rom. xiv. 9). O my God! who would be so ungrateful a wretch as to believe it an Article of Faith that God died to secure his love, and yet refuse to love Him, and, renouncing His friendship, choose voluntarily to make himself a slave of hell?

O Lord, give me that life which Thou hast purchased for me by Thy death, and henceforth mayst Thou have entire dominion over my heart. Never let the devil have possession of it again; he is not my God, he does not love me, and has not suffered anything for me. In past times he was not the true sovereign, but the robber of my soul; Thou alone, my

Jesus, art my true Lord, who hast created and redeemed me with Thy Blood; Thou alone hast loved me, and oh, how much! It is therefore only just that I should be Thine alone during the life that remains to me. Tell me what Thou wouldst have me to do; for I will do it all. Chastise me as Thou wilt; I accept everything Thou sends me; only spare me the chastisement of living without Thy love; make me love Thee, and then dispose of me as Thou wilt. Most holy Mary, my refuge and consolation, recommend me to thy Son; His death and thy intercession are all my hope.

Monday--Second Week of Advent

Morning Meditation

CONSIDERATIONS ON THE RELIGIOUS STATE. I.

Consider that salvation is assured to souls who enter the Religious state.

God has placed us in the world and keeps us here in life, not to acquire the perishable goods of earth, but the eternal goods of Heaven. The end is life everlasting (Rom. vi. 22). But the misfortune is that in the world men think very little indeed, if at all, of eternal life, and only dream of acquiring honors and pleasures, and this is the reason why so many souls perish.

I.

To understand the importance of our eternal salvation it is enough to have Faith and to consider we have only one soul, and if that is lost, all is lost were a man even master of the whole world. What doth it profit a man if he gain the whole world, and suffer the loss of his soul? (Matt. xvi. 26). This great maxim of the Gospel has induced many youths to shut themselves up in cloisters, others to live in deserts, and others to give up their lives for Jesus Christ. For, said they, what does it profit us to possess the whole world, and all the goods of this world, in this present life, which must soon finish, and then be damned and be miserable in the life to come, which will never end? All those rich men, all those princes and emperors, who are now in hell -- what have they now of all they enjoyed in this life but greater torment and a greater despair? Miserable beings! They lament now and say: All those things have passed away like a shadow (Wis. v. 9). For them all is passed like a shadow, like a dream, and that lamentation, which is their lot has lasted already many years, and will last throughout all eternity. The fashion of this world passes away (1 Cor.

vii. 51). This world is a scene which lasts but a short time; happy he who plays in this scene that part which will afterwards make him happy in the life which will never end. When he shall then be contented, honored, and a prince in Paradise, so long as God shall be God, little will he care for having been in this world -- poor, despised and in tribulation. For this end alone God has placed us on this earth, and keeps us here in life, not to acquire transitory but eternal goods: The end is life everlasting.

O my God! How have I ever deserved this great mercy, that, having left so many others to live in the midst of the world, Thou hast willed to call me, who have offended Thee more than others, and deserved, more than they, to be deprived of Thy divine light, to enjoy the honor of living as a friend in Thy own house! O Lord, grant that I may understand this exceeding grace, which Thou hast bestowed on me, that I may always thank Thee for it, as I purpose and hope to do always during my life and throughout eternity, and do not permit me to be ungrateful for it. Since Thou hast been so liberal towards me, and hast in Thy love preferred me to others, it is but just that more than others I should serve and love Thee.

II.

With desolation is all the land made desolate, because there is none that considered in the heart (Jer. xii. 11). How few are they who reflect on death, by which for us the scene is closed; on the eternity which awaits us; on what God has done for our sake! And hence it comes that these miserable beings live in blindness and carelessly, far from God, having their eyes, like the beasts, intent only on earthly things, without remembering God, without desiring His love, and without a thought of eternity. Therefore, they die afterwards an unhappy death, which will be the beginning of eternal death and endless misery. Then it is they will open their eyes; but it will be only to lament over their own foolishness.

This is the great means of salvation, which is found in Religion, namely, continual meditation on the eternal truths. Remember thy last end and thou shalt never sin (Eccles. vii. 40). In well-regulated Religious houses this is done every day, and even several times a day. And therefore, in the light of divine things, which there shines continually, it is morally impossible to live, at least for a long time, far from God, and without keeping one's account ready for eternity.

O my Jesus! Thou wouldst have me to be wholly Thine, and to Thee I give myself entirely. Accept me, and henceforward keep me as Thy own, since I am no longer mine. Finish Thou the work which Thou hast begun. Thou hast called me to Thy house because Thou wilt have me become a Saint. Make me then what Thou wilt have me. Do it, O Eternal Father! for the love of Jesus Christ, in Whom is all my confidence. I love Thee, my sovereign Good, I love Thee. O infinite Goodness! I love Thee alone and will love Thee forever. O Mary, my hope, succor me, and obtain for me to be always faithful and thankful to my Lord.

Spiritual Reading

COUNSELS CONCERNING A RELIGIOUS VOCATION

I. HOW IMPORTANT IT IS TO FOLLOW A VOCATION TO THE RELIGIOUS LIFE

It is evident our Eternal Salvation depends principally upon the choice of a state of life. Father Louis of Granada calls the choice of a state the main spring of the whole life. Just as in a clock when the main spring is out of order the whole clock goes wrong, so in the order of our salvation, if we fail to enter the state to which we are called, the whole life, as St. Gregory Nazianzen says, is in disorder.

If then, we wish to make our eternal salvation secure we must, in our choice of a state, embrace the Divine Vocation in which God has prepared for us the efficacious means of salvation. For, as St. Cyprian says: "the grace of the Holy Ghost is given according to the order of Divine Providence and not according to our own caprice." And in this sense St. Paul writes: Everyone has his proper gift from God (1 Cor. vii. 7). That is, God gives to each one his Vocation, chooses the state in which He wills him to be saved. And this is the order of predestination described by the same Apostle: Whom he predestinated, them he also called: and whom he called them he also justified ... and them he also glorified (Rom. viii. 30).

And here we must remark that in the world there are some who pay little attention to this question of Vocation. They think it to be all the same, whether they live in the state to which God calls them, or in that which they themselves choose, following their own inclinations, and this is why so many lead a bad life and lose their souls. It is certain that this is the principal point with regard to the acquisition of eternal life. Vocation is followed by justification, and justification by glorification, that is, eternal life. He who disturbs this order and breaks this chain of salvation shall not save his soul. With all his labors and with all the good he may do, the words of St. Augustine apply to him: "Thou run well, but off the road," that is, out of the way in which God called you to walk for attaining salvation. The Lord does not accept sacrifices, which are purely of our own making: But to Cain and his offerings he had no respect (Gen. iv. 5). Rather He threatens with great chastisement those who, when He calls them, turn their backs on Him to follow the counsels of their own caprice. Woe to you apostate children, He says through Isaias, that you would take counsel and not from me, and would begin a web and not by my spirit (Is. xxx. 1).

A divine call to a more perfect life is undoubtedly a special and a very great grace which God does not give to all; hence He has much reason to be displeased with those who despise it. How greatly would a prince not think himself offended, if he should call one of his vassals to serve near his person, and he should refuse to obey! And should God not resent like conduct? Ah! He resents it very much indeed, and threatens, saying: Woe to him that gainsay his Maker (Ib. xiv. 9). The word "Woe" in Scripture signifies eternal damnation. The chastisement of the disobedient will begin even in this life, in which he will always be unquiet, for, says Job, Who hath resisted him and hath had peace? (Job ix. 4). He will be deprived of those abundant and efficacious helps necessary to lead a good life. For which reason the Theologian, Habert, writes "He will with great difficulty be able to work out his salvation." He will with great difficulty save himself; for, being like a member out of its proper place, he will with great difficulty be able to live well. "In the body of the Church," adds the learned author, "he will be like a limb of the human body out of its place, which may be able to perform its functions, but only with difficulty and in an awkward manner." Hence, he concludes: "And although, absolutely speaking, he may be saved, he will with difficulty enter upon and advance in the road and use the means of salvation." The same thing is taught by St. Bernard and St. Leo. St. Gregory, writing to the Emperor Maurice, who by an Edict had forbidden soldiers to become Religious, says that this was an unjust law, which shut the gates of Paradise to many, because many would save themselves in Religion who would otherwise perish in the world.

Father Lancicius tells us there was in the Roman College a youth of great talents. While he was doing the Religious Exercises, he asked his confessor whether it was a sin not to correspond to a Vocation to the Religious life. The confessor replied that it was not a grievous sin, because a call to perfection is a counsel and not a precept, but he would expose his salvation to great danger as had happened to many who, not following their Vocation, were in the end, lost. He did not obey the call. He went to study in Macerata, where he soon began to omit prayer and Holy Communion, and finally gave himself up to a bad life. Soon after, coming one night from the house of a wicked woman, he was mortally wounded by a rival. Some priests ran to his assistance, but he had expired before they arrived, just in front of the college. By this circumstance God wished to show that this chastisement came upon him for having neglected his Vocation.

Father Pinamonti relates in his treatise, Victorious Vocation, that a Novice who had resolved to leave the Novitiate had a vision. He saw Christ on a throne in wrath, ordering his name to be blotted out of the Book of Life. He was so terrified that he persevered in his Vocation.

How many similar examples are there not to be found in books! And how many unhappy youths shall we not see damned on the Day of Judgment for not having followed their Vocation! Such are rebels against the divine light, as the Holy Ghost says: They have been rebellious to the light, they have not known his ways (Job xxiv. 13), and they will be justly punished by losing the light; and because they would not walk in the way shown them by the Lord, they shall walk without light in that chosen by their own caprice and perish. Behold I will declare my spirit to you (Prov. i. 23). Behold the Call of God -- but because they fail to follow it, God adds: Because I called you and you refused ... you have despised all my counsel ... I also will laugh at your destruction, and I will mock when that shall come upon you which you feared. Then shall you call upon me, and I will not hear; they shall rise in the morning and shall not find me. Because they have hated instruction and received not the fear of the Lord, nor consented to my counsel, but despised all my reproof (Ib. i. 24, 26, 28, 80). And this signifies that God will not hear the prayers of him who has neglected to obey His voice. St. Augustine says: "They who have despised the will of God which invited them, shall feel the will of God when it becomes its own avenger."

Evening Meditation

THE LOVE THAT THE SON OF GOD HAS SHOWN US IN THE REDEMPTION

I.

He hath loved us, and hath delivered himself for us (Eph. v. 2).

Consider that the Eternal Word is that God Who is so infinitely happy in Himself that His happiness cannot be greater than it is, nor could the salvation of all mankind have added anything to it; nor could the loss of souls have diminished it; and yet He has done and suffered so much to save us miserable worms that if His beatitude, as St. Thomas says, had depended on that of man, He could not have done or suffered more: "As if without him He could not be happy." And, indeed, if Jesus Christ could not have been happy without redeeming us, how could He have humbled Himself more than He has done, in taking upon Himself our infirmities, the miseries of infancy, the troubles of human life, and a death so barbarous and ignominious?

None but God could love to so great an excess such wretched sinners as we are, and who are so unworthy of being loved. A devout author says: "If Jesus Christ had permitted us to ask of Him to give us the greatest proof of His love, who would have ventured to ask of Him that He should become a Childlike unto us, that He should clothe Himself with all our miseries, and make Himself of all men the most poor, the most despised, and the most ill-treated, even to being put to death by the hands of executioners, and in the greatest torments upon an infamous gibbet, cursed and forsaken by all, even by His own Father, Who abandoned His Son that He might not abandon us in our ruin?"

But that which we should not have had the boldness even to think of, the Son of God has thought of and accomplished.

My Jesus, I should, indeed, do great injustice to Thy mercy and Thy love, if, after Thou hast given me so many proofs of the love Thou barest me, and the desire Thou hast to save me, I should still distrust Thy mercy and Thy love. My beloved Redeemer, I am a poor sinner; but Thou hast said that Thou didst come to seek sinners: I am not come to call the just, but sinners. (Matt. ix. 13). I am a poor infirm creature -- Thou came to cure the infirm, and Thou didst say: They that are whole need not the physician, but they that are sick (Luke v. 31). I was lost through my sins, but Thou didst come to save the lost: The son of man is come to save that which was lost (Matt. xviii. 11). What, then, can I fear, if I am willing to amend my life and to become Thine? I have only myself and my own weakness to fear; but my own weakness and poverty ought to increase my confidence in Thee, who hast declared Thyself to be the refuge of the destitute: The Lord is become a refuge for the poor (Ps. ix. 10).

II.

Even from His childhood He sacrificed Himself for us to sufferings, to opprobrium, and to death: He hath loved us, and hath delivered himself for us (Eph. v. 2). He loved us, and out of love He gave us Himself, in order that we, by offering Him as a Victim to the Father, in satisfaction for our debts, might through His merits obtain from the divine goodness all the graces that we desire; a Victim dearer to the Father than if we offered Him the lives of all men and of all the Angels. Let us therefore continually offer to God the merits of Jesus Christ, and through them let us seek and hope for every good.

I implore this favor of Thee, O my Jesus! Give me confidence in Thy merits, and grant that I may always recommend myself to God through Thy merits. Eternal Father, save me from hell, and first from sin, for the love of Jesus Christ; for the sake of the merits of this Thy Son enlighten my mind to obey Thy will; give me strength against temptations; grant me the gift of Thy holy love; and, above all, I beseech Thee to give me the grace to pray to Thee to help me, for the love of Jesus Christ, Who hast promised that Thou wilt grant to him who prays in His name whatever he asks of Thee. If I continue to pray to Thee in this way, I shall certainly be saved; but if I neglect it, I shall certainly be lost. Most holy Mary, obtain for me this great gift of prayer, and that I may persevere in recommending myself constantly to God, and also to thee, who dost obtain from God whatever thou wills.

Feast of the Immaculate Conception (8 December)

Morning Meditation

IT WAS BECOMING THAT THE ETERNAL FATHER SHOULD PRESERVE MARY FROM ORIGINAL SIN.

As the lily among thorns, so is my love among the daughters (Cant. ii. 2).

Great indeed was the injury entailed on Adam and on all his posterity by his accursed sin. But from this general misfortune God was pleased to exempt the Blessed Virgin, as the predestined Mother of His only begotten Son and the first-born of Grace. She was to crush the serpent's head and to be the sinless Mediatress of peace between men and God. Hence the Eternal Father could well say of His beloved Daughter: As the lily among thorns, so is my beloved among the daughters, always immaculate and always beloved.

I.

It was most becoming that God should preserve Mary from original sin for He destined her to crush the head of the infernal spirit which, by seducing our First Parents, brought death upon all men. This the Lord foretold: I will put enmities between thee and the woman, and thy seed and her seed; she shall crush thy head (Gen. iii. 15). But if Mary was that Valiant Woman brought into the world to conquer Lucifer, certainly it was not becoming that he should first conquer her and make her his slave. Reason would indeed demand that she should be preserved from all stain and even momentary subjection to her opponent. How then could God permit that she should first be the slave of the infernal serpent? Praised and ever blessed be God, Who, in His infinite goodness, pre-endowed

Mary with such great grace that, remaining always free from guilt of sin, she was ever able to beat down and confound the serpent's pride.

Besides this it was wholly becoming that the Eternal Father should create Mary, "the one and only daughter of life," free from the stain of original sin and always possessed by His grace, destined as she was to be the repairer of a lost world, Mediatress of peace between men and God. "O Blessed Virgin," says St. John Damascene, "thou was born that thou might minister to the salvation of the whole world." "Hail, reconciler of the whole world!" cries out St. Ephrem. "Hail, thou, who art appointed umpire between God and man!" cries St. Basil of Silucia.

Now it certainly would not be becoming to choose an enemy to treat of peace with the offended person, and still less an accomplice in the crime itself. St. Gregory says that "an enemy cannot undertake to appease his judge who is at the same time the injured party; for if he did, instead of appeasing him, he would provoke him to greater wrath." And, therefore, as Mary was to be the Mediatress of peace between men and God, it was of the utmost importance that she should not herself appear as a sinner and an enemy of God, but that she should appear in all things as a friend, and free from every stain. Hence it was becoming that God should preserve her from sin, that she might not appear guilty of the same fault as the men for whom she was to intercede.

Ah, my Immaculate Lady, I rejoice with thee on seeing thee enriched with so great purity. I thank our common Creator for having preserved thee from every stain of sin. Thou art all fair and there is not a spot in thee! (Cant. iv. 7). O most pure dove, all fair, all beautiful, always the friend of God! Ah, most sweet, most amiable, immaculate Mary, disdain not to cast thy compassionate eyes upon the wounds of my soul. Behold me, pity me, heal me! The happy day when I shall go to behold thy beauty in Paradise seems a thousand years off, so much do I long to praise and love thee more than I now do, my Mother, my Queen, my beloved, most sweet, most pure, immaculate Mary! Amen.

II.

But above all it was becoming that the Eternal Father should preserve this His daughter unspotted from Adam's sin, because He predestined her to be the Mother of His only-begotten Son. As Jesus was the first-born of God, the first-born of every creature (Col. i. 15), so was Mary, the destined Mother of God, always considered by Him as His first-born by adoption, and therefore He always possessed her by His grace. The Lord possessed me in the beginning of his ways (Prov. viii. 22). For the honor, therefore, of His Son, it was becoming that the Father should preserve the Mother from every stain of sin. When David was planning the Temple of Jerusalem, on a scale of magnificence worthy of God, he said: For a house is being prepared not for man but for God (1 Par. xxix. 1). How much more reasonable, then, is it not, to suppose that the Sovereign Architect, who destined Mary to be the Mother of His own Son, adorned her soul with all the most precious gifts that she might be a dwelling worthy of a God!

We know that a man's highest honor is to be born of noble parents. And the glory of children are their fathers (Prov. xvii. 6). How, then, can we suppose that God Who could cause His Son to be born of a noble Mother by preserving her from sin, would, on the contrary, permit Him to be born of one infected by it, and thus leave it always in Lucifer's power to reproach Him with the shame of having a mother who had once been his slave and the enemy of God. No, certainly, the Eternal Father did not permit this; but He well provided for the honor of His Son by preserving His Mother always immaculate, that she might be a Mother worthy of such a Son. And the Holy Church herself assures us of this: "O Almighty and Eternal God Who by the co-operation of the Holy Ghost, didst prepare the body and soul of the glorious Virgin Mother Mary, that she might become a worthy habitation for Thy Son."

Ah, my most beautiful Lady, I rejoice in seeing thee, by thy purity and thy beauty, so dear to God. I thank God for having preserved thee from every stain. O thou, who from the first moment of thy life didst appear pure and beautiful before God, pity me, who not only was born in sin, but have again since Baptism stained my soul with crimes. What grace will God ever refuse thee? Immaculate Virgin, thou hast to save me. Amen.

Spiritual Reading

IT WAS BECOMING THAT THE SON SHOULD PRESERVE HIS MOTHER FROM ORIGINAL SIN.

In the second place it was becoming that the Son should preserve Mary from sin, as being His Mother. No man can choose his mother; but should such a thing ever be granted to anyone, who is there who, if able to choose a queen, would wish for a slave? Or if able to choose a friend of God, would wish for an enemy? If, then, the Son of God alone could choose a Mother according to His own Heart and His own liking, we must consider, as a matter of course, that He chose one worthy of God. St. Bernard says, "that the Creator of men becoming man, must have Himself selected a Mother who He knew would be worthy of Him." As it was becoming that a most pure God should have a Mother pure from all sin, He created her spotless. Here we may apply the words of the Apostle to the Hebrews: For it was fitting that we should have such a high priest; holy, innocent, undefiled, separated from sinners (Heb. vii. 26). A learned author observes that, according to St. Paul, it was fitting that our Blessed Redeemer should not only be separated from sin, but also from sinners; according to the explanation of St. Thomas, who says, "that it was necessary that He, who came to take away sins, should be separated from sinners, as to the fault under which Adam lay." But how could Jesus Christ be said to be separated from sinners, if He had a Mother who was a sinner?

St. Ambrose says, "that Christ chose this vessel into which He was about to descend, not of earth, but from Heaven; and He consecrated it a temple of purity." This agrees with that which St. John the Baptist revealed to St. Bridget, saying: "It was not becoming that the King of Glory should repose otherwise than in a chosen vessel exceeding all men and angels in purity." And to this we may add that which the Eternal Father Himself said to the same Saint: "Mary was a clean, and an unclean vessel: clean, for she was all fair; but unclean because she was born of sinners, though she was conceived without sin, that My Son might be born of her without sin." And remark these last words: "Mary was conceived without sin." Not that Jesus Christ could have contracted sin; but that He might not be reproached with even having a Mother infected with it, who would consequently have been the slave of the devil.

The Holy Ghost says that the glory of a man is from the honor of his father, and a father without honor is the disgrace of the son (Ecclus. iii. 13). "Therefore, it was," says an ancient writer, "that Jesus preserved the body of Mary from corruption after death; for it would have been to His dishonor had that virginal flesh with which He had clothed Himself become the food of worms." For, he adds: "Corruption is a disgrace of human nature; and as Jesus was not subject to it, Mary was also exempted; for the flesh of Jesus is the flesh of Mary." But since corruption of her body would have been a disgrace for Jesus Christ, because He was born of her, how much greater would the disgrace have been, had He been born of a mother whose soul was once infected by the corruption of sin? For not only is it true that the flesh of Jesus is the same as that of Mary, "but," adds the same author, "the flesh of our Savior, even after His Resurrection, remained the same that He had taken from His Mother. The flesh of Christ is the flesh of Mary; and though it was glorified by the glory of His Resurrection, yet it remains the same that was taken from Mary." And now if this is true, supposing that the Blessed Virgin had been conceived in sin, though the Son could not have contracted its stain, nevertheless His having united flesh to Himself which once had been infected with sin, a vessel of uncleanness and subject to Lucifer, would always have been a dishonor to Him.

Mary was not only the Mother, but the worthy Mother of our Savior. She is called so by all the holy Fathers. St. Bernard says: "Thou alone was found worthy to be chosen as the one in whose virginal womb the King of kings should have His first abode." St. Thomas of Villanova says: "Before she conceived, she was already worthy to be the Mother of God." The Holy Church herself attests that Mary merited to be the Mother of Jesus Christ, saying: "The Blessed Virgin, who merited to bear in her womb Christ our Lord"; and St. Thomas Aquinas, explaining these words, says, that "the Blessed Virgin is said to have merited to bear the Lord of all; not that she merited His Incarnation, but that she merited, by the graces she had received, such a degree of purity and sanctity, that she could worthily be the Mother of God"; that is to say, Mary could not merit the Incarnation of the Eternal Word, but by divine grace she merited such a degree of perfection as to render her worthy to be the Mother of a God; according to what St. Augustine says: "Her singular sanctity, the effect of grace, merited that she alone should be judged worthy to receive a God."

And now, supposing that Mary was worthy to be the Mother of God, "what excellence and what perfection was there that did not become her?" asks St. Thomas of Villanova. St. Thomas says: "that when God chooses any one for a particular dignity, He renders him fit for it"; hence he adds: "that God, having chosen Mary for His Mother, He also by His grace rendered her worthy of this highest of all dignities." "The Blessed Virgin was divinely chosen to be the Mother of God, and therefore we cannot doubt that God had fitted her by His grace for this dignity; and we are assured of it by the Angel: For thou hast found grace with God; behold thou shalt conceive (Luke i. 50). And thence the Saint argues that "the Blessed Virgin never committed any actual sin, not even a venial one. Otherwise," he says, "she would not have been a mother worthy of Jesus Christ; for the ignominy of the Mother would also have been that of the Son, for He would have had a sinner for His mother." And now if Mary, on account of a single venial sin, which does not deprive a soul of divine grace, would not have been a mother worthy of God, how much more unworthy would she have been had she contracted the guilt of original sin, which would have made her an enemy of God and a slave of the devil? And this reflection it was that made St. Augustine utter those memorable words, that, when speaking of Mary for the honor of Our Lord, Whom she merited to have for her Son, he would not entertain even the question of sin in her; "for we know," he says, "that through Him, Who it is evident was without sin, and Whom she merited to conceive and bring forth, she received grace to conquer all sin."

It was no shame to Jesus Christ that He was contemptuously called by the Jews the Son of Mary, meaning that He was the Son of a poor woman: Is not his mother called Mary? (Matt. xiii. 55). He came into this world to give us an example of humility and patience. But, on the other hand, it would undoubtedly have been a disgrace should He have heard the devil say: "Was not His mother a sinner? Was He not born of a wicked mother, who was once our slave?" It would even have been unbecoming had Jesus Christ been born of a woman whose body was deformed, or crippled, or possessed by devils; but how much more would it not have been so, had He been born of a woman whose soul had been once deformed by sin, and in the possession of Lucifer!

Ah! indeed, God, who is Wisdom itself, well knew how to prepare Himself a becoming dwelling, in which to reside on earth: Wisdom hath built herself a house (Prov. ix. 1). The Most High has sanctified his own tabernacle. God will help it in the morning early (Ps. xlv. 5, 6). David says our Lord sanctified this His dwelling in the morning early; that is to say, from the beginning of her life, to render her worthy of Himself; for it was not becoming that a Holy God should choose Himself a dwelling that was not holy: Holiness becometh thy house (Ps. xcii. 5). The Holy Church sings: "Thou, O Lord, hast not disdained to dwell in the Virgin's Womb." Yes, for He would have disdained to have taken flesh in the womb of an Agnes, a Gertrude, a Teresa, because these virgins, though holy, were nevertheless for a time stained with original sin; but He did not disdain to become Man in the womb of Mary, because this beloved Virgin was always pure and free from the least shadow of sin, and was never possessed by the infernal serpent. And therefore, St. Augustine says: "the Son of God never made Himself a more worthy dwelling than Mary, who was never possessed by the enemy, nor despoiled of her ornaments." On the other hand St. Cyril of Alexandria asks: "Who ever heard of an architect who built himself a temple, and yielded up the first possession of it to his greatest enemy?"

Yes, says St. Methodius, speaking on the same subject, that Lord Who commanded us to honor our parents, would not do otherwise, when He became Man, then observe it, by giving His Mother every grace and honor: "He Who said, honor thy father and thy mother, that He might observe His own decree, gave all grace and honor to His Mother." Therefore, we must certainly believe that Jesus Christ preserved the body of Mary from corruption after death; for if He had not done so, He would not have observed the law, which, while it commands us to honor our mother, forbids us to show her disrespect. But how little would Jesus have guarded His Mother's honor, had He not preserved her from Adam's sin! "Certainly, that son would sin," says the Augustinian Father Thomas of Strasburg, "who, having it in his power to preserve his mother from original sin did not do so." "But that which would be a sin in us," continues the same author, "would certainly have been considered un-becoming in the Son of God, Who, whilst He could make His Mother immaculate, did it not." "Ah, no," exclaims Gerson, "since Thou, the supreme Prince, chooses to have a Mother, certainly Thou owes her honor. But now if Thou didst permit her, who was to be the dwelling-place of the all-pure God, to be in the abomination of original sin, certainly it would appear that the law was not well fulfilled."

"Moreover, we know," says St. Bernardine of Sienna, "that the Divine Son came into the world to redeem Mary more than all other creatures." There are two means by which a person may be redeemed, as St. Augustine teaches us: the one by raising him up after having fallen, and the other by preventing him from falling; and this last means is doubtless the more honorable. "He is more honorably redeemed," says the learned Suarez, "who is prevented from falling, than he who, after falling, is raised up"; for thus the injury or stain, which the soul always contracts in falling, is avoided. This being the case, we ought certainly to believe that Mary was redeemed in the more honorable way, and the one more becoming to the Mother of God, as St. Bonaventure remarks, "for it is to be believed that the Holy Ghost, as a very special favor, redeemed and preserved her from original sin by a new kind of sanctification, and this in the very moment of her Conception; not that sin was in her, but that it might otherwise have been." On the same subject Cardinal Cusano beautifully remarks, that "others had Jesus as a liberator, but to the most Blessed Virgin He was a pre-liberator"; meaning, that all others had a Redeemer Who delivered them from sin with which they were already defiled, but that the most Blessed Virgin had a Redeemer Who, because He was to become her Son, preserved her from ever being defiled by sin.

In fine, to conclude in the words of Hugo of St. Victor, the tree is known by its fruits. If the Lamb was always immaculate, the Mother must also have been always immaculate: "Such the Lamb, such the Mother of the Lamb; for the tree is known by its fruits." Hence this same Doctor salutes Mary, saying: "O worthy Mother of a worthy Son"; meaning, that no other than Mary was worthy to be the Mother of such a Son, and no other than Jesus was a worthy Son of such a Mother; and then he adds these words: "O fair Mother of Beauty itself, O high Mother of the Most High, O Mother of God!" Let us then address this most Blessed Mother in the words of St. Ildephonsus: "Suckle, O Mary, thy Creator, give milk to Him Who made thee, and Who made thee such that He could be made of thee." Amen.

Evening Meditation

IT WAS BECOMING THAT THE HOLY GHOST SHOULD PRESERVE MARY FROM ORIGINAL SIN.

I.

My sister, my spouse, is a garden enclosed, a fountain sealed up (Cant. iv. 12).

Since it was becoming that the Eternal Father should preserve Mary from sin as His daughter, and the Son as His Mother, it was also becoming that the Holy Ghost should preserve her as His Spouse. St. Augustine says that "Mary was that only one who merited to be called the Mother and Spouse of God." For St. Anselm asserts that the Divine Spirit, the Love itself of the Father and the Son, came corporally into Mary, and enriching her with singular grace above all creatures, rested in her and made her the Queen of Heaven and earth. The Holy Ghost shall come upon thee (Luke i. 35).

And now, had an excellent artist the power to make his bride in reality such as he would represent her in his picture, what pains would he not take to render her as beautiful as possible! Who, then, can say that the Holy Ghost did otherwise with Mary, when He could make her, who was to be His Spouse, as beautiful as it was becoming that she should be? Ah no, the Holy Ghost acted as it became Him to act, for this same Lord declares: Thou art all fair, O my love, and there is not a spot in thee (Cant. iv. 7).

The Holy Ghost signifies the same thing when He called this His Spouse an enclosed garden and a sealed fountain: My sister, my spouse, is a garden enclosed, a fountain sealed up -- a Spouse into whom no guile could enter, against whom no fraud of the enemy could prevail, and who was always holy in mind and body. "Thou art," says St. Bernard, "an enclosed garden into which has never entered the hand of sinners to pluck its flowers."

Ah, my immaculate Queen, fair dove, beloved of God, disdain not to cast thine eyes on the many stains and wounds of my soul. See me and pity me. God Who loves thee much, denies thee nothing, and thou knowest not how to refuse those who have recourse to thee. O Mary conceived without sin, pray for us who have recourse to thee.

II.

In Proverbs we read: Many daughters have gathered together riches, thou hast surpassed them all (Prov. xxxi. 29). If Mary has surpassed all others in the riches of grace, she must have had original justice as Adam and the Angels had it. In the Canticles we read: There are young maidens without number. One is my dove, my perfect one (in the Hebrew it is my entire, my immaculate one) is but one. She is the only one of her mother (Cant. vi. 7). All souls are daughters of divine grace, but amongst these Mary was the dove without the gall of sin, the perfect one without spot in her origin, the one conceived in grace.

Hence it is that the Angel, before she became the Mother of God, found her already full of grace, and saluted her: Hail, full of grace! (Luke i. 28). Grace was given partially to other Saints, but to the Blessed Virgin all grace was given. So much so that St. Thomas says: "Grace rendered not only the soul but even the flesh of Mary holy, so that the Blessed Virgin might be able to clothe the Eternal Word with it."

O immaculate and entirely pure Virgin Mary, Mother of God, Queen of the Universe, our own good Lady, thou art the advocate of sinners, the consolation of the world, the ransom of captives, the joy of the sick, the comfort of the afflicted, the refuge and salvation of the whole world. O most pure Virgin Mary, I venerate thy most holy heart which was the delight and resting place of God, thy heart overflowing with humility, purity, and divine love. Ah, my Mother, for the love of Jesus, take charge of my salvation. O Lady, deny not thy compassion to one to whom Jesus has not denied His Blood. O my Mother, abandon me not! Never, never cease to pray for me until thou see me safe in Heaven at thy feet, blessing and thanking thee forever. Amen.

Tuesday--Second Week of Advent

Morning Meditation

CONSIDERATIONS ON THE RELIGIOUS STATE. II.

Consider the happy death of a Religious.

Blessed are the dead who die in the Lord (Apoc. xiv. 13). And who are those blessed dead who die in the Lord if not Religious, who, at the end of their lives are found already dead to the world, since they have by their Vows already detached themselves from the world and all its goods. I leave all and choose Thee alone for my Treasure, O most pure Lamb of God and my most ardent Lover!

I.

Consider, my brother, your contentment, if following your Vocation, it will be your good fortune to die in the House of God. The devil will certainly represent to you that if you retire into the House of God, you may perhaps afterwards repent of having left your own house and your own country, and deprived your parents of the advantages which they might have expected from you. But ask yourself: Shall I, at the point of death, be sorry, or shall I rejoice at having followed my resolution? I beseech you therefore to imagine yourself already at the point of death, about to appear before the Tribunal of Jesus Christ. Reflect what, when reduced to that state, you would wish to have done. Perhaps to have pleased your parents, to have worked for your own family and your country, and then to die surrounded by brothers, and nephews, and relatives in your own house with the title of Pastor, Parish Priest, Canon, Bishop or a Minister of State, having done your own will? Or, on the other hand, to die in the House of God, assisted by your good brethren in Religion, who would encourage you in the passage to eternity, after having lived many years in Religion, humble, mortified, poor, far from parents, deprived of your own will and under obedience, and detached from everything in the world -- all which render death sweet and agreeable? "He who has been accustomed to deprive himself of the delights of the world," says St. Bernard. "Will not regret having done so when he has to leave it." Pope Honorius II., when dying, wished that he had remained in his monastery, occupied in washing the plates, and had not been Pope. Philip II. wished at his death that he had been a lay brother in some Religious Order, intent on serving God, and had not been a king. Phillip III, also King of Spain, said when he was dying: "Oh, that I had been in a desert, there to serve God, and that I had never been a monarch! For, had such been the case, I should now appear with more confidence before the Tribunal of Jesus Christ."

O my Lord Jesus Christ! Who, in order to obtain a happy death for me, hast chosen so bitter a death for Thyself -- since Thou hast loved me to such an extent as to have chosen me to follow more closely Thy holy life, to have me thus more intimately united with Thy loving Heart, bind me, I beseech Thee, wholly to Thee with the sweet cords of Thy love, that I may no more separate myself from Thee. O my beloved Redeemer! I wish to be grateful to Thee, and to correspond with Thy grace, but I fear my weakness may render me unfaithful. O my Jesus! Do not permit this. Let me die rather than abandon Thee or forget the peculiar affection Thou hast shown me.

II.

When then, hell tempts you about your Vocation, think of the hour of death, and set before your eyes that all-important moment upon which eternity depends. Thus, you will overcome all temptations; you will be faithful to God; and certainly you will not repent of it at the point of death, but will give thanks to the Lord, and die contented. Gerard, brother of St. Bernard, died singing at the very thought of dying in the House of God. Father Suarez, of the Society of Jesus, felt at his death so great consolation and sweetness at dying in Religion that he said: "I never thought it would be so sweet to die." Another good Religious, of the same Society, laughed when at the point of death; and being asked why he laughed, answered: "And why should I not laugh? Has not Jesus Christ Himself promised Paradise to him who leaves everything for His sake? Was it not He Who said: Everyone that has left house, or brethren, or sisters, or father, or mother, or wife or children or lands for my name's sake, shall receive a hundred-fold, and shall possess life-everlasting? (Matt. xix. 29). I have left all for God; God is faithful, He cannot fail in His promises; and so," he said, "why should I not rejoice and laugh, seeing myself assured of Paradise?" A certain

Lay-brother, who died some years ago, was asked, at his death, what he desired most? He answered: "I desire nothing but to die and to be united with God."

Father Januarius Sarnelli, a short time before his death, when conversing with God, was heard saying: "O Lord, thou knows that all I have done and all I have thought, has been for Thy glory; now I wish to go to see Thee face to face, if it please Thee so." And then, desiring his departure, he said: "Courage, I wish to enter into a sweet agony." He then began to converse affectionately with God, and shortly after placidly expired. There was a smile on his lips, and from his body came a sweet odor, which, as many attested, remained for several days in the room in which he had died.

St. Bernard, speaking of the happy state of Religious, had good reason to exclaim: "O secure life, in which death is expected without fear -- yea, sweetly desired and devoutly accepted!"

I love Thee, O my Savior! Thou art and shalt always be the only Lord of my heart and of my soul. I leave all and choose Thee alone for my Treasure, O most pure Lamb of God. O my most ardent Lover! My beloved is white and ruddy, chosen out of thousands (Cant. v. 10). Begone, ye creatures, my only Good is my God, He is my Love, my All. I love Thee, O my Jesus! and in loving Thee I will spend the remainder of my life, be it short, or be it long. I embrace Thee, I press Thee to my heart, and I wish to die united to Thee. I wish nothing else. Make me live always burning with Thy love, and when I shall have arrived at the end of my life, make me expire in an ardent act of love towards Thee.

Immaculate Virgin Mary, obtain this grace for me, I hope it from thee.

Spiritual Reading

COUNSELS CONCERNING A RELIGIOUS VOCATION

II. THE CALL OF GOD MUST BE OBEYED AND OBEYED WITHOUT DELAY.

Whenever, therefore, God calls us to a more perfect state, he who does not wish to expose his eternal salvation to great risk must then obey and obey promptly. Otherwise, he will hear from Jesus Christ the reproach of that young man who, when invited to follow Him, said: I will follow thee, Lord, but let me first take my leave of them that are at my house (Luke ix. 61). Upon which, Jesus told him he was not fit for Paradise: No man putting his hand to the plough and looking back is fit for the kingdom of God (Ib. 62). The lights which God gives are transient, not permanent gifts. Hence St. Thomas Aquinas says that the call of God to a more perfect state must be obeyed as quickly as possible -- quanto citius. He proposes in his Summa the question whether it would be praiseworthy to enter Religion without having asked the counsel of many and without long deliberation. He answers in the affirmative, saying that counsel and deliberation are necessary in doubtful matters, but not in this, which is certainly good, because Jesus Christ has counselled it in the Gospel, and the Religious State embraces most of the Counsels of Jesus Christ. What a wonderful thing! When there is question of entering Religion to lead a more perfect life, and one more free from the dangers of the world, men of the world will say that it is necessary to deliberate a long time before putting such a resolution into execution, to ascertain whether the Vocation comes from God or from the devil! But they do not talk thus when it is a question of accepting a place in the Magistracy, or a Bishopric, and so on, where there are so many dangers of losing one's soul. Then these men of the world do not say that many proofs are required that it is a true call from God.

But the Saints do not speak thus. St. Thomas says that even should a Vocation to Religion come from the devil, we should follow it as a good counsel, though coming from an enemy. St. John Chrysostom, as quoted by the same St. Thomas, says that God, when He gives such Vocations, wills that we should not delay, even for a moment, to follow them. Christ requires from us such an obedience that we should not delay an instant. And why this? Because, as God is much pleased to see a soul prompt in obeying Him, He opens His hand and fills that soul with His blessings. On the contrary, He is displeased with tardiness in obeying Him; He shuts His hand and withdraws His lights. Hence, the soul will follow its Vocation with difficulty, and will easily abandon it. Therefore, St. John Chrysostom says that when the devil cannot bring one to give up his resolution of consecrating himself to God, he at least seeks to make him defer the execution of it and esteems it a great gain if he can obtain the delay of one day, or even of an hour. And why? Because a day later, or even an hour later, other occasions presenting themselves, it will be less difficult for him to obtain still greater delay, until he who has been called, finding himself more feeble and less assisted by grace, gives way altogether and loses his Vocation. Therefore, St. Jerome gives to those who are called to quit the world this advice: "Make haste, I beseech you, and cut rather than untie the cable by which your barque is bound fast to the land." The Saint wished to say that as a man who should find himself in a boat on the point of sinking would seek to cut the rope rather than to untie it, so he who finds himself in the midst of the world ought to seek to get out of it as quickly as possible, in order to free himself from the danger which is so great in the world, of losing his soul.

Let us also hear what St. Francis de Sales writes, concerning Religious Vocation. It will confirm what has already been said, and what will be said hereafter: "To have a sign of a true Vocation, it is not necessary that our constancy be sensible, it suffices if it be in the superior part of our soul. And therefore, we must not judge that a Vocation is not true if, before it is actually followed, a person no longer feels those sensible movements which he felt in the beginning, and even should he feel a repugnance and coldness, which sometimes makes him waver, and it appears to him that all is lost. It is enough that the will remains constant in not abandoning the divine call, and that there remains some affection for this call. To know whether God wills one to become a Religious, one ought not to expect that God Himself should speak or send an Angel from Heaven to signify His will. And as little necessary is it that ten or twelve Doctors should examine whether the Vocation is to be followed or not. But it is necessary to correspond with the first movement of the inspiration, and to cultivate it, and then not to grow weary if disgust or coldness should follow; for, in acting thus, God will not fail to make all succeed to His glory.

Nor ought we to care much about what quarter the first movement comes. The Lord uses many means to call His servants. Sometimes He makes use of a sermon, at other times of the reading of good books. Some, as St. Anthony and St. Francis, have been called by hearing the words of the Gospel; others by means of afflictions and troubles that came upon them in the world, and which suggested to them the motive for leaving it. These persons, although they come to God only because they are disgusted with the world or have lost its favor, nevertheless, because they give themselves to Him with their whole will, become sometimes greater Saints than those who entered Religion with a more apparent Vocation. Father Platus relates that a nobleman, riding one day on a fine horse, and striving to make a great display in order to please some ladies whom he saw, was thrown from the horse into the mire from which he rose besmeared and covered with mud. He was so full of confusion at this accident that at the same moment he resolved to become a Religious, saying: "Treacherous world, thou hast mocked me, but I will mock thee. Thou hast played me a game, I will play thee another; for I will have no more peace with thee, and from this hour I resolve to forsake thee and to become a friar." And, in fact, he became a Religious and lived a holy life in Religion.

Evening Meditation

JESUS, THE MAN OF SORROWS FROM THE WOMB OF HIS MOTHER

I.

A man of sorrows, acquainted with infirmity. (Is. liii. 8).

Thus does the Prophet Isaias designate our Lord Jesus Christ -- the man of sorrows. Yes, because this Man was created on purpose to suffer, and from His infancy began to endure the greatest sorrows that any man had ever suffered. The first man, Adam, enjoyed for some time upon this earth the delights of the earthly Paradise; but the second Adam, Jesus Christ, did not pass a moment of His life without sorrows and anguish; for even as a Child He was afflicted by the foresight of all the sufferings and ignominy that He would have to endure during His life, and especially at His death, when He was to close that life immersed in a tempest of sorrow and opprobrium, as David had predicted: I am come into the depth of the sea, and a tempest hath overwhelmed me (Ps. lxviii. 3).

My sweetest Redeemer, when shall I begin to be grateful to Thy infinite goodness? When shall I begin to acknowledge the love that Thou hast borne me, and the sorrows Thou hast endured for me? Hitherto, instead of love and gratitude, I have returned Thee offences and contempt; shall I then continue to live always ungrateful to Thee, my God, Who hast spared nothing to acquire my love? No, my Jesus, it shall not be so. During the days that may yet remain to me I will be grateful to Thee; and Thou wilt, I trust, help me to be so. If I have offended Thee, Thy sufferings and Thy death are my hope. Thou hast promised to forgive the penitent. I repent with my whole soul of having despised Thee. Fulfil, therefore, Thy promise, my Beloved, and forgive me. O dearest Infant, I behold Thee in the manger already nailed to Thy Cross, which is constantly present to Thee, and which Thou dost already except for me. O my crucified Babe, I thank Thee for it, and I love Thee.

II.

Even from the womb of Mary, Jesus Christ accepted obediently the sacrifice which His Father had desired Him to make, even His Passion and Death: Becoming obedient unto death (Phil. ii. 8). So that even from the womb of Mary He foresaw the scourges and presented to them His flesh; He foresaw the thorns and presented to them His head; He foresaw the blows and presented to them His cheeks; He foresaw the nails and presented to them His hands and feet; He foresaw the Cross and offered His life. Hence it is true that even from His earliest infancy our Blessed Redeemer, every moment of His life, suffered a continual martyrdom; and He offered it every moment for us to His Eternal Father.

But what afflicted Him most was the sight of the sins which men would commit even after this painful Redemption. By His divine light He well knew the malice of every sin, and therefore did He come into the world to do away with all sins; but when He saw the immense number which would be committed, the sorrow that the Heart of Jesus felt was greater than all the sorrows that all men ever suffered or ever will suffer upon earth.

Stretched upon this straw, O my Jesus, suffering already for me, and preparing Thyself even now to die for the love of me, thou dost command and invite me to love Thee: Love the Lord thy God. And I desire nothing more than to love Thee. Since, therefore, thou wills that I should love Thee, give me all the love that Thou requires of me; love for Thee is Thy gift, and the very greatest gift Thou canst make to a soul. Accept, O my Jesus! for Thy lover a sinner Who has so greatly offended Thee. Thou didst come from Heaven to seek the lost sheep; do Thou, therefore, seek me, and I will seek none other but Thee. Thou desires my soul, and my soul desires nothing but Thee. Thou love him that loves Thee, and sayest: I love those that love me (Prov. viii. 17). I love Thee, do Thou also love me; and if Thou loves me, bind me to Thy love; but bind me so that I may never again be able to disengage myself from Thee. Mary, my Mother, do thou help me. Let it be thy glory also to see thy Son loved by a miserable sinner, who has hitherto so greatly offended Him.

WEDNESDAY--SECOND WEEK OF ADVENT

Morning Meditation

CONSIDERATIONS ON THE RELIGIOUS STATE. III

Consider the account which he will have to render to Jesus Christ on the Day of Judgment who does not follow his Vocation.

The grace of Vocation is a very rare grace which God grants only to a few. But the greater the grace, the greater will be the indignation of the Lord against him who does not correspond with it. He is the Lord. When He calls, He wishes to be obeyed, and obeyed promptly.

I.

The grace of Vocation to the Religious state is not an ordinary grace; it is a very rare one, which God grants only to a few. He hath not done so to every nation (Ps. cxlvii. 20). Oh, how much greater is this grace, to be called to a perfect life, and to become one of the households of God, than if one were called to be the king of any kingdom on this earth! For what comparison can there be between a temporal kingdom on this earth and the eternal kingdom of Heaven?

But the greater the grace, the greater will be the indignation of the Lord against him who has not corresponded with it, and the more rigorous will be His judgment on the day of account. If a king were to call a poor shepherd to his royal palace, to serve him among the noblemen of his court, what would not be the indignation of the king were he to refuse such a favor through unwillingness to leave his poor little hut and his little flock? God knows well the value of His graces, and therefore He chastises with severity those who despise them. He is the Lord; when He calls, He wishes to be obeyed, and obeyed promptly.

O Lord, thou hast shown me such an excess of bounty as to choose me from among so many others, to serve Thee in Thy own House with Thy most beloved servants. I know how great is that grace, and how unworthy of it I have been. Behold, I am now willing to correspond to so great a love. I will obey Thee. Since Thou hast been so liberal towards me as to call me when I did not seek Thee, and when I was so ungrateful, permit not that I should offer Thee that greater excess of ingratitude as to embrace again my enemy, the world, in which heretofore I have so oftentimes forfeited Thy grace and my eternal salvation, and thus to forsake Thee, Who hast shed Thy Blood and given Thy life for my sake. Since Thou hast called me, give me also the strength to correspond to the call. Already have I promised to obey Thee. I promise it again, but without the grace of perseverance I cannot be faithful to Thee. This perseverance I ask from Thee, and through Thy own merits it is that I wish it and hope to obtain it.

II.

When, therefore, by His inspiration, God calls a soul to a perfect life, if it does not correspond, He deprives it of His light, and abandons it to its own darkness. Oh, how many poor souls shall we see among the reprobate on the Day of Judgment for this very reason, that they were called and would not correspond!

Give thanks, then, to the Lord, who has invited you to follow Him; but if you do not correspond, tremble! Since God calls you to serve near His Person, it is a sign that He wishes to save you. But He will have you to be saved in that path only which He indicates to you and has chosen for you. If you wish to save yourself on a road of your own choosing, there is great danger that you will not be saved at all; for if you remain in the world, when God wishes you to be a Religious, He will not give you those efficacious helps prepared for you had you lived in His House, and without those you will not save yourself. *My sheep hear my voice* (Jo. x. 27). He who will not obey the voice of God shows that he is not, and will not be, one of His sheep, but in the Valley of Josaphat, he will be condemned with the goats.

Give me courage, O my Jesus, to vanquish the passions of the flesh, through which the devil seeks to induce me to betray Thee. I love Thee, O my Jesus! To Thee I consecrate myself entirely. I am already Thine; I will always be Thine. O Mary, my Mother and my hope, thou art the Mother of perseverance. This grace is only dispensed through thy hands; do thou obtain it for me. In thee do I confide.

Spiritual Reading

COUNSELS CONCERNING A RELIGIOUS VOCATION

III. THE MEANS TO BE EMPLOYED FOR PRESERVING A RELIGIOUS VOCATION

He, then, who wishes to be faithful to the Divine call, ought not only to resolve to follow it, but to follow it promptly, as soon as ever he can, if he does not wish to expose himself to the evident danger of losing his Vocation. Should he, of necessity, be forced to wait, he ought to use all diligence to preserve it, as the most precious jewel he could possess.

The means to preserve one's Vocation are three in number:

1. Secrecy;
2. Prayer;
3. Recollection.

A. Secrecy

Generally speaking, he must keep his Vocation secret from everybody except his spiritual Father, because, commonly, people of the world scruple not to say to young people who are called to the Religious state, that one may serve God anywhere, and therefore in the world also. And the wonder is that such propositions come sometimes out of the mouths of priests, and even of Religious, but of such only who have become Religious without a Vocation, or do not know what Vocation means. Most certainly he who is not called to the Religious state may serve God in every place, but not so he who is called to Religion, and then from his own inclination wishes to remain in the world; such a one, as I have said before, can with difficulty lead a good life, and serve God.

It is especially necessary not to speak about Vocation to parents.

It was, indeed, the opinion of Luther, as Bellarmine relates, that children entering Religion without the consent of their parents commit a sin. For, said he, children are bound to obey their parents in all things. But this opinion has generally been rejected by Councils and the Holy Fathers. The Tenth Council of Toledo expressly declares that it is lawful for children to become Religious without the consent of their parents, provided they have attained the age of fourteen years. Here are the words of the Council: "It shall not be lawful for parents to put their children in a Religious Order after they have attained their fourteenth year. After this age, it shall be lawful for children to take upon themselves the yoke of Religious observance, whether it be with the consent of their parents, or only the wish of their own hearts." The same is taught by St. Ambrose, St. Jerome, St. Augustine, St. Bernard, St. Thomas, and others, with St. John Chrysostom who writes: "When parents stand in the way of spiritual good, they ought not even to be recognized."

Some Doctors hold that when a child called by God to the Religious state can easily and securely obtain the consent of his parents, without any danger of their hindering him from following his Vocation, it is becoming that he should seek their blessing. This doctrine may be held speculatively, but not in practice, because in practice such a danger always exists. Hence it is well to discuss this point fully, in order to do away with the pharisaical scruples which some entertain.

It is certain that in the choice of a state of life, children are not bound to obey their parents. This is the common teaching of the doctors, with St. Thomas, who says: "Servants are not bound to obey their masters, or children their parents, with regard to contracting matrimony, preserving virginity, and such like things." Nevertheless, regarding the state of marriage, Father Pinamonti, in his Treatise on Religious Vocation, rightly holds the opinion of Sanchez, Comminchio, and others, who teach that a child is bound to take counsel of his parents, because in such matters they have more experience than the young, and generally do their duty. But, speaking of Religious Vocation, he adds that a child is not bound at all to take counsel of his parents, because in this matter they have no experience, and through interest, are commonly changed into enemies, as St. Thomas also remarks when speaking of Religious Vocation. "Frequently," he says "our friends according to the flesh are opposed to our spiritual good." For fathers often prefer that their children should be damned with them rather than be saved away from them. Hence, St. Bernard exclaims: "O hard father, O cruel mother, whose consolation is the death of their son, who wish rather that I perish with them than reign without them!"

God, says a grave author, Porrecta, when He calls a person to a perfect life wishes him to forget his father, saying: Hearken, O daughter, and see, and incline thine ear; and forget thy people and thy father's house (Ps. xliv. 11). By this, then, he adds, the Lord certainly admonishes us that he who is called ought by no means to allow the counsel of parents to intervene. "If God will have a soul, who is called by Him, to forget his father and his father's house, without doubt He suggests by this, that he who is called to the Religious state ought not, before he follows the call, to interpose the counsel of the carnal friends of his household."

St. Cyril, commenting on what Jesus Christ said to the youth mentioned above: No man putting his hand to the plough and looking back is fit for the kingdom of God (Luke ix. 61), says that he who asks for time to confer with his parents in reference to his Vocation is exactly the one who is declared by our Lord to be unfit for Heaven. "He looks back who seeks for delay that he may be able to confer with his parents." Hence, St. Thomas absolutely advises those who are called to Religion, to abstain from deliberating on their Vocation with their relatives: "From this deliberation, the relatives of the flesh are before all to be excluded; for it is said: Treat thy cause with thy friend (Prov. xxv. 9). Now our relatives are in this affair not our friends, but our enemies, according to the saying of our Lord: A man's enemies are they of his own household (Matt. x. 36)."

Evening Meditation

GRANDEUR OF THE MYSTERY OF THE INCARNATION

I.

And the Word was made flesh (St. John i. 14).

Our Lord sent St. Augustine to write upon the heart of St. Mary Magdalen de Pazzi the words, And the Word was made flesh. Oh, let us also pray the Lord to enlighten our minds, and to make us understand what an excess and what a miracle of love this is: that the Eternal Word, the Son of God, should have become Man for the love of us.

The Holy Church is struck with awe at the contemplation of this great Mystery: I considered thy works and was afraid. If God had created a thousand other worlds, a thousand times greater and more beautiful than the present, it is certain that this work would be infinitely less grand than the Incarnation of the Word: He hath showed might in his arm (Luke i. 51). To execute the great work of the Incarnation, it required all the omnipotence and infinite wisdom of God, to unite human nature to a Divine Person, and that a Divine Person should so humble Himself as to take upon Himself human nature. Thus God became Man, and Man became God; and hence, the Divinity of the Word being united to the soul and body of Jesus Christ, all the actions of this Man-God became divine: His prayers were divine, His sufferings divine, His infant cries divine, His tears divine, His steps divine, His members divine, His very Blood divine, which became, as it were, a fountain of health to wash out all our sins, and a Sacrifice of infinite value to appease the justice of the Father, Who was justly angered with men.

O Soul, O Body, O Blood of my Jesus! I adore you and thank you; you are my hope; you are the price paid to save me from hell, which I have so often merited. O my God! What a miserable and hopeless life would await me in eternity, if Thou, my Redeemer, hadst not thought of saving me by Thy sufferings and death! But how is it that souls, redeemed by Thee with so much love, knowing all this, can live without loving Thee, and can despise the grace which Thou hast acquired for them with so much suffering? And did not I also know all this? How, then, could I have offended Thee, and offended Thee so often? But I repeat it, Thy Blood is my hope. I acknowledge, my Savior, the great injuries that I have done Thee. Oh, that I had rather died a thousand times! Oh, that I had always loved Thee!

II.

And who, then, are these men? Miserable, ungrateful, and rebellious creatures! And yet for these God becomes Man; subjects Himself to human miseries; suffers and dies to save these unworthy sinners; He humbled himself, becoming obedient unto death, even to the death of the cross (Phil. ii. 8). O holy Faith! If Faith did not assure us of it, who would believe that a God of infinite majesty should abase Himself so far as to become a worm like us, to save us at the cost of so much suffering and disgrace, and of so cruel and shameful a death?

"O grace! O power of love!" cries out St. Bernard. O grace, which men could not even have imagined, if God Himself had not thought of granting it to us! O mercy! O infinite charity, worthy only of an infinite Bounty!

By Thy grace I now feel great sorrow for the offences I have committed against Thee; I feel within me an ardent desire of loving Thee; I feel fully resolved to lose everything rather than Thy friendship; I feel a love towards Thee that makes me abhor everything that displeases Thee. And this sorrow, this desire, this resolution, and this love, who is it that gives them to me? It is Thou, O Lord, in Thy great mercy. Therefore, my Jesus, this is a proof that Thou hast pardoned me; it is a proof that now Thou loves me, and that Thou wills me at all costs to be saved; Thou wills that I should be saved, and I will save myself principally to give Thee pleasure. Thou loves me, and I also love Thee; but my love is little indeed. Oh, give me more love; Thou deserves more love from me, for I have received from Thee more special favors than others: I pray Thee do Thou increase the flames of my love.

Most holy Mary, obtain for me that the love of Jesus may consume and destroy in me every affection that has not God for its object. Thou dost listen to the prayers of all that call on thee; listen to me also and obtain for me love and perseverance.

Thursday--Second Week of Advent

Morning Meditation

CONSIDERATIONS ON THE RELIGIOUS STATE. IV.

Consider the torments of the soul of one in hell who lost his Vocation.

He will say: O fool that I was! I might have become a great Saint! And if I had obeyed the Call of God I should certainly have become a Saint, and now I am damned without remedy! Make your choice, for God leaves it in your own hands, to be a great king in Paradise, or a reprobate in hell.

I.

The remorse for having lost, by one's own fault, some great good, or for having been the voluntary cause of some great evil to us, is so great that even in this life it is an insupportable torment. But what torment will that youth, called by the singular favor of God to the Religious state, feel in hell when he perceives that if he had obeyed God, he would have attained a high place in Paradise, and sees himself nevertheless confined in that prison of torments, without hope of remedy for this his eternal ruin! *Their worm dieth not* (Mark ix. 43).

This will be that worm, which, living always, will always gnaw his heart by continual remorse. Fool that I was! He will say, I might have become a great Saint. And if I had obeyed, I should certainly have become a Saint; and now I am damned without remedy.

Unfortunate man! For his greater torment, on the Day of Judgment, he will see and recognize at the right hand of God and crowned as Saints, those who followed their Vocation, and, leaving the world, retired to the House of God, to which he also had been called. He shall see himself separated from the company of the Blessed and placed during that innumerable and miserable crew of the damned, for his disobedience to the voice of God.

No, my God, permit me not to disobey Thee and to be unfaithful. I see Thy goodness, and thank Thee, for instead of casting me away from Thy face, and banishing me to hell, as I have so often deserved, thou calls me to become a Saint, and preparest for me a high place in Paradise. I see that I should deserve a double torment, should I not correspond with this grace -- a grace not given to all. I will obey Thee. Behold, I am Thine, and always will be Thine. I embrace with joy all the pains and discomforts of the Religious life, to which Thou invited me. And what are these pains in comparison with the eternal pains, which I have deserved? I was entirely lost through my sins; now I give myself entirely to Thee. Dispose of me and my life as Thou pleases.

II.

We know well, as we have considered above, that to this most unhappy lot he exposes himself, who, to follow his own caprice, turns a deaf ear to the call of God. Therefore, my brother, you who have already been called to become a Saint in the House of God, consider that you will expose yourself to a great danger should you lose your Vocation through your own fault. Consider that this very Vocation which God in His Sovereign Bounty has given you, in order, as it were, to take you out from among the crowd, and place you among the chosen princes of His Paradise, will, through your own fault, should you be unfaithful to it, become a special hell for you. Make your own choice, then, for now God leaves it in your own hands, either to be a great king in Paradise, or a reprobate in hell, fuller of despair than the rest.

Accept, O Lord, of one already at the gates of hell, as I have been, to serve Thee and love Thee in this life and in the next. I will love Thee as much as I have deserved to be doomed to hate Thee in hell, O God, worthy of an infinite love! O my Jesus Thou hast broken those chains by which the world held me captive; Thou hast delivered me from the servitude of my enemies. I will love Thee much, then, O my Love! and for the love I bear thee, I will always serve Thee and obey Thee. I will always thank thee, O Mary, my advocate, who hast obtained this mercy for me. Help me and suffer me not to be ungrateful to that God Who has loved me so much. Obtain for me that I may die rather than be unfaithful to so great a grace. This is my hope.

Spiritual Reading

COUNSELS CONCERNING A RELIGIOUS VOCATION

IV. THE MEANS TO BE EMPLOYED TO PRESERVE A RELIGIOUS VOCATION

Secrecy (continued)

If, then, it would be a great mistake to ask the advice of parents in following one's Vocation, it would be a greater error still to ask their permission to follow it, and wait for their consent; for there would be an evident danger of losing the Vocation in so doing when there is a likely suspicion that parents would exert themselves to prevent it. Thus St. Thomas Aquinas acted, and St. Francis Xavier, St. Philip Neri, and St. Louis Bertrand. And we know that the Lord approved, even by miracles, of their glorious flight.

St. Peter of Alcantara, when he went to the monastery to become a Religious and was fleeing from the house of his mother under whose obedience he had lived since the death of his father, found himself prevented by a wide river from advancing any further. He recommended himself to God, and at the same instant saw himself transported to the other side.

In like manner, when St. Stanislaus Kotska fled from home, without the permission of his father, his brother set out after him in great haste in a carriage, but having almost overtaken him, the horses, despite all the violence used against them, would not advance a step further, till turning back towards the city, they began to travel at full speed.

In like manner the Blessed Oringa of Valdarno, in Tuscany, being promised in marriage to a young man, fled from the house of her parents in order to consecrate herself to God; but she was stopped by the river Arno. After a short prayer she saw it divide and form, as it were, two walls of crystal, to let her pass through with dry feet.

Therefore, my very beloved brother, if you are called by God to leave the world, be very careful not to make your resolution known to your parents, and, content to be thus blessed by God, seek to execute it as promptly as you can, and without their knowledge, if you would not expose yourself to the great danger of losing your Vocation. For relatives, as has been said before, especially fathers and mothers, oppose the execution of such resolutions; and although they may be endowed with piety, nevertheless, interest and passion render them so blind that under various pretexts they scruple not to thwart with all their might the Vocation of their children.

We read in the Life of Father Paul Segneri the Younger, that his mother, though a matron much given to prayer, left, nevertheless, no means untried to prevent her son from entering the Religious state to which he was called. We also read in the life of Mgr. Cavalieri, Bishop of Troja, that his father, although a man of great piety, used every means to prevent his son from entering the Congregation of Pious Workers (which, notwithstanding, he afterwards did), and even went so far as to bring against him a lawsuit in the Ecclesiastical Court. And how many other fathers, even though they were men of piety and prayer, have not in such cases been seen to change, and to become possessed, as it were, by the devil! For under no other circumstances does hell seem to employ more formidable arms than when there is a question of preventing those who are called to the Religious state from executing their resolution.

For this reason, be also very careful not to communicate your design to your friends, who will not scruple to dissuade you from it, or at least, to divulge the secret, so that the knowledge of it will easily come to the ears of your parents.

Evening Meditation

JESUS SUFFERS DURING HIS WHOLE LIFE.

I.

My sorrow is continually before me (Ps. xxxvii. 18).

Consider that all the sufferings and ignominy that Jesus endured in His life and death were present to Him from the first moment of His life: *My sorrow is continually before me*; and even from His childhood He began to offer them in satisfaction for our sins, beginning even then to fulfil His office as Redeemer. He revealed to one of His servants that from the commencement of His life even unto His death He suffered continually; and suffered so much for each of our sins that if He had had as many lives as there are men, He would as many times have died of sorrow, if God had not preserved His life that He might suffer more.

Oh, what a martyrdom did not the loving Heart of Jesus constantly endure in beholding all the sins of men! He held every single fault. Even whilst He was in the womb of Mary every sin passed in review before Jesus, and each sin afflicted Him immeasurably. St. Thomas says that this sorrow which Jesus Christ felt at the knowledge of the injury done to His Father, and of the evil that sin would occasion to the souls that He loved, surpassed the sorrows of all the contrite sinners that ever existed, even of those who died of pure sorrow; because no sinner ever loved God and his own soul as much as Jesus loved His Father and our souls.

Behold, my Jesus, at Thy feet, the ungrateful sinner, the persecutor who kept Thee in continual affliction during all Thy life. But I will say to Thee with Isaias: But thou hast delivered my soul that it should not perish; thou hast cast all my sins behind thy back (Is. xxxviii. 17). I have offended Thee. I have wounded Thee by so many sins; but Thou hast not refused to take upon Thy shoulders all my offences. I have voluntarily cast my soul into the fire of hell every time that I have consented to offend Thee gravely; and Thou, at the cost of Thy own Blood, hast continually liberated me and prevented me from being entirely lost. My beloved Redeemer, I thank Thee.

II.

Wherefore that agony which our Redeemer suffered in the Garden at the sight of our sins was endured by Him even from His Mother's womb: I am poor, and in labors from my youth (Ps. lxxxvii. 16). Thus, through the mouth of David did our Savior prophesy of Himself that all His life would be a continual suffering. From this St. John Chrysostom deduces that we ought not to afflict ourselves for anything but for sin alone; and that since Jesus was afflicted all His life long on account of our sins, so we who have committed them ought to feel a continual sorrow for them, remembering that we have offended God Who has loved us so much. St. Margaret of Cortona never ceased to shed tears for her sins. One day her confessor said to her: "Margaret, no more tears! It is enough -- Our Lord has already forgiven thee." "What!" answered the Saint, "how can my tears and my sorrows suffice for the sins for which my Jesus was afflicted all His life long!"

O my Jesus, I could wish to die of sorrow when I think how I have abused Thy infinite goodness; forgive me, my Love, and come and take entire possession of my heart. Thou hast said that Thou wouldst not disdain to enter the abode of him that opens to Thee, and to remain in his company: If any man shall open to me the door, I will come into him, and will sup with him (Apoc. iii. 20). If I had hitherto driven Thee away from me, I now love Thee and desire nothing but Thy favor. Behold, the door is open, enter Thou into my heart, but enter never to depart from it again. I am poor; but if Thou enter, thou wilt make me rich. I shall always be rich so long as I possess Thee, the Sovereign Good. O Queen of Heaven, sorrowful Mother of this suffering Son, I also have been a cause of sorrow to thee, because thou hast participated, in great measure, in the sufferings of Jesus. My Mother, do thou also forgive me, and obtain for me the grace to be faithful to thee, now that I hope my Jesus has returned into my soul.

Friday--Second Week of Advent

Morning Meditation

CONSIDERATIONS ON THE RELIGIOUS STATE. V.

Consider the immense glory that Religious will enjoy in Heaven.

He will render to everyone according to his works (Matt. xvi. 27).

From this you can judge how exceeding great will be the reward that God will give in Heaven to good Religious on account of the great merits they acquire every day. *Going, they went and wept casting their seeds; but coming, they shall come with joyfulness, carrying their sheaves* (Ps. cxxv. 6, 7).

I.

Consider, in the first place, what St. Bernard says: that it is difficult for Religious who die in the Religious state to be damned. "From the cell to heaven the way is easy. One scarcely ever descends from the cell into hell." The reason the Saint adduces is: "because one scarcely ever perseveres in it until death unless he be predestinated." For it is with difficulty a Religious perseveres until death, if he be not of the number of the Elect of Paradise. Therefore, St. Laurence Justinian called the Religious state the gate of Paradise: "Of that heavenly city this is the gate." And he said that, therefore, "Religious have a great sign of predestination."

Consider, moreover, that the reward of Heaven, as the Apostle says, is a crown of justice (2 Tim. iv. 8). Wherefore, God, though He rewards us for our works more abundantly than we deserve, rewards us nevertheless in proportion to the works we have done. *He will render to everyone according to his works*. From this you can judge how exceedingly great will be the reward which God will give in Heaven to good Religious, in consideration of the great merits they daily acquire.

The Religious gives to God all his earthly goods and is content to be entirely poor, without possessing anything. The Religious renounces all attachment to his parents, friends, and country, to unite himself more closely to God. The Religious continually mortifies himself in many things which he would enjoy in the world. The Religious, finally, gives to God his whole self, by giving him his will through the Vow of Obedience.

The dearest thing that we must give is our own will, and what God, of all other things, requires of us most is the heart, that is to say, the will. My son, give me thy heart. He who serves God in the world will give Him his possessions, but not himself; he will give Him a part and not the whole, for he will give Him indeed his goods by alms-deeds, his food by fasting, his blood by disciplines, etc. But he will always reserve for himself his own will, fasting when he pleases, praying when he likes. But the Religious, giving Him his own will, gives himself and gives all; gives not only the fruits of the tree, but the whole tree itself. Whence he may then truly say to Him: O Lord! Having given Thee my will, I have nothing more to give Thee.

Is it possible, O my God and my true Lover! that Thou so much desires my good, and to be loved by me, and that I, miserable that I am, desire so little to love and to please Thee? For what end hast Thou favored me with so many graces, and taken me out of the world? O my Jesus! I understand thee. Thou loves me much, Thou wilt have me love Thee much, and be all Thine, in this life and in the next. Thou wishes that my love should not be divided with creatures, but wilt have it be wholly for Thyself, the only Good, the only lovely One, and worthy of infinite love. Ah! my Lord, my Treasure, my Love, my All! Yes, I pant and truly desire to love Thee, and to love no other but Thee.

II.

And, therefore, in all that the Religious does through Obedience, he is sure to do the will of God perfectly, and merits by all he does, not only when he prays, when he hears confessions, when he preaches or fasts, or practices other mortifications, but also when he takes his food; when he sweeps his room, when he makes his bed, when he takes his rest, when he recreates himself; for, doing all this through Obedience, in all he does the will of God. St. Mary Magdalen de Pazzi said that everything done through Obedience is a prayer. Hence, St. Anselm, speaking of those who love Obedience, asserted that all that Religious do is meritorious for them. St. Aloysius Gonzaga said that in Religion one travels, as it were, in a vessel in which even he who does not labor advances.

Oh, how much more will a Religious gain in one month by observing his Rule than a secular, with all his penance and prayers, in a year! Of that disciple of Dorotheus called Dositheus, it was revealed that for the five years he had lived under Obedience, there was given to him in Heaven the glory of St. Paul the Hermit, and of St. Anthony the Abbot, both of whom had, for so many years, lived in the desert. Religious, it is true, must suffer the inconvenience of regular observance: Going, they went and wept. But when they are called to the other life they will go to Heaven, and ... with joyfulness, carrying their sheaves (Ps. cxxv. 6, 7). Whence they will sing: The lines have fallen unto me in goodly places, for my inheritance is goodly to me (Ps. xv. 6). These bonds which have bound me to the Lord have become for me exceedingly precious, and the glory they have acquired for me is exceedingly great.

I thank Thee, Jesus, for this desire Thou hast given me; preserve it in me, always increase it in me, and grant that I may please Thee, and love Thee on this earth as Thou desires, so that I may come hereafter to love Thee face to face, with all my strength in Paradise. Behold, this is all that I ask from Thee. Thee will I love, O my God! I will love Thee; and for Thy love I offer myself to suffer every pain. I will become a Saint, not that I may enjoy great delight in Heaven, but to please Thee much, O my beloved Lord! and to love Thee much forever. Graciously hear me, O Eternal Father for the love of Jesus Christ.

My Mother Mary, for the love of this thy Son, help thou me. Thou art my hope; from thee I hope for every good.

Spiritual Reading

COUNSELS CONCERNING A RELIGIOUS VOCATION

V. THE MEANS TO BE EMPLOYED FOR PRESERVING A RELIGIOUS VOCATION

B. Prayer

In the second place, it is necessary to remember that these Vocations are only preserved by prayer; he who gives up prayer will certainly lose his Vocation. It is necessary to pray, and to pray much; and, therefore, let him who feels himself called, not omit to make every morning after rising, an hour's Meditation, or at least one for half an hour, in his own room, if he can do so without molestation, and, if not, in the church; and likewise for half an hour in the evening.

Let him not omit also to make every day a Visit to the Most Holy Sacrament, and to the Most Blessed Virgin Mary, to obtain the grace of perseverance in his Vocation and let him not omit to receive Holy Communion three times, or at least, twice a week.

His Meditations ought almost always to be on his Vocation, considering how great a favor he has received from God, in being thus called by Him; how much more easily he will secure his eternal salvation, if he be faithful in following it; and on the contrary, to how great a danger of being lost he exposes himself, if he be unfaithful. Let him then especially keep before his eyes the hour of death and consider the contentment that he will then feel if he shall have obeyed God, and the pains and the remorse he will experience if he should die in the world. To this end I shall add some considerations on which he may make his meditation.

It is, moreover, necessary that all his prayers to Jesus and Mary, and especially those after Communion and in the Visits, be directed to obtain perseverance. In these prayers and Communions let him always renew the offering of himself to God, saying: "Behold, O Lord! I am no longer mine own. I am Thine. Already have I given myself to Thee, and now I renew this my offering of my whole self. Accept of me and give me strength to be faithful to Thee and to retire as quickly as possible into Thy House."

C. Recollection

In the third place, it is necessary to be recollected. This will not be possible unless he withdraws from worldly reunions and secular amusements. And, indeed, if we are in the world, what suffices to cause the loss of Vocation? A mere nothing. One day of dissipation, a word from a friend, a passion not mortified, a little attachment, some groundless fear, some slothfulness not overcome -- any one of these suffices to bring to nought all one's good resolutions of retiring from the world, and of giving oneself entirely to God. Wherefore, he who is called to Religion ought to keep perfectly recollected, detaching himself from everything of this world. His occupation while waiting should be prayer and frequenting the Sacraments; and he should pass his time at home or in church. Let him who will not act thus, but who distracts himself by pastimes, be persuaded that he will undoubtedly lose his Vocation. He will, indeed, feel remorse for not following his Vocation, but he certainly will not follow it. Oh, how many by neglecting these precautions have lost their Vocation, and afterwards their souls!

A PRAYER FOR PERSEVERANCE

(To be said often and fervently)

My Lord Jesus Christ, Who didst choose for Thyself the most bitter death of the Cross that I might die a happy death -- ah, since Thou hast so loved me as to call me out of the world to follow in Thy footsteps and be thus always united to Thy loving Heart, bind me, I beseech Thee, dear Jesus, with the sweet chain of Thy love wholly to Thyself that I may never more be separated from Thee. O my beloved Redeemer, I do desire to be grateful, and faithful to Thy grace and to my Vocation, but I fear lest, through my own weakness, I should be faithless. My Jesus do not allow that it should be so. No! Let me die rather than that I should ever abandon Thee. May I never forget the special love which Thou hast shown me. I love Thee, my dear Savior. Thou art now and wilt ever be the only Master of my heart and soul. I quit all and chose Thee alone for my only Treasure.

Go, creatures -- go far away! My God is my only Good. He is my Love. He is my All! My Jesus, I love Thee, and in loving Thee I wish to spend my whole life, be it long or short. I embrace Thee. I clasp Thee to my heart. In Thy loving arms I wish to die. This grace I ask for, and I care for nothing else.

Make me live always burning with Thy love, and when my end shall have at length come, let me give forth my last breath in an ardent act of love to Thee. O Mary Immaculate, do thou obtain for me this grace. My hope is in thy powerful intercession. Help me to forsake the world. Come to my rescue now. Succor me and obtain for me the grace to overcome myself and to become a Saint. Amen.

Evening Meditation

JESUS WISHED TO SUFFER SO MUCH IN ORDER TO GAIN OUR HEARTS.

I.

I have a baptism wherewith I am to be baptized and how am I straitened until it be accomplished? (Luke xii. 50).

Consider how Jesus suffered even from the first moment of His life, and all for love of us. During the whole of His life, He had no other interest, after the glory of God, than our salvation. He, as the Son of God, had no need to suffer to deserve Paradise; but whatever He suffered of pain, of poverty, of ignominy, He applied it all towards meriting for us eternal salvation. And even though He could have saved us without suffering, yet He chose to embrace a life of nothing but sufferings, poor, despised, and deprived of every comfort, with a death the most desolate and bitter that was ever endured by any Martyr or penitent, only to make us understand the greatness of the love He bore us, and to gain our affections.

He lived thirty-three years, and He lived sighing for the hour in which He was to sacrifice His life, which He desired to offer up to obtain for us divine grace and eternal glory, in order that He might have us with Him forever in Paradise.

My beloved Redeemer, I am also one of those ungrateful wretches who have repaid Thy immense love, Thy sorrows, and Thy death, with offences and contempt. O my dearest Jesus! How is it possible that, seeing as Thou didst the ingratitude that I should show Thee for all Thy mercies, Thou couldst yet love me so much, and resolve to endure so much contempt and suffering for me! But I will not despair. The evil is already done. Give me, therefore, O my Savior, that sorrow which Thou hast merited for me by Thy tears; but let it be a sorrow equal to my iniquities. O loving Heart of my Savior, once so afflicted and desolate for my sake, and now all burning with love for me, I beseech Thee change my heart, give me a heart that will make reparation for the offences I have committed against Thee -- a love that will equal my ingratitude!

II.

It was this desire which made Jesus say: I have a baptism wherewith I am to be baptized; and how am I straitened until it be accomplished? He desired to be baptized with His own Blood, not to wash out His own sins, since He was innocent and holy, but the sins of men whom He loved so much: He loved us, and washed us in his own blood (Apoc. i. 5). Oh, excess of the love of God, which all the men and Angels that ever existed will never succeed in understanding or praising as it deserves.

St. Bonaventure weeps at seeing the great ingratitude of men for so great a love: "It is a cause for wonder that the hearts of men do not break for love of Thee." It is a marvel, says the Saint, to see a God endure such sufferings, shedding tears in a stable, poor in a workshop, languishing on a Cross; in short afflicted and tormented; the whole of His life for the love of men; and then to see these men, who not only do not burn with love towards such a loving God, but even have the boldness to despise His love and His grace. O Lord, how is it possible to conceive that a God should have given Himself up to so much suffering for men, and yet that there should be men who can offend, and not love this merciful God!

I give Thee thanks, my Savior, because I see that Thy mercy has already changed my heart. I hate, above every evil, the insults I have offered Thee; I detest them, I abhor them. I now esteem Thy friendship above all the riches and kingdoms of the world. I desire to please Thee as much as it is possible for me; I love Thee, who art infinitely amiable; but I see that my love is too feeble. Do Thou increase the flame, give me more love. Thy love for me ought to be responded to by a greater degree of love in me, who have so much offended Thee, and who, instead of chastisement, have received so many special favors from Thee. O Sovereign Good, permit me not to be any longer ungrateful for all the favors Thou hast bestowed upon me. I will say with St. Francis: "May I die, Lord, for the love of Thy love, who for the love of my love didst design to die!" Mary, my hope, help me; pray to Jesus for me!

Saturday--Second Week of Advent

Morning Meditation

THE OFFERING MARY MADE OF HERSELF TO GOD WAS PROMPT AND WITHOUT DELAY.

Arise, make haste, my love, my dove, my beautiful one, and come! (Cant. ii. 10). Mary well understood the voice of God calling her to devote herself to His love. And thus, enlightened, she at once offered herself to her Lord. Behold, O Mary, I this day present myself to thee, and in union with thee I renounce all creatures and devote myself entirely to the love of my Creator.

I.

Hearken, O daughter, and see, and incline thine ear; and forget thy people and thy father's house (Ps. xliv. 11). The holy Virgin obeyed this divine call with promptitude and with generosity. From the first moment that the heavenly child was sanctified in her mother's womb, which was at the instant of her Immaculate Conception, she received the perfect use of reason, and she began to merit. And immediately, as an Angel revealed to St. Bridget, our Queen determined to sacrifice her will to God, and to give Him all her love for the whole of her life.

Mary, hearing that her holy parents, St. Joachim and St. Anne, had consecrated her by Vow to God, requested them with earnestness to take her to the Temple, and accomplish their promise. At the age of three years, as St. Epiphanius tells us -- an age at which children are the most desirous and stand in the greatest need of their parents' care -- Mary desired to consecrate herself to God.

Behold, then, Joachim and Anne, generously sacrificing to God the most precious treasure they possessed in the world, and the treasure dearest to their hearts. They set forth from Nazareth carrying their well-beloved little daughter in turn, for she could not otherwise have undertaken so long a journey as that from Nazareth to Jerusalem, a distance of eighty miles. They were accompanied by few relatives, but choirs of Angels escorted and served the Immaculate little Virgin, who was about to consecrate herself to the Divine Majesty. How beautiful are thy steps ... O prince's daughter. (Cant. vii. 1). "O how beautiful," must the Angels have sung, "how acceptable to God is thy every step taken on the way to present and offer thyself to Him, O noble daughter, most beloved of our common Lord!"

O beloved Mother of God, most amiable child, Mary, who didst present thyself in the Temple, and with promptitude and without reserve didst consecrate thyself to the glory and love of God; O that I could offer thee this day the first years of my life, to devote myself without reserve to thy service, my holy and most sweet Lady! But it is now too late to do this, for I have lost many years in the service of the world. Woe to that time in which I did not love thee! But it is better to begin, now at last than not at all. O Mary, I this day present myself to thee, and in union with thee I renounce all creatures and devote myself entirely to the love of my Creator. Do thou help my weakness by thy powerful intercession.

II.

God Himself with the whole Heavenly Court made great rejoicings on the day that Mary presented herself to be His Spouse in the Temple. For He never saw a more holy creature, or one He so tenderly loved, come to offer herself to Him.

When the holy company reached the Temple, the fair child turned to her parents and, on her knees, kissed their hands and asked their blessing; and then without turning back, she ascended the steps of the Temple. She bade farewell to the world, and renouncing all the pleasures it promises to its votaries, she offered and consecrated herself to her Creator.

At the time of the Deluge a raven sent out by Noe, remained to feed on the dead bodies; but the dove, without resting her foot, quickly returned to him into the ark (Gen. vii. 9). Many who are sent by God into this world unfortunately remain to feed on earthly goods. It was not thus our heavenly dove, Mary, acted. She knew that God should be our only Good, our only Hope, our only Love; and she knew that the world is full of dangers, and that he who leaves it the soonest is most free from its snares. Hence, she sought to do this from her tenderest years, and as soon as possible shut herself up in the sacred retirement of the Temple, where she could the better hear God's voice, and honor and love Him more. Rejoice with me, all ye who love God, for when I was a little one, I pleased the Most High. (Off. B.V.M.).

O happy Virgin Mary, who didst begin so soon to serve God, and who didst always serve Him so faithfully! Ah, cast a look on me who has returned to Him with such tardiness, after so many years lost in the love of creatures. Obtain for me the grace to give God at least the remainder of my life, be it long or short. Teach me, O Lady, what I should now do to belong entirely to God, and thus to repair the time I have lost. Thou hast already done so much for me, finish the work of my salvation. Do not abandon me till thou see me safe at thy feet in Paradise. Amen.

Spiritual Reading

COUNSELS CONCERNING A RELIGIOUS VOCATION

VI. DISPOSITIONS REQUIRED FOR ENTERING RELIGION

He who is called by God to a Religious Institute in which regular observance reigns should understand that the end of every such Institute is that its members walk in the footsteps and imitate as exactly as possible the example of the most holy life of Jesus Christ -- a life entirely detached and mortified, full of sufferings and humiliations. I have said an Institute in which regular observance reigns, for it would be better, perhaps, to remain in the world than to enter a Religious Institute that is relaxed. He, then, who resolves to enter such a Religious Institute must, at the same time, resolve to enter in order to suffer and deny himself in everything, as Jesus Christ has Himself declared to those who wish to follow Him perfectly: If any man will come after me let him deny himself and take up his cross and follow me. He must be firm in his resolution to suffer, and to suffer much, so that afterwards he may not give way to temptations, when, having entered Religion, he feels pressed down under the hardships and privations of the poor and mortified life which is led in Religion.

There are many who, on entering a fervent Community, do not take the proper means of finding peace therein, and of becoming Saints, because they only place before their eyes the advantages of Community life, such as the solitude, the quiet, the freedom from the troubles caused by relatives, from strife and other disagreeable matters, and from the cares consequent on being obliged to think of one's lodging, food, and clothing.

There is no doubt that a Religious is, indeed, much indebted to his Institute, which delivers him from so many troubles, and thus procures for him so great a facility to serve God perfectly in peace, continually furnishing him with so many means for the welfare of his soul, with the good example of his companions, and good advice from his Superiors, who are watchful for his benefit, and with so many exercises conducive to eternal salvation. All this is true; but in order not to be deprived of so blessed a lot, he must resolve to embrace all the sufferings he may, on the other hand, meet with in Religion; for if he does not embrace these with love, he will never obtain that full peace which God gives to those who overcome themselves: To him that overcomes I will give the hidden manna (Apoc. ii. 17). For the peace which God gives His faithful servants to taste is hidden; nor is it known to men of the world, who, seeing their mortified life, far from envying, pity them and call them the unhappy ones of this earth! But "they see the Cross, the unction they do not see," says St. Bernard. They see their mortification, but they do not see the contentment which God gives them to enjoy.

It is true that in the spiritual life one must suffer, but, as St. Teresa says, when one resolves to suffer the pain ceases. Nay, the pains themselves turn into joy. "My daughter," so the Lord said one day to St. Bridget, "the treasure-house of My graces seems to be surrounded with thorns; but for him who overcomes the first prickles, all is changed into sweetness." And then those delights which God gives to His beloved souls in their prayers, in their Communions, in their solitude; those lights, those holy ardors and that intimate union with God, that quiet of conscience, that blessed hope of eternal life -- ah, who can understand them, if he does not experience them? "One drop of the consolations of God," says St. Teresa, "is worth more than all the consolations and the delights of the world." Our most gracious God knows well how, even in this valley of tears, to give him who suffers something for His sake, a foretaste of the glory of the Blessed; for in this is truly verified that which David says: Thou who feigns labor in commandment (Ps. xciii. 20). In the spiritual life, God, when announcing pains, tediousness, death, seems to feign labor, but, in fact, there is no labor; for the spiritual life brings to them who entirely give themselves to God that peace which, St. Paul says, surpasses all understanding (Phil. iv. 7). It surpasses all the pleasures of the world and of worldlings. Hence, we see a Religious more content in a poor cell than all the monarchs in their royal palaces. O taste and see that the Lord is sweet (Ps. xxxiii. 9). He who has not made the trial cannot understand it.

On the other hand, he who does not resolve to suffer and to overcome himself in what is distasteful, must be persuaded that he will never enjoy this true peace, though he should have already entered Religion. To him that overcomes, I will give the hidden manna (Apoc. ii. 17). It is then necessary that he who wishes to be admitted into an Institute of observance should enter with a mind determined to overcome himself in everything, by expelling from his heart every inclination and desire that is not from God, or for God. Hence, he must detach himself from all things, and especially from the following: Comforts, Parents, Self-esteem, and Self-will.

Evening Meditation

THE GREATEST SORROW OF JESUS

I.

What profit is there in my blood, whilst I go down to corruption (Ps. xxix. 10).

Jesus Christ revealed to the Venerable Agatha of the Cross that whilst He was in His Mother's womb, that which afflicted Him more than any other sorrow was the hardness of the hearts of men, who would, after His Redemption, despise the graces which He came into the world to diffuse. And He had expressed this sentiment before, by the mouth of David, in the words just quoted, which are generally thus understood by the holy Fathers: What profit is there in my blood, whilst I go down to corruption? St. Isidore explains whilst I descend into corruption "whilst I descend to take the nature of man, so corrupted by vices and sins"; as if He had said: "O my Father, I am indeed going to clothe Myself with human flesh, in order to shed My Blood for men; but what profit is there in my blood? The greater part of the world will set no value on My Blood, and will go on offending Me, as if I had done nothing for the love of them."

This sorrow was the bitter chalice which Jesus begged the Eternal Father to remove from Him, saying: Let this chalice pass from me. (Matt. xxvi. 39). What chalice? The sight of the contempt with which His love was treated. This made Him exclaim again on the Cross: My God, my God, why has thou forsaken me? (Matt. xxvii. 46). Our Lord revealed to

St. Catherine of Sienna that this was the abandonment of which He complained -- the knowledge, namely, that His Father would have to permit that His Passion and His love should be despised by so many men for whom He died.

O my most amiable Jesus, how much have I, too, caused Thee to suffer during Thy lifetime! Thou hast shed Thy Blood for me with so much sorrow and love, and what fruit hast Thou hitherto drawn from me but contempt, offences, and insults? But, my Redeemer, I will no longer afflict Thee; I hope that in future Thy Passion will produce fruit in me by Thy grace, which I feel is already assisting me. I will love Thee above every other good; and to please Thee, I am ready to give my life a thousand times.

II.

And this same sorrow tormented the Infant Jesus in the womb of Mary, the foresight of such a prodigality of sorrows, of ignominy, of blood-shedding, and of so cruel and ignominious a death, and all to so little purpose. The holy Child saw, even there, what the Apostle says: that many, indeed the greater number, would trample under foot His Blood and despise His grace, which this Blood would obtain for them: *Treading underfoot the Son of God ... and offering an affront to the Spirit of grace* (Heb. x. 29). But if we have been of the number of those ungrateful men, let us not despair. Jesus, at His birth, came to offer peace to men of goodwill, as He made the Angels sing: *And on earth peace to men of good-will* (Luke ii. 14). Let us, then, change our will, repent of our sins, and resolve to love this good God, and we shall find peace, that is, the Divine friendship.

Eternal Father, I should not have the boldness to appear before Thee to implore either pardon or grace, but Thy Son has told me, that whatever grace I ask of Thee in His Name Thou wilt grant it to me: *If ye shall ask anything of the Father in my name, he will give it to you* (Jo. xvi. 23). I offer Thee, therefore, the merits of Jesus Christ, and in His Name, I ask of Thee first a general pardon for all my sins; I ask holy perseverance even unto death; I ask of Thee, above all, the gift of Thy holy love, that it may make me always live according to Thy divine will. As to my own will, I am resolved to choose a thousand deaths sooner than offend Thee, and to love Thee with my whole heart, and to do everything that I possibly can to please Thee. But to do all this, I beg of Thee, and hope to receive from Thee, grace to execute what I propose. My Mother Mary, if Thou wilt pray for me, I am safe. Oh, pray for me, pray; and cease not to pray until thou see that I am changed, and made what God wishes me to be.

Third Sunday of Advent

Morning Meditation

THE JOY OF JESUS' COMING

Rejoice in the Lord always: again, I say, rejoice! The Lord is nigh. (Epistle of Sunday. Philip. iv. 4, 7).

Take comfort, take comfort, O men, saith the Lord, by the mouth of Isaias: Be comforted; be comforted, my people, saith your God. Speak ye to the heart of Jerusalem and call to her; for her evil is come to an end; her iniquity is forgiven (Is. xl. 1). God hath discovered a way of saving man, while at the same time His Justice and His Mercy shall both be satisfied. Justice and Peace have kissed (Ps. lxxxiv. 11).

I.

Speaking of the coming of the Redeemer, Isaias made this prediction: The land that was desolate and impassable shall be glad, and the wilderness shall rejoice and shall flourish like the lily (Is. xxxv. 1). The Prophet had been speaking of the pagans (among whom were our own unfortunate ancestors) who were living in heathendom, as in a desert land void of a single man that knew or worshipped the true God, but peopled only with those who were slaves of the devil -- a land desolate and impassable, because there was no path of salvation known to those wretched people. He foretold that the world, though so miserable then, would yet rejoice at the coming of the Messias and would see itself filled with followers of the true God, strengthened by His grace against all the enemies of their salvation; and that the whole land would blossom as the lily by purity of morals and the sweet odor of all virtues. Wherefore Isaias proceeds to say: Say to the faint hearted: Take courage and fear not! God himself will come and save you! (Ibid. 4).

This very event, foretold by Isaias, has already happened. Let me, then, acclaim with gladness: Go on joyfully, O children of Adam! Go on joyfully! Be no longer faint-hearted! Even though you perceive yourselves weak and unable to stand against so many enemies, Fear not! God himself will come and save you. God Himself has come on earth, and has redeemed us, by imparting to us strength sufficient to combat and to vanquish every enemy of our salvation.

Oh, happy me, if from this day forward I shall be able always to say with the Sacred Spouse: My beloved to me and I to him! (Cant. iii. 16). My God, my Beloved has given Himself all to me. It is but reasonable for me to give myself all to my God, and to say: What have I in heaven and besides thee what do I desire on earth! (Ps. lxxii. 25). Oh, my beloved Infant, my dear Redeemer, since Thou hast come down from Heaven to give Thyself to me what else shall I care for or seek in Heaven or on earth besides Thee, Who art my Sovereign Good, my only Treasure, the Paradise of souls! Be Thou, then, the sole Lord of my heart and do Thou possess it wholly. May my heart obey Thee alone! May my soul love Thee alone and mayst Thou alone be its portion! Amen.

II.

You have no grounds for being sad anymore, says St. Leo, on account of the sentence of death fulminated against you, now that Life itself is born for you; "nor is there any lawful room for sadness when it is the Birthday of Life." And St. Augustine exclaims: "O sweet day for penitents! Today sin is taken away and shall the sinner despair!" Speed on then with gladness, O ye souls that love God and hope in God, speed on your way with gladness! What if Adam's sin and still more our own sins, have wrought sad ruin on us? Let us understand that Jesus Christ, by the Redemption, has infinitely more than repaired our ruin. Where sin abounded, grace did more abound (Rom. v. 20).

The Lord said: I am come that they may have life and may have it more abundantly (Jo. x. 10). I am come to give life to men and a more abundant measure than that which they had lost by sin. Not as the offence, so also the gift (Rom. v. 15). Great has been man's sin; but greater, says the Apostle, has been the gift of Redemption. And with him plentiful redemption (Ps. cxxix. 7). For this reason, the Church styles the fault of Adam a happy fault: "O happy fault which deserved to have such and so great a Redeemer!"

Oh, how much more are we bound to thank God for having brought us into life after the coming of the Messias! How did the Prophets and the Patriarchs of the Old Testament long to see the Redeemer born! But they saw Him not! Drop down dew, ye heavens, from above, and let the clouds rain the Just! (Is. xlv. 8), was their incessant exclamation. Send forth, O Lord, the Lamb, the Ruler of the earth! Such were the longing exclamations of the Saints! But for all that, during the space of four thousand years they did not have the happy lot to see the Messias born. We, however, have had this happiness! But what are we doing? Do we know how to love this amiable Redeemer? Very great would be your ingratitude to your God, O Christian soul, if you were not to love Him, after He has been pleased to be bound in swaddling-clothes that you may be released from the chains of hell; after He has become poor that you may be made partaker of His riches; after He has made Himself weak to give you strength against your enemies; after He has chosen to suffer and weep, that by His tears your sins may be washed away.

O sweet Infant, give me Thy love and then do with me what Thou wilt. I was once a slave of hell, but now that I am free from those unhappy chains, I consecrate myself entirely to Thee. I give Thee my body, my goods, my life, my soul, my will and my liberty. I desire no longer to belong to myself, but only to Thee, my only Good! Ah, bind my heart to Thy feet, that it may no more stray from Thee! O most holy Mary, obtain for me the grace of living united to thy Son by the blessed chains of love. He grants all that thou ask. Pray to Him! Pray to Him for me! This is my hope. Amen.

Spiritual Reading

"THE WAY OF THE LORD"

In his preaching, St. John the Baptist exclaimed: Make straight the way of the Lord (Jo. i. 23). To be able to walk always in the way of the Lord, without turning to the right or to the left, it is necessary to adopt the proper means. There are two very important means about which we will speak to you here.

1. To put away confidence in self.
2. To have confidence in God.

I. WE MUST PUT AWAY ALL SELF-CONFIDENCE.

With fear and trembling, says the Apostle, St. Paul, work out your salvation (Phil. ii. 12). To secure eternal salvation we must be always penetrated with fear, we must be afraid of ourselves -- with fear and trembling -- and distrust altogether our own strength; for without divine aid we can do nothing. Without me, says Jesus Christ, you can do nothing (Jo. xv. 5). We can do nothing for the salvation of our souls. St. Paul tells us that of ourselves we are not capable of even a good thought. Not that we are sufficient to think anything of ourselves as of ourselves, but our sufficiency is from God (2 Cor. iii. 5). Without the aid of the Holy Ghost, we cannot even pronounce the Name of Jesus to deserve a reward. And no one can say the Lord Jesus, but by the Holy Ghost (I Cor. xii. 3).

Miserable the man who trusts to himself in the way of God! St. Peter experienced the sad effects of self-confidence. Jesus Christ said to him: In this night before the cock crow, thou wilt deny me thrice (Matt. xxvi. 34). Trusting in his own strength and his goodwill, the Apostle replied: Yea, though I should die with thee, I will not deny thee (Ib. 35). What was the result? On the night on which Jesus Christ had been taken, Peter was reproached in the court of Caiphas with being one of the disciples of the Savior. The reproach filled him with fear; he thrice denied his Master and swore that he had never known Him! Humility and diffidence in ourselves are so necessary for us, that God permits us sometimes to fall into sin, that by our fall we may acquire humility and a knowledge of our own weakness. Through want of humility David also fell hence, after his sin, he said: Before I was humbled, I offended (Ps. cxviii. 67).

Hence the Holy Ghost pronounces the man blessed who is always in fear: Blessed is the man who is always fearful (Prov. xxviii. 14). He who is afraid of falling distrusts his own strength, avoids as much as possible all dangerous occasions, and recommends himself often to God, and thus preserves his soul from sin. But the man who is not fearful, but full of self-confidence, easily exposes himself to the danger of sin: he seldom recommends himself to God, and thus he falls. Let us imagine a person suspended over a great precipice by a cord held by another. Surely, he would constantly cry out to the person who supports him: "Hold fast, hold fast; for God's sake, do not let go." We are all in danger of falling into the abyss of every crime if God does not support us. Hence, we should constantly beseech Him to keep His hand over us, and to succor us in all dangers.

On rising from bed, St. Philip Neri used to say every morning: "O Lord, keep Thy hand this day over Philip; if Thou do not, Philip will betray Thee." And one day, as he walked through the city reflecting on his own misery, he frequently said: "I despair, I despair." A certain Religious who heard him, believing that the Saint was really tempted to despair, corrected him, and encouraged him to hope in divine mercy. But the Saint replied: "I despair of myself, but I trust in God." Hence, during this life, in which we are exposed to so many dangers of losing God, it is necessary for us to live always in great diffidence of ourselves, and full of confidence in God.

II. WE MUST HAVE GREAT CONFIDENCE IN GOD.

St. Francis de Sales says that mere self-diffidence on account of our own weakness would only render us pusillanimous and expose us to great danger of abandoning ourselves to a tepid life, or even to despair. The more we distrust our own strength, the more we should confide in divine mercy. This is a balance, says the same Saint, in which the more the scale of confidence in God is raised, the more the scale of diffidence in us descends.

Listen to me, O sinners who have had the misfortune of having hitherto offended God, and of being condemned to hell: If the devil tells you that but little hope remains of your eternal salvation, answer him in the words of the Scripture: No one hath hoped in the Lord, and hath been confounded (Ecclus. ii. 11). No sinner has ever trusted in God and been lost. Make, then, a firm purpose to sin no more; abandon yourselves into the arms of the divine goodness; and rest assured that God will have mercy on you and save you from hell. Cast thy care upon the Lord and he shall sustain thee (Ps. liv. 23). The Lord one day said to St. Gertrude: "He who confides in Me does Me such violence that I cannot but hear all his petitions."

But, says the Prophet Isaias, they that hope in the Lord shall renew their strength; they shall take wings as eagles; they shall run, and not be weary; they shall walk, and not faint (Is. xl. 31). They who place their confidence in God shall renew their strength; they shall lay aside their own weakness and shall acquire the strength of God; they shall fly like eagles in the way of the Lord, without fatigue and without ever failing. David says that Mercy shall encompass him that hopes in the Lord (Ps. xxi. 10). He who hopes in the Lord shall be encompassed by His mercy, so that he shall never be abandoned by it.

St. Cyprian says that the divine mercy is an inexhaustible fountain. They who bring vessels of the greatest confidence, draw from it the greatest graces. Hence, the Royal Prophet has said: Let thy mercy, O Lord, be upon us, as we have hoped in thee (Ps. xxxii. 22).

Whenever the devil terrifies us by placing before our eyes the great difficulty of persevering in the grace of God despite all the dangers and sinful occasions of this life, let us, without answering him, raise our eyes to God, and hope that in His goodness He will certainly send us help to resist every attack. *I have lifted my eyes to the mountains, from whence help shall come to me* (Ps. cxx. 2). And when the enemy represents to us our weakness, let us say with the Apostle: *I can do all things in him who strengthened me* (Phil. iv. 13). Of myself I can do nothing; but I trust in God, that by His grace I shall be able to do all things.

Hence, during the greatest dangers of perdition to which we are exposed, we should continually turn to Jesus Christ and, throwing ourselves into the hands of Him Who redeemed us by His death, and say: *Into thy hands I commend my spirit: thou hast redeemed me, O Lord, the God of truth* (Ps. xxx. 6). This prayer should be said with great confidence of obtaining eternal life, and to it we should add: *In thee, O Lord, I have hoped; let me not be confounded forever* (Ib. 1).

Evening Meditation

THE LOVE OF JESUS FOR US IN BECOMING MAN

I.

The charity of Christ pressed us (2 Cor. v. 14). It was not enough, says St. Augustine, for the Divine Love to have made us to His own Image in creating the first man, Adam, but He must also Himself be made to our image in redeeming us. Adam partook of the forbidden fruit, beguiled by the serpent which suggested to Eve that if she ate of that fruit, she should become like to God, acquiring the knowledge of good and evil; and therefore, the Lord then said: *Behold, Adam is become one of us!* (Gen. iii. 2). God said this ironically, and to upbraid Adam for his vast presumption. But after the Incarnation of the Word, we can truly say: "Behold, God has become one of us!"

"Look, then, O man," exclaims St. Augustine, "thy God is made thy brother!" Thy God is made like to thee, a Son of Adam, as thou art; He has put on the self-same flesh, has made Himself passible, liable as thou art to suffer and to die. He could have assumed the nature of an Angel, but no, He would take upon Himself thy very flesh, that thus He might give satisfaction to God with the very same flesh, though sinless, of Adam the sinner. And He even gloried in this, oftentimes styling Himself the Son of Man. Hence, we have every right to call Him our brother.

II.

It was an immeasurably greater humiliation for God to become a Man than if all the princes of the earth, and all the Angels and Saints of Heaven, with the divine Mother herself, had been turned into a blade of grass, or into a handful of clay; yes, for grass, clay, princes, Angels, Saints, are all creatures; but between the creature and God there is an infinite difference. Ah, exclaims St. Bernard, the more God has humbled Himself for us in becoming Man, so much the more has He made His goodness known to us: "The smaller He has become by humility, the greater He has made Himself in bounty." But the love which Jesus Christ bears to us, exclaims the Apostle, irresistibly urges, and impels us to love Him: The charity of Christ presses us.

Let us say with St. Augustine: "O Fire, ever burning, inflame me." O Word Incarnate, thou wert made Man to enkindle divine love in our hearts: and how could Thou have met with such a want of gratitude in the hearts of men? Thou hast spared nothing to induce them to love Thee; Thou hast even gone so far as to give Thy Blood and Thy life for them: and how, then, can men remain so ungrateful? Do they, perchance, not know it? Yes, they know it, and they believe that for them Thou didst come down from Heaven to put on mortal flesh, and to load Thyself with our miseries; they know that for their love Thou didst lead a painful life, and embrace an ignominious death; and how, then, can they live forgetful of Thee? They love relatives, friends; they love even animals: if from them they receive any token of good-will they are anxious to repay it; and yet towards Thee alone are they so loveless and ungrateful. But alas! in accusing them, I am my own accuser; I have treated Thee worse than anyone else.

O God! did not Faith assure us of it, who could ever believe that a God, for love of such a worm as man is, should Himself become a worm like him? A devout author says: Suppose, by chance, that, passing on your way, you should have crushed to death a worm in your path; and then someone, observing your compassion for the poor reptile, should say to you: 'Well, now, if you would restore that dead worm to life, you must first yourself become a worm like it, and then must shed all your blood, and make a bath of it in which to wash the worm, and it shall revive' -- what would you reply? You would surely say: 'And what matters it to me whether the worm be alive or dead, if I should have to purchase its life by my own death?' And the more would you say so if it was not a harmless worm, but an ungrateful asp, which, in return for all your benefits, had tried upon your life. But even should your love for that reptile reach so far as to induce you to suffer death to restore it to life, what would men say then? And what would not that serpent do for you whose death had saved it, supposing it were capable of reason? But this much has Jesus Christ done for you, most vile worm; and you, with the blackest ingratitude, have tried oftentimes to take away His life; and your sins would have done so, were Jesus liable to die again. How much viler are you in the sight of God than is a worm in your own sight! What difference would it make to God had you remained dead and forever reprobate in your sins, as you well deserved? Nevertheless, this God had such a love for you that, to release you from eternal death, He first became a worm like you; and then, to save you, would lavish upon you His Heart's Blood, even to the last drop, and endure the death which you had justly deserved, Yes, all this is of Faith: *And the Word was made Flesh* (Jo. i. 14). *He hath loved us and washed us from our sins in his own blood* (Apoc. i. 5).

O my Jesus, Thy Goodness encourages me! I am aware, my Redeemer, that my heart is no longer worthy of Thy acceptance, since it has forsaken Thee for the love of creatures; but, at the same time, I see that Thou art willing to have it, and with my entire will I dedicate it and present it to Thee. Inflame it, then, wholly with Thy divine love, and grant that from this day forward it may never love any other but Thee, O infinite Goodness, worthy of an infinite love. I love Thee, my Jesus; I love Thee, O Sovereign Good! I love Thee, O only Love of my soul!

O Mary, my Mother, thou who art *the mother of fair love* (Ecclus. xxiv. 24), do thou obtain for me this grace to love my God; I hope it of thee.

Monday--Third Week of Advent

Morning Meditation

CONSIDERATIONS ON THE RELIGIOUS STATE. VI.

Consider the peace that God gives to good Religious.

St. Teresa used to say that one drop of heavenly consolation is worth more than all the delights of the world. Oh, what contentment does he not find, who, having left all for God, is able to say with St. Francis: "Deus meus et omnia!" -- My God and my All! -- free from the world's slavery and enjoying the liberty of the Children of God.

I.

The promises of God cannot fail. God has said: Every one that has left house, or brethren, or sisters, or father or mother, or wife, or children, or lands for my name's sake, shall receive an hundredfold, and shall possess life everlasting (Matt. xix. 29). A hundredfold on this earth, and life everlasting in Heaven.

Peace of the soul is of greater value than all the kingdoms of the world. And what avails it to have dominion over the whole world without interior peace? Better is it to be the poorest peasant in the land and content, than to be the lord of the whole world, and to live a discontented life. But who can give this peace? The world? Oh no, peace is a blessing that is obtained only from God. "O God!" the Church prays, "give to Thy servants that peace which the world cannot give." He is called the God of all consolation (2 Cor. i. 3). But if God be the sole Giver of peace, to whom, think you, will He give that peace if not to those who leave all, and detach themselves from all creatures, to give themselves entirely to their Creator? And therefore, we see good Religious shut up in their cells, mortified, despised and poor, yet living a more contented life than the great ones of the world, with all the riches, the pomp, and diversions they enjoy.

St. Scholastica said that if men knew the peace good Religious enjoy, the whole world would become a monastery; and St. Mary Magdalen de Pazzi said that if men knew it they would scale the walls in order to get into the monasteries. The human heart having been created for an infinite Good, finite creatures cannot content it. God alone, who is an Infinite Good can content it: Delight in the Lord and he will give thee the request of thy heart (Ps. xxxvi. 4). Oh no; a good Religious united with God envies none of the princes of the world who possess kingdoms, riches, and honors. "Let the rich," he will say with St. Paulinus, "have their riches, the kings have their kingdoms, to me Christ is my kingdom and my glory." He will see lovers of the world foolishly glory in pomp and vanity; but he, seeking to detach himself more from earthly things, and to unite himself more closely to God, will live contented in this life, and may well say: Some trust in chariots, and some in horses, but we call upon the name of the Lord, our God (Ps. xix. 8).

O my Lord and my God, my All! I know that Thou alone canst make me contented in this life and in the next. But I will not love Thee for my own contentment; I will love Thee to content Thy divine Heart. I wish this to be my peace, my only satisfaction during my whole life, to unite my will to Thy holy will, even should I have to suffer pain to do this. Thou art my God, I am Thy creature.

II.

St. Teresa used to say that one drop of heavenly consolation is worth more than all the delights of the world. Father Charles of Lorraine, having become a Religious, said that God, by one moment of the happiness that He gave him to feel in Religion, superabundantly paid him for all he had left for God. Hence his jubilation was sometimes so great that, when alone in his cell, he could not help dancing for very joy. The Blessed Seraphino of Ascoli, a Capuchin Lay-brother, said that he would not exchange a foot length of his cord for all the kingdoms of the world.

Oh, what contentment does he not find, who, having left all for God is able to say with St. Francis: "My God and my All!" and to see himself thus freed from the servitude of the world, from the thralldom of worldly fashion, and from all purely earthly affections. This is the liberty enjoyed by the children of God, and such good Religious are. It is true that in the beginning, the deprivation of the reunions and pastimes of the world, the observances in Community and of the Rules, seem to be thorns; but these thorns, as Our Lord said to St. Bridget, will all become flowers and delights of Paradise to him who courageously bears their first prickles, and then he will taste on earth that peace which, St. Paul says, surpasses all the gratification of the senses, the enjoyments of feasts, of banquets, and other pleasures of the world: The peace of God which surpasses all understanding (Phil. iv. 7). And what greater peace can there be than to know that one pleases God?

And what greater good can I hope for than to please Thee, my Lord and my God, Who hast been so partial in Thy love towards me. Thou, O my Jesus, hast left Heaven to live for love of me a poor and mortified life. I leave all to live only for Thee, my most Blessed Redeemer. I love Thee with my whole heart. If only Thou wilt give me the grace to love Thee, treat me as Thou pleases.

O Mary, Mother of God, protect me and render me like to thee, not in thy glory which I do not deserve, but in pleasing God, and obeying His Holy Will, as thou didst. Amen.

Spiritual Reading

COUNSELS CONCERNING A RELIGIOUS VOCATION

VII. DETACHMENT

I. From Comforts

In Religion, after the year's Novitiate, besides the Vows of Chastity and Obedience, a Vow of Poverty is made, in consequence of which, if solemn, one can never possess anything as one's own, not even a pin, or income, or money, or any other things. The Community will provide him with all that he needs. But the Vow of Poverty alone will not make one a true follower of Jesus Christ if he does not embrace with joy of spirit all the inconveniences of Poverty. "Not poverty but the love of poverty, is a virtue," says St. Bernard, and he means to say that to become holy it is not enough to be simply poor -- one must also love the inconveniences of poverty. "Oh, how many wish to be poor and like to Jesus Christ," says Thomas a Kempis, "but without wanting for anything!" They would have, in a word, the honor and reward of Poverty, but not the inconveniences of Poverty. It is easy to understand that in Religion no one will seek things that are superfluous -- garments of silk, choice dishes, valuable furniture, and the like; but he will desire to have all things that are necessary, and these he may be unable to get. It is then he gives proof that he truly loves Poverty, when things that are necessary -- such as the usual clothing, bedcovering or food -- happen to be wanting, if he remains content and is not troubled. And what kind of Poverty would that be never to suffer the want of anything necessary? Father Balthasar Alvarez says that in order truly to love Poverty, we must also love the effects of poverty; that is, as he specifies them: cold, hunger, thirst, and contempt.

A Religious must not only be content with that which is given to him, without ever asking for anything which the officials of the Community may have forgotten to furnish him with -- which would be a great defect -- but he must be prepared to suffer, now and then, the want even of those simple things that the Rule allows. For it may happen that sometimes he is in want of clothing, bedcovering, linen, food, and such-like things, and then he must be satisfied with that little which can be given him, without complaining or being disquieted at seeing himself in want even of what is necessary. He who has not this spirit, ought not to think of entering Religion, because it is a sign that he is not called thereto, or that he has not the will to embrace the spirit of a Religious Institute. "He who goes to serve God in His House," says St. Teresa, "ought to consider that he is going, not to be well treated for God, but to suffer for God."

II. From Relations

He who would enter Religion should be detached from and forget his relations, for, in Religious houses of exact observance, detachment from relations is enforced in the highest degree, in order to follow perfectly the teaching of Jesus Christ Who said: I came not to send peace but the sword: I came to set a man at variance with his father (Matt. x. 34, 35); and He added the reason: A man's enemies shall be they of his own household (Ib. 36). And this is especially the case, as has been remarked already, where there is a question of a Religious Vocation. When a person called by God wishes to leave the world, there are no worse enemies than parents, who, either through interest or passion, prefer to become enemies of God, by turning their children away from their Vocation, rather than give their consent. Oh! how many parents shall we see in the Valley of Josaphat damned for having made their children lose their Religious Vocation! and how many youths shall we see lost who, to please their parents, and by not detaching themselves from them, have lost their Vocation and afterwards their souls! Hence, Jesus declares to us: If any man hates not his father and mother and wife and children and brethren and sisters, yea, and his own life, he cannot be my disciple (Luke xiv. 26). Let him, then, who wishes to enter a Religious Institute of perfect observance, and to become a true disciple of Jesus Christ, resolve to detach himself from his parents.

And should he have already entered Religion, let him remember that he must practice this same detachment. Let him know that he cannot go to visit his parents in their own house, except in the case of some dangerous illness of his father or mother, or of some urgent necessity, and always with the permission of the Superior. To go to the house of one's parents without this permission would be considered in Religion a most notable and scandalous fault. In Religion it is considered a defect even to ask permission or to show a desire to see parents or of speaking with them.

St. Charles Borromeo said that when he visited his family he always, on his return, found himself less fervent in spirit. And let him who goes to his relations by his own will and not through a positive obedience to his Superiors, be persuaded that he will return either tempted or lukewarm.

St. Vincent de Paul could only be induced once to visit his country and his parents, and this out of pure necessity. He said that the love of home and country was a great impediment to his spiritual progress. He narrated how many, on account of having visited their home, had become so tender towards their relatives that they were like flies, which being once entangled in a cobweb, cannot extricate themselves from it. He added: "For that one visit of mine, though it was for a short time only, and though I took care to remove from my relatives every hope of help from me, I, nevertheless, felt at leaving them such pain that I ceased not to weep all along the road, and was for three months harassed by the thought of succoring them. Finally, God in His mercy, took the temptation from me."

Let him know, moreover, that no one can write letters without permission, and without showing them to the Superior. He who would act otherwise would be guilty of a fault that is not to be tolerated in Religion, and he should be punished with severity; for from this might come a thousand disorders tending to destroy the religious spirit. But they especially who have just entered should know that this rule is enforced with the greatest rigor; for novices, during their year of Novitiate, do not easily obtain permission to talk to their parents, or to write to them.

Finally, let it be remembered that should a subject fall ill, it would be a notable defect in him to ask or to show an inclination to go to his own home for his restoration to health, under the plea of better attendance, or of enjoying the benefit of his native air. The air of his own country is almost always, if not indeed always, hurtful, and pestilential to the spirit of the subject. And if he should say that he wishes to be cured at home to save the Institute expense for remedies, this is no excuse, for he should know that the sick is treated with all care and charity in Religion. As for change of air, the Superiors will think of that; and if the air of one house is not beneficial to him, they will send him to another. And as for remedies, they will even sell their books, if need be, to provide for the sick. And thus, he need not fear that Divine Providence will fail him. And if the Lord does not wish his recovery, he ought to conform to the will of God, without even mentioning the word "home." The greatest grace that he who enters Religion can desire is to die, when God wills it, in the House of God, assisted by his brethren in Religion, and not in his home in the world during his relatives.

Evening Meditation

JESUS IS THE FOUNTAIN OF GRACE.

I.

Ye shall draw waters with joy out of the Savior's fountains (Is. xii. 3).

Consider the four Fountains of grace that we have in Jesus Christ, as contemplated by St. Bernard.

The first is that of Mercy, in which we can wash ourselves from all the filthiness of our sins. This fountain was provided for us by our Redeemer with His tears and His Blood: He loved us and washed us from our sins in his own blood (Apoc. i. 5).

The second Fountain is that of Peace and Consolation in our tribulations: Call upon me in the day of trouble, and I will console thee (Ps. xlix. 15). He that thirsted, let him come to me, says Jesus (Jo. vii. 37). He thirsted for true consolations even in this world, let him come to me, for I will satisfy him. He that once tastes the sweetness of My love will forever disdain all the delights of the world: But he that shall drink of the water that I will give him shall not thirst forever (Jo. iv. 13). And thoroughly contented will he be when he shall enter the kingdom of the blessed, for the water of My grace shall raise him from earth to Heaven. It will become in him a fountain of water springing up into life everlasting (Ibid. 14). The peace which God gives to souls that love Him is not the peace that the world promises from sensual pleasures, which leave behind more bitterness than peace: the peace which God bestows exceeds all the delights of the senses: Peace which surpasses all understanding. Blessed are those who long for this divine fountain. Blessed are they that hunger and thirst for justice (Matt. v. 6).

O my sweet and dearest Savior, how much do I not owe Thee? How much hast Thou did not oblige me to love Thee, since Thou hast done for me what no servant would have done for his master, no son for his father. If Thou, therefore, hast loved me more than any other, it is just that I should love Thee above all others. I could wish to die of sorrow at the thought that Thou hast suffered so much for me, and that Thou even didst except for my sake the most painful and ignominious death that a man could endure, and yet I have so often despised Thy friendship. But Thy merits are my hope.

The third Fountain is that of Devotion. Oh, how devoted and ready to follow the divine inspiration and increase always in virtue does not he become who often meditates on all that Jesus Christ has done for our sake! He will be like the tree planted by a stream of water. He shall be like a tree that is planted near the running waters (Ps. i. 3).

The fourth Fountain is that of Charity. In my meditation a fire shall flame out (Ps. xxxviii. 4). It is impossible to meditate on the sufferings and ignominy borne by Jesus Christ for the love of us and not to feel inflamed by that blessed fire which He came upon earth to kindle. How true it is then, that he who betakes himself to these blessed Fountains of Jesus Christ will always draw from them waters of joy and salvation! You shall draw waters with joy out of the Savior's Fountains.

Ah, my dear Jesus, I too desire to be reckoned amongst the number of Thy lovers. I now esteem Thy grace above all the kingdoms of the earth. I love Thee, and for Thy love I accept every suffering, even death itself. And if I am not worthy to die for Thy glory by the hand of executioners, I accept willingly, at least, that death which Thou hast determined for me; I accept it in the manner and at the time that Thou shalt choose. My Mother Mary, do thou obtain for me the grace always to live and die, loving Jesus.

Tuesday--Third Week of Advent

Morning Meditation

CONSIDERATIONS ON THE RELIGIOUS STATE. VII.

Consider the harm done to Religious by tepidity.

Negligent souls are commonly abandoned by God. St. Teresa saw the place prepared for her in hell had she not detached herself from a certain worldly affection which, however, was but slightly culpable. *He that contemned small things shall fall by little and little* (Ecclus. xix. 1).

I.

Consider the misery of the Religious who, after having left his home, his parents, and the world with all its pleasures, and after having given himself to Jesus Christ, consecrating to Him his will and his liberty, exposes himself to the danger of being damned by leading a lukewarm and negligent life. Alas! such a Religious is not far from perdition, who, called into the House of God to become a Saint, leads a lukewarm life. God threatens to reject and abandon such Religious if they do not amend: *But because thou art lukewarm I will begin to vomit thee out of my mouth* (Apoc. iii. 16).

St. Ignatius of Loyola, seeing that a Lay brother of the Society had become lukewarm in the service of God, called him one day and said to him: "Tell me, my brother, why did you come into Religion?" He answered, "To serve God." "O my brother!" replied the Saint, "what have you said? If you had answered that you had come to serve a Cardinal, or a prince of this earth, you would be more excusable; but you say that you came to serve God, and is it thus you serve Him?" Father Nieremberg says that some are called by God to be saved as Saints, and that if they do not take care to live as Saints, but thinking to be saved as imperfect Christians, they will not be saved at all. And St. Augustine says that such are, in most cases, abandoned by God: "God is accustomed to abandon negligent souls." And how does He abandon them? By permitting them from lighter faults, which they see and do not amend, to fall into grievous ones, lose divine grace and their Vocation. St. Teresa of Jesus saw the place prepared for her in hell, had she not detached herself from an earthly, though not a grievously sinful affection. He that contemned small things shall fall by little and little.

Many wish to follow Jesus Christ as St. Peter did, who, when his Master was arrested in the garden, says St. Matthew, followed him afar off (Matt. xxvi. 58). But by doing so that will easily happen to them which happened to St. Peter, namely, when the occasion came, he denied Jesus Christ. A lukewarm Religious will be contented with the little he does for God; but God, who called him to a perfect life, will not be contented, and, in punishment for his ingratitude, will not only deprive him of special favors, but will sometimes permit his fall. "When you say: 'It is enough,' you are lost," says Augustine. The fig-tree of the Gospel was cast into the fire, only because it brought forth no fruit.

O my God, reject me not, as I deserve, for I will amend my life. I know full well that a life negligent as mine cannot satisfy Thee. I know that I have, by my lukewarmness, shut the door of my heart against the graces which Thou didst desire to bestow upon me. O Lord! do not abandon me yet awhile; I will rise from my miserable state. I will for the future be more careful to overcome my passions, to follow Thy inspirations, and I will never through slothfulness omit my duties; I will perform them with greater diligence. In short, I will, from this time forward, do all I can to please Thee, and I will neglect nothing which I know to be pleasing to Thee.

II.

Father Louis de Ponte said: "I have committed many faults, but I have never made peace with them." Miserable is the Religious who, being called to perfection, makes peace with his defects. If we detest our imperfections, there is hope that we may become Saints; but when we commit faults and make little of them, then, says St. Bernard, the hope of becoming Saints is lost. He who soweth sparingly shall also reap sparingly (2 Cor. ix. 6). Ordinary graces do not suffice to make one a Saint; extraordinary ones are necessary. But how shall God be liberal with His favors to one who acts sparingly and with reserve in his Love for Him?

Moreover, to become a Saint, one must have courage and strength to overcome all repugnances; and let no one ever believe, says St. Bernard, that he will be able to attain to perfection unless he distinguishes himself in the practice of virtue: "What is perfect, cannot but be singular." Reflect, my brother, for what have you left the world and all it can give? It was to become a Saint. But that lukewarm and imperfect life which you lead, is that the way of becoming a Saint? St. Teresa animated her daughters by saying to them: "My sisters, you have done the principal thing necessary to become Saints; the lesser remains yet to be done." The same I say to you; you have, perhaps, done the chief part already; you have left your country, your parents, and home, your property and your amusements, the lesser part now remains to be done to become a Saint. Do it.

Since Thou, O my Jesus! hast been so liberal with Thy graces towards me, and hast deigned to give Thy Blood and Thy life for me, why should I act with such reserve towards Thee? Thou art worthy of all honor and love, and to please Thee one ought gladly to undergo every labor and suffer every pain. But, O my Redeemer, thou know my weakness, help me by Thy powerful grace; in Thee I confide. O immaculate Virgin Mary, thou who hast helped me to leave the world, help me to overcome myself and to become a Saint.

Spiritual Reading

COUNSELS CONCERNING A RELIGIOUS VOCATION

VIII. DETACHMENT (continued)

III. From Self-Esteem

He who enters Religion must be entirely detached from all self-esteem. There are many who leave their home, their comforts, their relations, but arrive bringing with them a certain esteem for themselves: such attachment would be the worst of all. Here is the greatest sacrifice we have to offer to God, namely the giving up, not only of our goods, our pleasures, our home, but of our own selves to Him. This is that denial of self which Jesus recommended more than anything else to His followers. And to deny himself, a man must tread under foot all self-esteem, by desiring and embracing every imaginable contempt that he may meet with in Religion; as, for instance, seeing others, whom perhaps he thinks less deserving, preferred to himself, or himself considered unfit to be employed, or only employed in lower or more laborious occupations. It must be understood that in the House of God those charges are the highest and the most honorable that are imposed by obedience. God forbid that anyone should seek for or aspire to any office or charge of pre-eminence. This would be a strange thing in Religion, and would mark a Religious as proud and ambitious, and as such he should receive a penance, and be mortified especially on this very point. Better would it be, perhaps, that a Religious Order were destroyed than there should enter in that accursed pest of ambition which, when it enters, disfigures the most perfect Communities, and the most beautiful works of God.

On the contrary, he ought to feel interiorly consoled who sees himself made fun of and despised by his companions. I say interiorly consoled, for as to nature, this is not possible, nor need the Religious be uneasy at the resentment of his feelings, for it is enough that the spirit embraces such things, and that he rejoices in the superior part of the soul. Thus, also when he sees himself continually reprimanded and mortified, not only by Superiors, but also by equals and inferiors, he ought heartily, and with a tranquil mind, to thank those who thus reprimand him, and have the charity to admonish him, answering that he will be more careful not to fall into that fault again.

One of the most ardent desires of the Saints in this world was to be despised for the love of Jesus Christ. It was this St. John of the Cross asked for, when Jesus Christ appeared to him with a Cross on His shoulder, and said: "John, ask from Me what thou wish," and St. John answered: "O Lord, to suffer and to be despised for Thee." The Doctors of the Church teach, with St. Francis de Sales, that the highest degree of humility is to be pleased with objections and humiliations. And in this consists also our greatest merit before God. Some insult suffered in peace for the love of God is of greater value in His sight than a thousand disciplines and a thousand fasts.

We must know that occasions to suffer some slight, either from Superiors or from companions, are to be found even in the most holy Communities. Read the Lives of the Saints, and you will see how many mortifications fell to the lot of a St. Francis Regis, St. Francis of Jerome, Father Torres, and others. The Lord sometimes permits that even among Saints there should exist, without any fault of theirs, certain natural antipathies, or at least, a certain diversity of character among subjects of the greatest piety, which will cause them to suffer many contradictions. At other times things will be believed that are not true.

God Himself will permit this in order that the subjects may have occasion to exercise themselves in patience and humility.

In short, he will gain little in Religion and lose much who cannot quietly put up with contempt and contradictions; and, therefore, he who enters Religion to give himself entirely to God should feel ashamed not to know how to bear contempt when he appears before Jesus Christ, who was filled with opprobrium for love of us. Let each one be attentive to this, and resolve to take pleasure in abjections, and to prepare himself to suffer many in Religion, for without the least doubt he will have many to bear. Otherwise, the disquiet caused by contradictions and contempt badly endured would trouble him to such a degree as to bring him to lose his Vocation and make him abandon the Religious life. Oh, how many have lost their Vocation on account of impatience in humiliations! But of what service to an Institute, or to God, can be he who does not know how to bear contempt for God's love? And how can one ever be said to be dead to himself, according to that promise which he made to Jesus Christ on entering Religion, if he remains still alive to resentment and disquiet, when he sees himself humbled? Away then with such subjects so full of self-esteem! Yes, far away! It is well that they go as soon as possible, lest they infect the rest with their pride. In Religion each one ought to be, as it were, dead, and especially to self-esteem, otherwise it was better for him not to enter, or to depart if he had already entered.

Evening Meditation

JESUS THE CHARITABLE PHYSICIAN OF OUR SOULS

I.

But unto you the sun of justice shall rise, and health in his wings (Mal. iv. 2).

Your Physician shall come, says the Prophet, to cure the infirm; and He will come swiftly like the bird that flies, and like the sun, which, on rising above the horizon, instantly sends its light to the other pole. But behold Him, He has already come. Let us console ourselves and return thanks to Him.

St. Augustine says: "He descends even to the bed of the sick"; that is to say, even to taking our flesh, for our bodies are the beds of our infirm souls.

Physicians, if they love their patients, do indeed make every possible effort to cure them; but what physician, to cure the sick man, ever took upon himself his disease? Jesus Christ is truly that Physician, who took on Himself our infirmities in order to cure them. Neither would He content Himself with sending another in His place, but He chose to come Himself to fulfil this charitable office to gain to Himself all our love.

Praised and blessed forever be Thy Charity, O my Redeemer! And what would become of my soul, so infirm and afflicted with the many wounds of my sins, if I had not Thee, my Jesus, who art both able and willing to heal me? O Blood of my Savior, I trust in Thee! Wash me and heal me.

II.

He hath borne our infirmities and carried our sorrows (Is. liii. 4). He was pleased to heal our wounds with His own Blood, and by His death deliver us from eternal death which we had deserved. In short, He chose to take the bitter medicine of a life of continual sufferings and a painful death to obtain life for us, and to deliver us from our many ills.

The chalice which my Father hath given me, shall I not drink it? (Jo. xviii. 11), He said to Peter. It was necessary then that Jesus Christ should embrace so many ignominies to heal our pride; that He should embrace such a life of poverty to cure our covetousness; that He should suffer a sea of torments, to die of pure agony to cure our eagerness for sensual pleasures.

O my Love, I repent of having offended Thee. Thou hast led a life of such tribulations and hast died such a bitter death to prove to me the love which Thou barest me! I would fain show Thee also how much I love Thee, but what can I do -- I am so infirm, so miserable and so weak? O God of my soul Thou art Omnipotent; Thou canst cure me and make me holy. Oh, kindle in me a great desire of pleasing Thee. I renounce all my satisfactions to please Thee my Redeemer, who dost deserve to be pleased at all cost. O Sovereign Good, I esteem Thee and love Thee above every good; make me love Thee with all my heart, and always implore Thy love. Hitherto I have offended Thee, and have not loved Thee, because I have not sought Thy love. I now beg this love of Thee, and the grace always to ask it of Thee. Hear me, by the merits of Thy Passion.

O Mary, my Mother, thou art always prepared to listen to him that prays to thee. Thou loves him that loves thee. I love thee, my Queen. Obtain for me the grace to love God, and I ask for nothing more. Amen.

Wednesday--Third Week of Advent

Morning Meditation

CONSIDERATIONS ON THE RELIGIOUS STATE. VIII.

Consider how dear to God is a soul that gives itself entirely to Him.

The Son of God has already given Himself entirely to us. A Child is born to us, and a Son is given to us. He has given Himself to us through the love He bears us. When St. Teresa gave herself to Jesus the Lord said to her: "Now because thou art all Mine, I am all thine."

I.

One is my dove, my perfect one (Cant. vi. 8). God loves all who love Him. I love them that love me (Prov. viii. 17). Many indeed give themselves to God but keep in their hearts some attachment to creatures which prevents them from belonging entirely to Him. How then will God give Himself to a soul that divides its love between Him and creatures? It is just He should act with reserve towards those who act with reserve towards Him. On the other hand, He gives Himself entirely to those souls who drive from their hearts everything that is not for God, and who can truly say: My God and my All!

St. Teresa, if she entertained an inordinate affection, though not an impure one, towards a certain person, could not hear from Jesus Christ what she afterwards heard, when, freeing herself from every attachment, she gave herself entirely to Divine Love, and God said to her: "Since now thou art all Mine, I am all thine!"

My beloved to me and I to him! (Cant. ii. 16). Since then, O my God, thou have given Thyself entirely to me, I should be ungrateful, indeed, were I not to give myself entirely to Thee; since Thou wouldst have me belong wholly to Thee, behold, O my Lord, I give myself entirely to Thee. Accept me through Thy mercy and disdain me not. Grant, O Lord, that my heart, which once loved creatures, may turn now wholly to Thy infinite goodness. "Let me at last die," said St. Teresa, "and let another live in me. Let God live in me and give me life. Let Him reign, and let me be His slave, for my soul wishes no other liberty." My heart is too small, O God most worthy of love, and it is too little able to love Thee, Who art deserving of an infinite love. I should then be guilty of too great an injustice were I to divide it by loving anything besides Thee. I love Thee, my God, above everything. I love only Thee; I renounce all creatures, and give myself entirely to Thee, my Jesus, my Savior, my Love, my All.

II.

Consider that the Son of God has not hesitated to give Himself all to us. A Child is born to us, and a Son is given to us (Is. ix. 6). He has given Himself to us through the love He bears us. He hath loved us and hath delivered himself for us (Eph. v. 2). It is, then, just, says St. Chrysostom, that as God has given Himself to you without reserve -- "He has given thee all, nothing has He left for Himself" -- you should give yourself to God without reserve, and burning with divine love should henceforth sing to Him:

Thine wholly will I always be;
Thou has bestowed Thyself on me;
Myself I wholly give to Thee.

St. Teresa, appearing after her death, revealed to one of her nuns that God loves a soul that, as a spouse, gives herself entirely to Him, more than a thousand who are tepid and imperfect. The choir of Seraphim is completed from these generous souls belonging entirely to God. The Lord Himself says that He loves a soul that tends to perfection so much that He seems not to love any other: One is my dove, my perfect one is but one (Cant. vi. 8). Hence Blessed Giles exhorts us: "One for one -- una uni," by which he wishes to say that this one soul of ours we ought to give wholly, undivided, to that One Who alone deserves all love, on Whom depends on all our good, and Who loves us more than all others love us. "Leave all and you shall find all," says Thomas a Kempis. Leave all for God and in God you will find all. "O soul!" concludes St. Bernard, "be alone, that you may keep yourself for Him alone." Keep yourself alone, give no part of your affections to creatures, that you may belong alone to Him Who alone deserves an infinite love, and Whom alone you ought to love.

What have I in heaven, and besides Thee, what do I desire on earth?... Thou art the God of my heart, and the God that is my portion forever (Ps. lxxii. 25). I desire nothing, either in this life or in the next, but to possess the treasure of Thy love. I am unwilling that creatures should any longer have a place in my heart; Thou alone must be its Master. To Thee alone shall it belong for the future. Thou only shalt be my God, my repose, my desire, all my love. "Give me only Thy love and Thy grace, and I am rich enough." O most holy Virgin Mary obtain for me that I may be faithful to God, and never recall the gift which I have made of myself to Him. Amen.

Spiritual Reading

COUNSELS CONCERNING A RELIGIOUS VOCATION

IX. DETACHMENT (continued).

IV. From Self-Will.

He who enters Religion must absolutely give up his own will and consecrate it without reserve to holy obedience. This condition is the most necessary of all. Of what use is it to leave comforts and relations and honors, and then bring into Religion one's own will? Renouncement of self consists especially in this: in dying spiritually and in giving oneself entirely to Jesus Christ.

The gift of the heart -- that is, of the will -- is what pleases Him most, and what He seeks from His sons and daughters in Religion. All our mortifications, all our meditations and prayers, and all other sacrifices, will be of little avail if there be not an entire detachment from and renouncement of self-will.

It is, then, evident that in this is the greatest merit before God. It is the only sure way of pleasing God in all things, because then each one can say what Jesus our Savior said: I do always the things that please Him (Jo. viii. 29). He who in Religion lives without any will of his own may say and hope that in all he does, he pleases God; whether he studies or prays, or hears confessions; whether he goes to the refectory or to recreation, or to rest; for in Religion there is scarcely a step made, or a breath drawn, but in obedience to the Rule, or to Superiors.

The world does not understand, and even certain pious people have little idea of, the great value of Community life under obedience. It is true that outside of Religious Communities there are found many persons who do much, and may be, more than those who live under obedience -- they preach, do penance, pray and fast, but in all this they follow more or less their own will. God grant that at the Day of Judgment they may not have to lament as those mentioned in Scripture: Why have we fasted and Thou hast not regarded, have we humbled our souls and Thou hast not taken notice? Behold, in the day of your fast, your own will is found (Is. lviii. 3). On which passage St. Bernard remarks: "Self-will is a great evil, for through it that which is good in itself may be for you no good at all." This is to be understood when in all our exercises we seek not God, but ourselves. On the contrary, he who acts by obedience is sure that in all he does he pleases God. The Venerable Mother Mary of Jesus said that she valued exceedingly her Religious Vocation, principally for two reasons: the first was that in the monastery she always enjoyed the presence and company of Jesus in the Blessed Sacrament, and the other, that there she belonged entirely to God, sacrificing her own will to Him by obedience.

It is related by Father Rodriguez that after the death of Dositheus, the disciple of St. Dorotheus, the Lord revealed that during the five years he had lived under obedience, though by reason of his infirmities he could not practice the austerities of the other monks, yet he had merited by virtue of obedience the reward of St. Paul the Hermit and of St. Anthony the Abbot.

He, then, who wishes to enter Religion, must resolve to renounce altogether his own will, and to will only what holy obedience wills. God preserve a Religious from ever letting escape from his lips the words "I will" or "I will not." But in all things, even when asked by Superiors what he desires, he should only answer: "I will that which holy obedience wills of me." And, provided there is no evident sin, he ought in every command imposed on him to obey blindly and without examination, because the duty of examining and deciding belongs not to him, but to his Superiors. Otherwise, even if in obeying, he does not submit his own judgment to that of the Superior, his obedience will be imperfect. St. Ignatius Loyola used to say that in matters of obedience prudence is not required in subjects, but in Superiors; and if prudence enters at all into obedience it is to obey without prudence. St. Bernard says: "Perfect obedience is indiscreet." And in another place: "For a prudent novice to remain in a Congregation is an impossible thing"; and he gives the reason, saying: "To judge belongs to the Superior, and to obey to the subject."

But to make progress in this virtue of obedience, on which all depends, he must always be ready to do all that for which he feels the greatest repugnance, and to be prepared to bear it peacefully when he sees that all he seeks or desires is refused him. It will happen that when he wishes for solitude, to apply himself to prayer or study, he will be the most employed in external labors. For though it is true that in Religion one leads as much as possible a solitary life when at home, and that for this end there are many hours of silence -- the Retreat each year of ten days, in perfect silence, and of one day each month, besides the fifteen days before the receiving of the habit, and one of fifteen before the Profession, when the Vows are made -- nevertheless, if it be an Institute of priests called to work and to be employed for the salvation of souls, the subject, if he is continually employed in this by obedience, ought to be content with the prayers and exercises of the community; he must be prepared sometimes to go even without these when obedience will have it so, without either excusing himself or being disquieted, being well persuaded of that of which St. Mary Magdalen de Pazzi was so confident when she said that "all the things which are done through obedience are so many prayers."

Evening Meditation

GOD HAS GIVEN HIS ONLY SON TO SAVE US.

I.

I have given thee to be the light of the Gentiles that thou mayest be my salvation even to the farthest part of the earth (Is. xlix. 6).

Consider how the Eternal Father addressed these words to the Infant Jesus at the instant of His Conception: I have given thee to be the light of the Gentiles that thou mayst be my salvation. My Son, I have given Thee to the world for the Light and Life of all people, in order that Thou mayst procure for them their salvation, which I have as much at heart as if it were My own. Thou must, therefore, employ Thyself entirely for the well-being of men. "Wholly given to man Thou must be wholly spent in his service." (St. Bernard). Thou must therefore, at Thy birth, suffer extreme poverty in order that men may become rich: "that Thou mayst enrich them by Thy poverty." Thou must be sold as a slave to acquire liberty for man; and Thou must be scourged and crucified as a slave to satisfy My justice for the punishment due to man. Thou must give Thy Blood and Thy Life to deliver man from eternal death. In a word, Thou art no longer Thine own, but Thou belongs to man:

A child is born to us, a son is given to us (Is. ix. 6). Thus, My beloved Son, man will be constrained to love Me, and to be Mine, when he sees that I give Thee, My only-begotten One, entirely to him, and that there is nothing left for Me to give him.

My dearest Jesus, if it is true (as the Law says) that dominion is acquired by gift, since Thy Father hath given Thee to me, thou art mine; for me Thou wert born, to me Thou hast been given: A child is born to us, a Son is given to us. Therefore, I may well say: "My Jesus and my all." Since Thou art mine, everything that belongs to Thee is also mine. Of this I am assured by Thy Apostle: How hath he not also with him given us all things (Rom. viii. 32). Thy Blood is mine, thy merits are mine, thy grace is mine, Thy Paradise is mine; and if Thou art mine who shall be able to take Thee from me? "No man can take God away from me," joyfully exclaimed the Abbot St. Anthony, and so, too, from this day forth, will I also continually say. It is only through my own fault that I can lose Thee and separate myself from Thee; but if in past times I have abandoned Thee and lost Thee, O my Jesus, I now repent of it with all my soul, and I am resolved to lose my life and everything sooner than lose Thee, O infinite Good, and only Love of my soul!

II.

God so loved the world! O infinite love, only worthy of an Infinite God! God so loved the world as to give his only begotten son! (Jo. iii. 16). The Infant Jesus, far from being sorrowful at this proposal, is pleased at it, accepts it with love, and exults in it: He hath rejoiced as a giant to run the way (Ps. lviii. 6), and from the first moment of His Incarnation He gives Himself entirely to man and embraces with pleasure all the sorrows and ignominy that He must suffer on earth for the love of man. These were, says St. Bernard, the mountains, and hills that Jesus Christ had to pass with so many labors in order to save man: Behold he cometh leaping upon the mountains, skipping over the hills (Cant. ii. 8).

Here consider that the Divine Father, in sending His Son to be our Redeemer and Mediator between Himself and man, has in a certain sense bound Himself to forgive us and love us, on account of the Covenant He made to receive us into His favor, provided His Son satisfied His Divine justice for us. On the other hand, the Divine Word, having accepted the decree of His Father, Who, by sending Him to redeem us, has given Him to us, has also bound Himself to love us; not, indeed, for our own merits, but to fulfil the merciful will of His Father.

I thank Thee, Eternal Father, for having given me Thy Son; and since Thou hast given Him entirely to me, I, a miserable sinner, give myself entirely to Thee. For the sake of this same Son, accept me, and bind me with the chains of love to my dear Redeemer; but bind me so strongly that I also may be able to say: Who shall separate me from the love of Christ? (Rom. viii. 35). What good shall there ever be in the world that shall separate me from my Jesus? And Thou, my Savior if Thou art all mine, know that I am all Thine. Dispose of me, and of all that belongs to me, as shall best please Thee. And how can I refuse anything to a God Who has not refused me His Blood and His life? Mary, my Mother, do thou guard me with thy protection. I will no longer be my own. I will be all my Savior's. Do thou help me to be faithful; I trust in thee.

Thursday--Third Week of Advent

Morning Meditation

CONSIDERATIONS ON THE RELIGIOUS STATE. IX.

Consider that to become a Saint it is necessary to have a great desire of holiness.

No Saint has ever become a Saint without having a great desire for sanctity. As wings are necessary to fly, holy desires are necessary to the soul in order to advance in the way of perfection. My heart is ready, O God, my heart is ready! Tell me what Thou desires of me. I will obey Thee in all things.

I.

Holy desires are necessary to the soul to advance in the way of perfection. To become a Saint, we must detach ourselves from creatures, conquer our passions, overcome ourselves, and love crosses. But to do all this much strength is required, and we must suffer much.

But what is the effect of this holy desire? St. Laurence Justinian answers: "It supplies strength and makes the pain easier to be borne." Hence the same Saint adds that he has already vanquished who has a great desire to vanquish. "A great part of the victory is the desire of vanquishing." He who wishes to reach the top of a high mountain will never reach it if he has not a desire to do so. This will give him courage and strength to undergo the fatigue of ascending; otherwise, he will halt at the foot, wearied, and discouraged.

St. Bernard asserts that we acquire perfection in proportion to the desire for it which we preserve in our hearts. St. Teresa said that God loves generous souls that have great desires; for which reason the Saint exhorted all, saying: "Let our thoughts be high, for thence will come our good. We must not have weak desires, but have confidence in God by which we shall, little by little, attain that perfection to which, by God's grace, the Saints attained." It was thus the Saints gained, in a short time, a great degree of perfection, and were able to do great things for God: Being made perfect in a short space, he fulfilled a long time (Wis. iv. 13). St. Aloysius Gonzaga attained in a few years (he was only twenty-three when he died) such a degree of sanctity that St. Mary Magdalen de Pazzi, beholding him in spirit in Heaven, said it seemed to her, in a certain way, that there was no Saint in Heaven who enjoyed greater glory than Aloysius. She understood while he had arrived at so high a degree by the great desire he had to love God as much as He deserved, and that, seeing this beyond his power, the holy youth had suffered on earth a martyrdom of love.

Behold, O my God! here I am. My heart is ready, O God, my heart is ready (Ps. lvi. 8). See, I am prepared to do all that Thou shalt require of me. O Lord, what wilt thou have me to do? (Acts ix. 6). Tell me what Thou desires of me. I will obey Thee in all things. I am sorry for having lost so much time in which I might have pleased Thee and have not done so. I thank Thee that still Thou gives me time to do it. Oh, no, I will not lose any more time. I will and I desire to become a Saint, not to obtain from Thee greater glory and more delights. I desire it that I may love Thee more, and that I may please Thee in this life and in the next.

II.

St. Bernard, when a Religious, was accustomed to say to himself to excite his fervor: Bernarde, ad quid venisti? -- "Bernard, for what hast thou come hither?" I say the same to you: What have you come to the House of God to do? Why have you left the world? To become a Saint? And what are you doing? Why do you lose time? Tell me -- do you desire to become a Saint? If you do not desire it, then, certainly, you will never become a Saint. If you have not this desire, ask Jesus Christ for it: ask Mary for it. And if you have it, take courage, says St. Bernard, for many there are who do not become Saints just because they are not courageous. And so, I repeat, let us take courage and great courage. Why should we fear? Why be cast down? Our Blessed Lord Who gave us strength to leave the world, will give us also the grace to embrace the life of a Saint. Everything comes to an end. Our life, be it a contented or a discontented one, will also come to an end, but eternity will never end. That little which we have done for God will alone console us at death and throughout eternity. The labor will be short, the crown, which is already in sight, will be immortal. How well pleased the Saints are now with all they have suffered for

God! If sorrow could enter Paradise, the blessed would be sorry only that they neglected to do more for God than they had done, and now they are unable to do it. Courage, then, make haste, for there is no time to lose; what can be done today we may not be able to do tomorrow. St. Bernardine of Sienna used to say that one moment of time is of as great value as God Himself, for at each moment we may gain God, His divine grace, and higher degrees of merit.

Make me, O Lord, to love and please Thee as much as Thou desires. Behold, this is all I ask from Thee, O my God! I will love Thee, I will love Thee; and, in order to love Thee, I offer myself to undergo every fatigue, and to suffer every pain. O my Lord, increase in me always this desire, and give me the grace to execute it. Of myself I can do nothing, but assisted by Thee I can do all things. Eternal Father, for the love of Jesus Christ graciously hear me. My Jesus, through the merits of Thy Passion, come to my succor. O Mary, my hope! for the love of Jesus Christ, protect me.

Spiritual Reading

COUNSELS CONCERNING A RELIGIOUS VOCATION

X. THE TRIALS WHICH WE MUST EXPECT TO HAVE IN THE RELIGIOUS LIFE

When then, a person has actually entered Religion, however genuine his Vocation may be, and though he may have conquered all his passions and his earthly affections, let him not imagine that he will be exempt from other temptations and trials, which God Himself will send him, such as tediousness, darkness, various fears, in order to establish him more firmly in his Vocation. We must remember that even the Saints, who loved their Vocation most, have sometimes suffered great darkness about it, and that it seemed to them that they were deceived, and would not be able to save themselves in that state. So it happened with St. Teresa, St. John of the Cross, St. Jane Frances de Chantal. But by recommending themselves to God, that darkness was dissipated, and they recovered their peace of mind. Thus, the Lord tests His most beloved children, as it was said to Tobias: Because thou was acceptable to God, it was necessary that temptation should prove thee (Tob. xii. 13). And in the Book of Deuteronomy, The Lord, your God, tries you, that it may appear whether you love him or not (Deut. xiii. 3). Let each one, therefore, prepare himself to suffer in Religion this obscurity. It will sometimes appear to him that he cannot bear the observance of the Order, that he will have no more peace of mind, or will not even be able to save himself. But, most of all, he must be on his guard when the temptation presents specious scruples or pretexts of greater spiritual good, to make him abandon his Vocation.

There are two principal remedies for such temptations:

First Remedy: To have Recourse to God.

Prayer is the first remedy: Come ye to him and be enlightened (Ps. xxxiii. 6). For, as it is not possible that temptation overcome one who has recourse to God by prayer, so he who does not recommend himself to God will surely be overcome. And let it be noted that sometimes it will not suffice to have recourse to God once, or for a few days, to be victorious. Perhaps the Lord will permit the temptation to continue, even after we have prayed for several weeks, months, and even years; but let us be assured that he who ceases not to recommend himself to God will certainly be enlightened and win the victory, and thereafter he will have more peace and be firmer in his Vocation.

Until we have passed through this storm, which for the most part comes to all, let none of us think himself secure. Let us be persuaded, however, that in this time of temptation it is vain to expect to feel fervor, or a clearness of reason sufficient to tranquilize ourselves; for during the darkness we see nothing but confusion. At such a time we can only cry out: O Lord, help me! O Lord, help me! We should also have frequent recourse to Most Holy Mary, who is the Mother of perseverance. Let us confide in that divine promise: Ask and you shall receive. It is certain that he who, with the help of divine grace, is victorious in such a combat finds afterwards a double calm and peace in his Vocation.

Second Remedy: To have Recourse to the Superiors.

The second remedy, and a principal and necessary one in such temptations, is to communicate to the Superiors, or to the Spiritual Father, the temptation which afflicts you, and this at once, before the temptation becomes strong. St. Philip Neri says that a temptation thus manifested is half conquered. On the contrary, there is no greater mistake than to conceal the temptation; for then, on the one hand, God withdraws His light because of the little fidelity shown by the subject in not disclosing it to those who hold His place, and, on the other, whilst the mine is not sprung, the temptation gains strength. Hence, it may be held for certain that he who is thus unfaithful when tempted against his Vocation, will surely lose it.

And let it be understood that in Religion these temptations against Vocation are the most pernicious that hell can raise against a subject, for, should he give way, the devil, with one stroke, will have gained many victories; for when a subject has lost his Vocation and left Religion, what good will he be able to do in the service of God? The enemy, it is true, will make him believe that out of Religion he will enjoy greater peace and be able to do better; nevertheless, let him hold for certain that as soon as he has left the House of God, he will feel such remorse that he will nevermore enjoy peace of conscience. And God grant that such a remorse may not torment him for all eternity in hell, into which, as has already been said, he who through his own fault loses his Vocation, may so easily fall. He will be so lukewarm and discouraged in doing good that he will not even have the strength to raise his eyes to Heaven. In such a state he will easily give up prayer altogether, because as often as he begins it, he will feel a hell of remorse, hearing his conscience reproach him and saying: "What hast thou done? Thou hast abandoned God; thou hast lost thy Vocation; and for what? To follow thine own caprice; to please thy parents." Let him be certain that he will have to feel this remorse through his whole life, and still more so at the hour of his death, when, in sight of eternity, instead of dying in the House of God, and in the midst of his Brethren in Religion, he will die out of Religion, perhaps in his own house, in the midst of his relatives, to please whom he has displeased God. A Religious should ever beseech God to let him die rather than permit so great a misfortune to befall him, the torments of which he will better understand at the point of death, because then there will be no remedy for the error. For him, then, who is tempted against his Vocation, the best Meditation he can make while it lasts, is to reflect what torment the remorse of having lost his Vocation, and of having to die out of Religion, through his own caprice, through his own fault, will cause him at the hour of his death.

Evening Meditation

GOD HAS MADE HIMSELF A CHILD TO GAIN OUR CONFIDENCE AND OUR LOVE.

I.

A child is born to us and a son is given to us (Is. ix. 6).

Consider how, after so many centuries, after so many prayers and sighs, the Messias Whom the holy Patriarchs and Prophets were not worthy to see, for Whom the nations sighed, the desire of the eternal hills, our Savior, is come! He is already born and has given Himself entirely to us. A child is born to us, and a son is given to us (Is. ix. 6).

The Son of God has made Himself little, to make us great; He has given Himself to us, in order that we may give ourselves to Him; He is come to show us His love, in order that we may respond to it by giving Him ours. Let us, therefore, receive Him with affection; let us love Him, and have recourse to Him in all our necessities.

"A child gives easily," says St. Bernard; children readily give anything that is asked of them. Jesus came into the world as a Child, in order to show Himself ready and willing to give us all good gifts: In whom are hid all treasures (Col. ii. 3). The Father hath given all things into his hands (Jo. iii. 35). If we wish for light, He comes on purpose to enlighten us. If we wish for strength to resist our enemies, He is come to give us comfort. If we wish for pardon and salvation, He is come to pardon and save us. If, in short, we desire the sovereign gift of Divine love, He is come to inflame our hearts with it; and, above all, for this very purpose, He has become a Child, and has chosen to show Himself to us worthy of our love, in proportion as He was poor and humble, in order to take away from us all fear, and to gain our affections. "Thus," says St. Peter Chrysologus "should He come Who willed to drive away fear and seek for love."

O my amiable Jesus, Whom I have treated with so much contempt, thou hast descended from Heaven to rescue us from hell, and to give Thyself entirely to us -- how can we, then, have so often despised Thee and turned our backs upon Thee? O God! men are so grateful to their fellow-creatures, that if anyone makes them a gift, if anyone comes from a distance to pay them a visit, if anyone shows them a mark of affection, they cannot forget it, and feel themselves obliged to make him a return. And yet they are so ungrateful towards Thee, who art their God, and so amiable, and Who for their love didst not refuse Thy Blood and Thy life. But alas! I have behaved worse than others towards Thee, because more loved by Thee, and yet I have been more ungrateful towards Thee. Ah, if Thou hadst bestowed the graces given to me on a heretic, on an idolater, he would have become a Saint! And yet I have only offended Thee! O Jesus, mercy!

II.

Jesus has, besides, chosen to become a little Child to make us love Him, not only with an appreciative but with a tender love. All infants attract the tender affections of those who behold them; but who will not, then, love with all tenderness a God Whom they behold as a little Child, in need of milk, trembling with cold, poor, abased, and forsaken, weeping and wailing, and lying on straw in a manger? It was this that made the enamored St. Francis exclaim: "Let us love the Child of Bethlehem! Let us love the Child of Bethlehem!" Come, ye souls, and love a God Who is become a Child and poor, who is so amiable, and Who has come down from Heaven to give Himself entirely to you.

Forget, O Lord, I pray Thee, the injuries I have done Thee. But Thou hast already said that when a sinner repents, thou forgets all the outrages Thou hast received from him: All his iniquities I will not remember (Ezech. xviii. 22). If in times past I have not loved Thee, in future I will do nothing but love Thee, thou hast given Thyself all to me, I will give Thee my entire will. With this will I love Thee, love Thee, love Thee; and I repeat it, I love Thee, I love Thee, I love Thee. While I live, I will constantly say this; and thus, shall I die, saying with my last breath those sweet words: "My God, I love Thee." And in the meantime, O my Lord, my only Good, my only Love, I intend to prefer Thy Will to every pleasure of my own. Let the whole world offer itself to me, I will refuse, for I will never cease to love Him Who has loved me so much. I will never again offend Him Who deserves from me an infinite love. Do Thou, O my Jesus, strengthen this my desire with Thy grace. Mary, my Queen, I acknowledge that all the graces that I have received from God are due to thy intercession. Cease not to intercede for me. Obtain for me perseverance, thou who art the Mother of perseverance.

Friday--Third Week of Advent

Morning Meditation

CONSIDERATIONS ON THE RELIGIOUS STATE. X.

Consider the love we owe to Jesus Christ in return for the love He has shown us.

In order to understand the love, the Son of God has borne us it is enough to consider what St. Paul says of Jesus Christ: *He emptied himself, taking the form of a servant ... he humbled himself, becoming obedient unto death, even the death of the cross.* O my Jesus, only too much, indeed, hast Thou obliged me to love Thee.

I.

He emptied himself, taking the form of a servant. He emptied Himself! O God! what astonishment to the Angels, through all eternity, to see a God become Man for the love of man and submit to all man's weaknesses and sufferings. *And the Word was made flesh!* What a marvel would it not be to see a king become a worm for the sake of worms! But it is an infinitely greater wonder to see a God become Man, and then humbled unto such a painful and ignominious death on the Cross upon which He ended His most sacred life.

Moses and Elias, on Mount Tabor, speaking of His death, as it is related in the Gospel, called it an "excess": *They spoke of his decease* (the Latin word is "excesses," which also means "excess") *that he should accomplish in Jerusalem* (Luke ix. 31). Yes, says St. Bonaventure, it is with reason the death of Jesus Christ was called an "excess," for it was an excess of suffering and of love -- *Excessus doloris, excesses amoris.* So much so that it would be impossible to believe it, if it had not already happened. It was truly an excess of love, adds St. Augustine, for to this end the Son of God wished to come on earth, to live a life so laborious and to die a death so bitter, namely, that He might make known to man how much He loved him. "Therefore, Christ came, that man should know how much God loved him."

The Lord revealed to His servant Armella Nicolas that the love He bore to man was the cause of all His sufferings and of His death. If Jesus Christ had not been God, but only man and our Friend, what greater love could He have shown us than to die for us? Greater love than this, no man hath, that a man lay down his life for his friends (Jo. xv. 13). At the thought of the love shown us by Jesus Christ, how little the Saints esteemed it to give their lives and their all for so loving a God! How many youths, how many noblemen, have left their house, their country, their riches, their parents, and all things to retire into cloisters, to live only for the love of Jesus Christ! How many young virgins, renouncing nuptials with princes and the great ones of the world, have gone joyfully to death, thus, to render some return for the love of a God Who had been executed on an infamous gibbet and died for their sake.

Indeed, O my Jesus, my Lord, and my Redeemer! only too much hast Thou obliged me to love Thee; too much has my love cost Thee. I should be too ungrateful if I should content myself to love with reserve a God Who has given me His Blood, His life, and His entire self. Oh, Thou Who hast died for me, thy poor servant, it is but just that I should die for Thee, my God, and my All. Yes, O my Jesus! I detach myself from all, to give myself to Thee. I put away from me the love of all creatures to consecrate myself entirely to Thy love.

II.

That Jesus Christ should die on the Cross for our sakes seemed to St. Mary Magdalen de Pazzi to be "foolishness." Hence, she said Jesus was foolish with love: "O my Jesus, Thou art foolish with love!" So, also, the Gentiles, as St. Paul attests, on hearing the death of Jesus Christ preached to them, considered it a folly that no one could believe. We preach Christ crucified, unto the Jews indeed a stumbling-block, and unto the Gentiles foolishness (1 Cor. i. 23). How is it possible, they said, that a God Who is in Himself most happy and is dependent on none, should die for the love of man, His own servant?

This would be as much as to believe that God became a fool for the love of men. Nevertheless, it is of Faith that Jesus Christ, the true Son of God, did, for love of us, deliver

Himself up to death. He hath loved us and hath delivered himself for us (Eph. v. 2). The same St. Mary Magdalen had reason than to exclaim, lamenting the ingratitude of men towards so loving a God: "O Love not known! O Love not loved!" Indeed, Jesus Christ is not loved by men, because they live in forgetfulness of His love.

And, in fact, a soul that considers a God Who died for her sake, cannot live without loving Him. The charity of Christ presses us (2 Cor. v. 14). The soul will feel herself inflamed, and as if constrained to love a God Who has loved her so much. Jesus Christ could have saved us, says Father Nieremberg, with one single drop of His Blood; but it was His will to shed all His Blood, and to give His Divine Life, that at the sight of so many sufferings and of His death, we might not content ourselves with an ordinary love, but be sweetly constrained to love with all our strength a God so full of love towards us. That they also who live may not now live to themselves, but unto him who died for them (Ib. v. 15).

O my Jesus, I choose Thee alone out of all things for my Good, my Treasure, and my only Love. I love Thee, O my Love! I love Thee. Thou art not satisfied that I should love Thee only a little. Thou art not willing to have me love anything besides Thee. I will please Thee in all things, and I will love Thee much. Thou shalt be my only Love. My God, my God, help me, that I may fully please Thee. Mary, my Queen, do thou also help me that I may have a great love for my God. Amen. So, I hope; so may it be.

Spiritual Reading

COUNSELS CONCERNING A RELIGIOUS VOCATION

XI. CONCLUSION

Finally, let him who wishes to enter Religion resolve to become a Saint, and to suffer every exterior and interior pain to be faithful to God, and not to lose his Vocation. And if he be not thus resolved, I exhort him not to deceive the Superiors and himself, and not to enter at all, for this is a sign that he is not called, or which is a still greater evil, that he has not the will to correspond as he ought, with the grace of his Vocation. Hence, with so bad a disposition, it is better to remain in the world, there to dispose himself better, to give himself entirely to God, and to suffer all for Him. Otherwise, he will do an injury both to himself and to Religion, for he will leave for the least cause, and then, besides being discredited before the world, he will be guilty before God of a still further infidelity to his

Vocation and will lose all hope of being able to take a single step in the way of God. God alone knows into what other misfortunes and sins he may fall.

To sum up. What a beautiful sight to see in Religion souls wholly given to God, who live in the world as if out of the world, without any other thought than that of pleasing God.

In Religion each one must live only for eternity. What happiness for us if we spend these few days of our life for God! And to this he is most especially obliged who has perhaps already spent much of his life in the service of the world. Let us set eternity before our eyes, and then we shall suffer everything in peace and joy.

Let us thank God Who gives us so much light and so many means to serve Him perfectly, since He has chosen us, from among so many, to serve Him in Religion -- having bestowed on us the gift of His holy love. Let us make haste to advance in virtue in order to please Him, reflecting that, perhaps, as St. Teresa said to her daughters, "we have already by His grace got over the chief difficulty in the way of becoming Saints when we turned our backs on the world and all its goods; that which is less difficult remains for us to do, and then we shall be Saints." I hold it for certain that for those who die in Religion, Jesus Christ has prepared a beautiful place in Paradise. In this world we shall be poor, despised, and looked upon as fools and imprudent people, but in the next our lot will be far different.

Let us always recommend ourselves to our most loving Redeemer, hidden in the Blessed Sacrament, and to the Blessed Virgin, for Religious must profess a most special love for Jesus in the Blessed Sacrament, and for His Immaculate Mother Mary. Let us have great confidence. Jesus Christ has chosen us to be princes of His court, and all Religious Orders, and each member of them, are indeed objects of His special care. *The Lord is my light and my salvation -- whom shall I fear?* (Ps. xxvi. 1).

O Lord! perfect Thy work, and, for Thy glory, make us all Thine own, so that all the members of Thy Orders may, until the Day of Judgment, be pleasing to Thee, and gain for Thee a countless number of souls. Amen, Amen.

Evening Meditation

JESUS OFFERED HIMSELF FOR OUR SALVATION FROM THE BEGINNING.

I.

He was offered because it was his own will (Is. liii. 7).

The divine Word, from the first instant that He was made Man and an Infant in Mary's womb, offered Himself of His own accord to suffer and to die for the ransom of the world: He was offered because it was his own will (Is. liii. 7). He knew that all the sacrifices of goats and bulls offered to God in times past had not been able to satisfy for the sins of men, but that it required a divine Person to pay the price of their redemption; wherefore He said, as the Apostle tells us: When he cometh into the world he saith: Sacrifice and oblation thou wouldst not, but a body thou hast fitted to me ... Then said I: Behold, I come (Heb. x. 5). "My Father," said Jesus, "all the victims hitherto offered to Thee have not sufficed, nor could they suffice, to satisfy Thy justice; Thou hast given Me this passible body, in order that by shedding my Blood I might appease Thee and save men: Behold, I come -- here I am ready, I accept everything, and I submit myself in everything to Thy will."

My Lord, ever since I began to have the use of reason, I began to despise Thy grace and Thy love. Nevertheless, thou hast borne with me, because Thou still dost love me. I fled from Thee, and Thou dost follow me and call me. The very same love that made Thee come down from Heaven to seek the lost sheep, has caused Thee to bear with me, and not to forsake me. My Jesus, thou seeks me now, and I seek Thee. I feel that Thy grace is assisting me: it assists me by giving me sorrow for my sins, which I abhor above every other evil; it assists me by making me feel a great desire to love Thee and to please Thee. Yes, my Lord, I will love Thee and please Thee as much as I can. On the one hand I feel afraid, it is true, at the thought of my frailty and the weakness which I have contracted by my sins; but greater is the confidence which Thy grace gives me, making me hope in Thy merits; so that I say, with great courage: I can do all things in him who strengthened me (Phil. iv. 13). If I am weak, thou wilt give me strength against my enemies: if I am infirm, I hope that Thy Blood will be my medicine; if I am a sinner, I hope thou wilt make me holy. I know that I have hitherto contributed to my own ruin, because I have neglected, in times of danger, to have recourse to Thee. But from this day forth, my Jesus and my Hope, I will always have recourse to Thee; and from Thee I hope for every assistance and every good.

II.

In Jesus the inferior part felt repugnance towards a life of suffering and a death so full of pain and shame; but the rational part, which was entirely subordinate to the will of His Father, conquered and accepted everything; and Jesus began from the Incarnation to suffer all the anguish and sorrows that He would have to suffer all the years of His life. Thus did our Redeemer act from the very first moment of His entrance into the world. But, O God, how have we conducted ourselves towards Jesus since we began as adults to know by the light of Faith the Sacred Mysteries of Redemption? What thoughts, what designs, what goods have we loved? Pleasures, amusements, vanities, resentments, sensuality -- these are the things that have engrossed the affections of our hearts. But if we have Faith, we must now at last change our lives and change our affections. Let us love a God Who has suffered so much for us. Let us place before ourselves the sufferings which the Heart of Jesus endured for us, even from His Infancy; for then we shall not be able to love anything else but this Heart which has loved us so much.

O my Jesus, now I love Thee above all things, and I will love none but Thee. In pity help me, through the merit of all those sufferings which from Thy infancy Thou hast endured for me. Eternal Father, for the sake of Jesus Christ accept my love. If I have provoked Thee let the tears of the Infant Jesus, Who is praying for me, appease Thy wrath: Look on the face of thy Christ (Ps. lxxxiii. 10). I do not deserve favors, but this Thy innocent Son deserves them, and offers Thee a life of sufferings, in order that Thou mayst be merciful to me. And thou, O Mother of mercy, Mary, cease not to intercede for me. Thou knows how much I confide in thee; and I well know that thou dost not forsake him that has recourse to thee.

Saturday--Third Week of Advent

Morning Meditation

CONSIDERATIONS ON THE RELIGIOUS STATE. XI.

Consider how much Religious ought to confide in the patronage of Mary.

I.

The divine Mother loves all men. How much, then, does not this great Queen love Religious who have consecrated their liberty, their life, and their all to the love of Jesus Christ, her Son? My happiness on this earth, O Mary, shall be to serve, bless and to love thee.

If it be true, and most true, indeed, it is, that, as St. Peter Damian teaches, the divine Mother, most holy Mary, loves all men with such an affection that, after God; there is not, nor can there be, anyone who surpasses or equals her in her love: "She loves us with an invincible love": how much must we think this great Queen loves Religious, who have consecrated their liberty, their life, and their all to the love of Jesus Christ? She well sees that the life of Religious is more conformable to her own life, and to that of her divine Son; she sees them often occupied in praising her, and continually attentive to honor her by their Novenas, Visits, Rosaries, Fasts, etc. She beholds them often at her feet, intent on invoking her aid, asking graces of her, and graces all conformed to her holy desires; that is, the grace of perseverance in the divine service, of strength in their temptations, of detachment from this world, and of love of God. Ah, how can we doubt that she employs all her power and mercy for the benefit of Religious, and especially of those who belong to this holy Congregation of the Most Holy Redeemer, in which, as it is well known, we make a special profession of honoring the Virgin Mother by Visits, by mortifications on

Saturdays and during her Novenas, etc. and by everywhere promoting devotion to her by sermons and Novenas!

I thank thee, O Mary, my advocate, for to thee do I owe this great mercy that I am consecrated to Jesus Christ in Religion. Help me that I may not be ungrateful to that God Who has loved me so much. Let me die rather than prove myself unfaithful to His holy grace. O Mary, I consign my soul to thee; thou hast to save it. I love thee, O my Queen, and I hope always to love thee. Behold, I place all my confidence in thy clemency; do not cease to assist me in all my wants. Thou art my hope, O Mary; I look for all things through thy powerful intercession.

II.

She, the great Mistress is grateful: I love those who love me (Prov. viii. 17). Yes, she is so grateful that, as St. Andrew of Crete says, "To him who does her the least service she is accustomed to return great favors." To those who love her, and who promote her honor among others, she graciously promises to save them from sin: Those that work by me shall not sin. She also promises them Paradise: Those that explain me shall have life everlasting (Office of the B. V. Mary).

For which reason we especially ought to thank God for having called us to this Congregation, where, by the usages of the Community and the example of our companions, we are often reminded, and in some way constrained, to have recourse to Mary, and continually to honor this, our most blessed Mother, who is called, and is, the joy, the hope, the life, and the salvation of those who invoke and honor her.

My most beloved, most lovely, amiable, and most loving Queen, I thank my Lord and thee, and will always thank thee, who hast not only drawn me out of the world, but also called me to live in this Congregation, in which a special devotion to thee is practiced. Accept me, then, my Mother, to serve thee. Among so many of thy beloved children, disdain not to let me serve thee also, miserable though I be. Thou after God shall always be my hope and my love. In all my wants, in all my tribulations and temptations I will have recourse to thee; thou shalt be my refuge and my consolation. I will not that anyone except God and thee should comfort me in my combats, in the sadness and the tediousness of this life. For thy service I renounce the kingdoms of the whole world! My kingdom on earth shall be to serve, bless, and love thee, O my most lovely Mistress, "whom to serve is to reign" as

St. Anselm says. Thou art the Mother of perseverance; obtain for me to be faithful unto death. By so doing I hope, and firmly hope, one day to come where thou reign, to praise and bless thee forever, and never more to depart from thy feet. "Jesus and Mary," I will say with thy loving servant, Alphonsus Rodriguez, "my sweetest Loves, let me suffer for You, let me die for You, let me be all Yours, and in nothing my own."

Spiritual Reading

ON DEVOTION TO THE BLESSED VIRGIN

My beloved reader and brother in Mary: Since the devotion that led me to write, and moves you to read what I write, makes us happy children of the same good Mother, should you hear it remarked that I might have spared myself the labor, as there are already so many celebrated and learned books on the same subject, I beg that you will reply that "the praise of Mary is an inexhaustible fount. The more it is enlarged the fuller it gets, and the more you fill it so much the more is it enlarged." In short, the Blessed Virgin is so great and so sublime, that the more she is praised the more there remains to praise; so much so, says an ancient writer, "that if all the tongues of men were put together, and even if each of their members were changed into a tongue, they would not suffice to praise her as much as she deserves."

Worldly lovers often speak of those whom they love and praise them in order that the object of their affections may be praised and extolled by others. There are some who pretend to be lovers of Mary, and yet seldom either speak of her or endeavor to excite others to love her; their love cannot be great. It is not thus that true lovers of this amiable Lady act; they desire to praise her on all occasions, and to see her loved by the whole world, and never lose an opportunity, either in public or in private, of enkindling in the hearts of others those blessed flames of love with which they themselves burn towards their beloved Queen.

That everyone may be persuaded how important it is, both for his own good and that of others, to promote devotion towards Mary, it is useful to know what Theologians say on the subject.

St. Bonaventure says that those who make a point of announcing to others the glories of Mary, are certain of Heaven; and this opinion is confirmed by Richard of St. Laurence, who declares, "that to honor this Queen of Angels is to gain eternal life"; and he adds, "that this most gracious Lady will honor in the next world those who honor her in this." And who is ignorant of the promise made by Mary herself, in the words of Ecclesiasticus, to those who endeavor to make her known and loved here below: they that explain me shall have life-everlasting; for this passage is applied to her by the Church, in the Office of the Immaculate Conception. "Rejoice, then," exclaims St. Bonaventure (who did so much to make the glories of Mary known), "rejoice, my soul, and be glad in her; for many good things are prepared for those who praise her." And he says that the whole of the Sacred Scriptures speak in praise of Mary: let us therefore always with our hearts and tongues honor this divine Mother, in order that we may be conducted by her into the kingdom of the Blessed.

We learn from the Revelations of St. Bridget, that the Blessed Bishop Emingo was in the habit of always beginning his sermons with the praises of Mary. One day the Blessed Virgin herself appeared to the Saint, and desired her to tell him that in consequence of his pious practice, "she would be his Mother, that he would die a holy death, and that she would herself present his soul to God." He died like a Saint in the act of praying, and in the most heavenly peace. Mary also appeared to a Dominican friar, who always concluded his sermons by speaking of her; when on his death bed, the Blessed Virgin defended him from devils, consoled him, and then she herself carried off his happy soul. The devout Thomas a Kempis, represents to us Mary recommending a soul who had honored her to her Son, saying: "My most loving Son, have mercy on the soul of this servant of Thine, who loved and extolled me."

Next, as to the advantage of this devotion for all, St. Anselm says, that as the most sacred womb of Mary was the means of salvation for sinners, the hearing of her praises must necessarily convert them, and thus be also a means of their salvation. "How can it be otherwise than that the salvation of sinners should come from the remembrance of her praises, whose womb was made the way through which the Savior came to save sinners?" And if the opinion is true, and I consider it as indubitably so, that all graces are dispensed by Mary, and that all who are saved are saved only by means of this divine Mother, it is a necessary consequence that the salvation of all depends upon preaching Mary, and exciting all to confidence in her intercession.

I find that Father Paul Segneri, the Younger, who was a very celebrated missioner, in every Mission preached a sermon on devotion to Mary, and always called it his beloved sermon.

And in our own Missions, in which it is an inviolable rule to do the same, we can attest, with all truth, that in most cases no sermon is more profitable, or produces so much compunction in the hearts of the people, as the one on the Mercy of Mary. I say, on her Mercy, for, in the words of St. Bernard: "we praise her Virginity, we admire her Humility; but because we are poor sinners, Mercy attracts us more and tastes sweeter; we embrace it more lovingly; we remember it oftener and invoke it more earnestly." Devout reader, should what I write on the Blessed Virgin prove acceptable to you, as I trust it will, I beg that you will recommend me to Mary, that she may give me great confidence in her protection. Ask this grace for me; and I promise you, whoever you may be, that I will ask the same for you who do me this charity. O blessed are they who bind themselves with love and confidence to those two anchors of salvation, Jesus and Mary. Certainly, they will not be lost. Let us then say with the pious Alphonsus Rodriguez: "Jesus and Mary, my sweetest Loves, for You may I suffer, for You may I die; grant that I may be in all things Yours and in nothing mine own." Let us love Jesus and Mary and become Saints; we can neither expect nor hope anything better.

Evening Meditation

JESUS A PRISONER IN THE WOMB OF MARY

I.

I am become as a man without help, free among the dead (Ps. lxxxvii. 5, 6).

Consider the painful life that Jesus led in the womb of His Mother, and the long, close, and dark imprisonment that He suffered there for nine months. Other infants are, indeed, in the same state, but they do not feel the miseries of it because they do not know them. But Jesus knew them well, because from the first moment of His life He had the perfect use of His reason, He had His senses, but He could not use them; eyes, but He could not see; a tongue, but He could not speak; hands, but He could not stretch them out; feet, but He could not walk -- so that for nine months He had to remain in the womb of Mary like a dead man shut up in the tomb: I am become as a man without help, free among the dead (Ps. lxxxvii. 5, 6). He was free, because He had of His own free-will made Himself a Prisoner of love in this prison; but love deprived Him of liberty and bound Him there so fast in chains that He could not move: Free among the dead! "Oh, great patience of our Savior!" says St. Ambrose, while he considered the sufferings of Jesus in the womb of Mary.

Forget not the kindness of thy surety (Ecclus. xxix. 19). Yes, my Jesus, the Prophet has reason to warn me not to forget the immense favor in that Thou the innocent One, Thou, O my God! hast chosen to satisfy for my sins by Thy sufferings and Thy death. But after all this kindness I have forgotten Thy favors and Thy love, and I have had the boldness to turn my back upon Thee, as if Thou hadst not been my Lord, and the Lord Who has loved me so much. But if in times past I have forgotten Thy mercies, O my dear Redeemer! I will in future never forget them again. Thy sufferings and death shall be the constant subjects of my thoughts because they will always recall to my mind the love that Thou hast borne me. Cursed be the days in which, forgetting what Thou hast suffered for me, I have made so bad a use of my liberty. Thou hast given it to me to love Thee, and I have used it to despise Thee. But I now consecrate entirely to Thee this liberty which Thou hast given me.

II.

The womb of Mary was, therefore, to our Redeemer, a voluntary prison, because it was a prison of love. But it was also not an unjust prison: He was, indeed, innocent Himself, but He had offered Himself to pay our debts and to satisfy for our crimes. It was, therefore, only reasonable for the divine justice to keep Him thus imprisoned, and so begin to exact from Him the satisfaction due.

Behold the state to which the Son of God reduces Himself for the love of men! He deprives Himself of His liberty and puts Himself in chains to deliver us from the chains of hell. What gratitude and love should we not show in return for the love and goodness of our deliverer and our surety, Who, not by compulsion, but only out of love, offered Himself to pay, and has paid for us, our debts, and our penalties by giving up His divine life! Forget not the kindness of thy surety; for he hath given his life for thee (Ecclus. xxix. 19).

I beseech Thee, my Savior, deliver me from the misery of seeing myself again separated from Thee, and again made the slave of Lucifer. I implore Thee to bind my poor soul to Thy feet by Thy holy love, so that it may never again be separated from Thee. Eternal Father, by the imprisonment of the Infant Jesus in the womb of Mary, deliver me from the chains of sin and hell. And thou, O Mother of God, help me! Thou hast in thy womb the Son of God imprisoned and confined; as, therefore, Jesus is thy Prisoner, He will do everything that thou tell Him. Tell Him to pardon me; tell Him to make me holy. Help me, my Mother, for the sake of the favor and honor Jesus Christ conferred upon thee by dwelling within thee for nine months.

Fourth Sunday of Advent

Morning Meditation

THE SALVATION OF THE LORD

And all flesh shall see the salvation of God (Gospel of Sunday. Luke iii. 1-6).

The Savior of the world, Whom, according to the Prophet Isaias, men were to see one day on the earth — *and all flesh shall see the salvation of God* — has come. And He came on earth, says St. Augustine, that men might know how much God loves them. And how is it, O my dear Jesus, that Thou dost meet with so much ingratitude from the greater number of men?

I.

Adam, our first father, sins, and is condemned to eternal death along with all his posterity. Seeing the whole human race doomed to perdition, God resolved to send a Redeemer to save mankind. Who shall come to be man's salvation? Perhaps an Angel or a Seraph? No, the Son of God, the supreme and true God, equal to the Father, offers Himself to come on earth, and there to take human flesh and die for the salvation of men. O prodigy of divine love! Man, says St. Fulgentius, despises God and separates himself from God, and through love for him God comes on earth to seek after rebellious man. Since we would not go to our Physician, He deigned to come to us, says St. Augustine. And why did Jesus resolve to come to us? Christ came, says the same holy Doctor, that man might know how much God loves him.

Hence the Apostle writes: *The goodness and kindness of God, our Savior, appeared* (Tit. iii. 4). The singular love of God towards men appeared, as the Greek Text has it. And what greater love and goodness could the Son of God show us than to become Man and a worm like us, to save us from perdition? What astonishment should we not feel if we saw a prince become a worm to save the worms of his kingdom! And what shall we say at the sight of a God made Man like us to deliver us from eternal death! The Word was made flesh (Jo. i. 14). A God made flesh! If Faith did not assure us of it, who could ever believe it?

O my sweet, amiable, holy Child, thou art at a loss to know what more to do to make Thyself loved by men! It is enough to say that from being the Son of God, Thou Wert made the Son of man, and that Thou didst choose to be born among men like the rest of infants, only poorer and more meanly lodged than the rest, selecting a stable for Thy abode, a manger for Thy cradle, a little straw for Thy bed. And yet few there are who know Thee! Few there are who love Thee!

II.

Tell me, O Christian, what more could Jesus Christ have done to win Thy love? If the Son of God had engaged to rescue from death His own Father, what lower humiliation could He have stooped to than to assume human flesh and to lay down His life in sacrifice for His salvation? Nay, I say more, had Jesus Christ been a mere man instead of One of the Divine Persons, and wished to gain by some token of affection the love of His God, what more could He have done than He has done for thee? If a servant of thine had given for thy love his very lifeblood, would he not have riveted thy heart to him, and obliged thee to love him out of mere gratitude? And how comes it that Jesus Christ, though He has laid down His very life for thee, has still failed to win thy love?

Men appreciate the good graces of a prince, of a prelate, a nobleman, of a man of letters, and even of a vile animal, and yet these same persons set no store by the grace of God — but renounce it for mere smoke, for a brutal gratification, for a handful of earth, for a whim, for a nothing! What sayest thou, my dear brother? Dost, thou wish still to be ranked among the ungrateful ones? Go, seek for thyself one who is better able than God to make thee happy in the present life and in the life to come. Go, find thyself a prince more courteous, a master, a brother, a friend more amiable, and who has shown thee a deeper love. O Lord, who is like to thee? (Ps. xxxiv. 10). O Lord, what greatness shall ever be found like Thine?

Love, then, love, O souls, love this little Child, exclaims St. Bernard, for He is exceedingly to be loved. Great is the Lord, and exceedingly to be praised! The Lord is a little One and exceedingly to be loved!

O my dear Jesus, how is it that Thou dost encounter such ingratitude from the greater number of men? In the time past, I, too, have not known Thee; but heedless of Thy love, I have sought my own gratification, making no account whatever of Thee and of Thy friendship. But now I am sorry for it. I grieve over it with my whole heart. O my sweet Child, and my God, forgive me for the sake of Thy Infancy. Thou knows my past treasons; for pity's sake do not abandon me or I shall fall away even worse than before. O Mary, great Mother of the Incarnate Word, do not thou abandon me! Thou art the Mother of perseverance and the stewardess of divine grace. With thy help, O my hope, I trust to be faithful to my God till death.

Spiritual Reading

JOSEPH AND MARY AT BETHLEHEM

Octavius Augustus, the Emperor of Rome, wishing to know the strength of his empire, decreed that there be a general numbering of all his subjects; and for this purpose he ordered the governors of all the provinces — and, among the rest, Cyrinus, governor of Judea — to make every one come to enroll himself, and at the same time pay a certain tribute as a sign of vassalage: There went out a decree ... that the whole world should be enrolled (Luke ii. 1). As soon as this decree was promulgated, Joseph obeys immediately; he does not even wait till his holy spouse should be delivered, though the time is near. I say he obeyed immediately, and set out on his journey with Mary, then pregnant with the Divine Word, to go and enroll himself in the City of Bethlehem: to be enrolled with Mary his espoused wife, who was with child (Luke ii. 5). The journey was a long one — for, according to some authors, it was ninety leagues; that is, four days' journey — long and difficult, for they had to traverse mountains and steep paths, through the wind, the rain, and the cold.

When a king makes his first entry into a city of his kingdom, what honors are not prepared for him! What preparations are not made, and triumphal arches erected! Do thou, then, O happy Bethlehem! prepare thyself to receive thy King with honor; for the Prophet Micheas has told thee that He is coming to thee, and that He is Lord, not only of all Judea, but of the whole world. And know, says the Prophet, thou, out of all the cities of the earth, art the fortunate one that has been chosen by the King of Heaven for His birthplace, that He may afterwards reign, not indeed in Judea, but in the hearts of men who live in Judea and in all the rest of the world: And thou, Bethlehem Ephrata, art a little one among the thousands of Juda: out of thee shall he come forth that is to be Ruler in Israel (Mich. v. 2). But behold these two illustrious pilgrims, Joseph and Mary, who bears within her womb the Savior of the world, are about to enter into Bethlehem. They enter and go to the house of the imperial minister to pay the tribute, and to enroll themselves in the book as subjects of Caesar, where they also inscribed the offspring of Mary, namely, Jesus Christ, who was the Lord of Caesar and of all the princes of the earth. But who acknowledges them? Who goes before them to show them honor? Who salutes them, and who receives them? He came unto his own, and his own received him not (John i. 11). They travel like poor people, and as such they are despised; they are treated even worse than the other poor and are driven away. Yes, for it came to pass when they were there her days were accomplished that she should be delivered (Luke ii. 6). Mary knew that the time of her delivery was come, and that it was here, and on this night, that the Incarnate Word willed to be born, and to manifest Himself to the world. She therefore told Joseph, and he hastened to procure some lodgings in the houses of the townspeople, so as not to take his spouse to the inn to be delivered, as it was not a becoming place for her to be besides which, it was then full of people. But Joseph found no one to listen to him; and very likely he was insulted, and perhaps called a fool by some of them, for taking his wife about at that time of night, and in such a crowd of people, when she was near her delivery; so that at last he was obliged, unless he would remain all night in the street, to take her to the public inn, where there were many other people lodging that night. He went there; but they were refused admittance even there, and they were told that there was no room for them: There was no room for them in the inn (Luke ii. 7). Room was found for all, even for the lowest, but not for Jesus Christ.

That inn was a figure of those ungrateful hearts where many find room for miserable creatures, but not for God. How many love their relatives, their friends, even animals, but do not love Jesus Christ, and care neither for His grace nor His love! But the ever-blessed Mary said once to a devout soul: "It was the dispensation of God that neither I nor my Son should find a lodging amongst men, that those souls who love Jesus might offer themselves as a lodging-place and might affectionately invite Him to come into their hearts."

These poor travelers, then, seeing themselves repulsed on every side, leave the city to try and find some place of refuge without its walls. They walk on in the dark; they go round about and examine, till at last they see a grotto, which was cut out of stone in the mountain under the city. Barradas, Bede, and Brocardus say that the place where Jesus Christ was born was a rock that had been excavated under the walls of Bethlehem, divided off from the city, and like a cavern, which served as a stable for cattle. When they came to it Mary said to Joseph: "There is no occasion to go any farther; let us go into this cave and remain here." "What!" replied Joseph, "my spouse, dost thou not see that this cave is quite exposed; that it is cold and damp, and that water is running down on all sides? Dost thou not see that it is no lodging for men, but it is a shed for beasts? How canst thou stop here all night and be delivered here?" Then Mary said: "It is nevertheless true that this stable is the royal palace in which the Eternal Son of God desires to be born on earth."

Oh, what must the Angels have said when they saw the divine Mother enter into this cave to bring forth her Son! The sons of princes are born in rooms adorned with gold; they have cradles enriched with precious stones, fine clothes, a retinue of the first lords of the kingdom; and has the King of Heaven nothing but a cold stable, without a fire, to be born in, some poor swaddling clothes to cover Him, a little straw for His bed, and a vile manger in which to lie? "Where is the palace," asks St. Bernard, "where is the throne?" Where, says the Saint, is the court, where is the royal palace for this King of Heaven? for I see nothing but two animals to keep Him company, and a manger for cattle, where He must be laid. O happy grotto, that witnessed the birth of the Divine Word! Happy manger to have had the honor of receiving the Lord of Heaven! Happy straw which served as a bed to Him Who sits on the shoulders of the Seraphim! Ah, when we think of the birth of Jesus Christ, and of the manner in which it took place, we ought all to be inflamed with love; and when we hear the names of cave, manger, straw, milk, tears, in reference to the birth of our Redeemer, these names ought to be so many incitements to our love, and arrows to wound our hearts. Yes, happy was that grotto, that crib, that straw; but still happier are those souls who love this amiable Lord with fervor and tenderness, and who receive Him in Holy Communion into hearts burning with love. Oh, with what desire and pleasure does not Jesus Christ enter and repose in a heart that loves Him!

Evening Meditation

THE ETERNAL WORD BECOMES LITTLE.

I.

He emptied himself, taking the form of a servant (Phil. ii. 7).

St. Paul says that Jesus Christ, coming on earth, emptied Himself. He annihilated Himself, so to say. And why? To save man and to be loved by man. "Where Thou didst empty Thyself," says St. Bernard, "there, did Mercy and Charity more brilliantly appear." Yes, my dear Redeemer, in proportion as Thy abasement was great in becoming Man and in being born an Infant, so were Thy mercy and love shown to be greater towards us, and this with a view to win over our hearts to Thyself.

Although the Jews, by so many signs and wonders, had a certain knowledge of the true God, they were not, however, satisfied; they wished to behold Him face to face. God found means to comply even with this desire of men; He became Man, to make Himself visible to them. "Knowing," says St. Peter Chrysologus, "that mortals felt an anguish of desire to see Him, God chose this method of making Himself visible to them." And to render Himself still more attractive in our eyes, He would make His first appearance as a little Child, that thus He might be the more charming and irresistible; He showed Himself an Infant, that He might make Himself more acceptable in our eyes. "Yes," adds St. Cyril of Alexandria, "He abased Himself to the humble condition of a little Child in order to make Himself more agreeable to our hearts." "For our advantage was this emptying made." For this, indeed, was the form most suitable to win our love.

The Prophet Ezechiel rightly exclaimed that the time of Thy coming on earth, O Incarnate Word, should be a time of love, the season of lovers: *Behold, thy time was the time of lovers* (Ezech. xvi. 8). And what object had God in loving us thus ardently, and of giving us such clear proofs of His love, other than that we might love Him? "God loves only in order to be loved," says St. Bernard. God Himself had already said as much: *And now, O Israel, what does the Lord, thy God require of thee, but that thou fear and love him* (Deut. x. 12).

O my sweet, amiable, holy Child, Thy first appearance before us is as a poor Infant, that even from birth Thou mightiest lose no time in attracting our hearts towards Thee. And so didst Thou go on through the remainder of Thy life ever showing us fresh and more striking tokens of Thy love, so that at length Thou didst shed the last drop of Thy Blood and die overwhelmed with shame upon the infamous tree of the Cross. And how is it,

O Jesus, that Thou could have encountered such ingratitude from most of mankind? I see few, indeed, that know Thee, and fewer still that love Thee. Ah, my dear Jesus, I, too, desire to be among this small number. O, my sweet Child and my God, forgive me. I love Thee! I love Thee!

II.

In order to force us to love Him God would not commission others but chose to come Himself in person to be made Man and to redeem us. St. John Chrysostom makes a beautiful reflection on these words of the Apostle: For nowhere doth he takes hold of the angels, but of the seed of Abraham he taketh hold (Heb. ii. 16). Why, asks the Saint, did he not say received, but rather taketh hold? Why did not St. Paul simply say that God assumed human flesh? Why would he affirm with marked emphasis that He took it, as it were, by force, according to the strict meaning of the Latin apprehendit? He answers that he spoke thus, making use of the metaphor of those who give chase to those who are fleeing away. By this he would convey the idea that God always longed to be loved by man, but man turned his back upon Him, and cared not even to know of His love; therefore God came from Heaven, and took human flesh, to make Himself known in this way, and to make Himself loved, as it were, by force by ungrateful man who fled from Him.

For this, then, did the Eternal Word become Man; for this He, moreover, became an Infant. He could, indeed, have appeared upon this earth as a full-grown Man, as the first man, Adam, appeared. No, the Son of God wished to present Himself under the form of a sweet little Child, that thus He might the more readily and the more forcibly draw to Himself the love of man. Little children of themselves are loved at once; to see them and to love them is the same thing. Ah, my dear Jesus, it is true that in time past I did not know Thee. Heedless of Thy love I sought only my own gratification, making no account whatever of Thee or of Thy friendship. But now I am conscious of the evil I have done. I am sorry for it and I grieve over it with my whole heart. I love Thee, Jesus, and that so dearly that even if I knew that all mankind were about to rebel against Thee and forsake Thee, yet would I not leave Thee though it should cost me a thousand lives. Accept, O Jesus, of my poor heart to love Thee. There was a time when it cared not for Thee, but now it is enamored of Thy goodness, O Divine Infant. O Mary, O great Mother of the Word Incarnate, neither do thou abandon me. Thou art the Mother of perseverance and the stewardess of divine grace. Help me, then, and help me always. With thy aid, O my hope, I trust to be faithful to my God for ever. Amen.

Monday--Fourth Week of Advent

Morning Meditation

CONSIDERATIONS ON THE RELIGIOUS STATE. XII.

I.

Consider the great happiness that Religious enjoy in dwelling in the same house with Jesus in the Blessed Sacrament.

If worldlings deem it so great a favor to be invited by kings to dwell in their palaces, how much more favored should we esteem ourselves who are admitted to dwell continually with the King of Heaven in His own house? O Lord, I thank Thee! How have I deserved this happy lot?

The Venerable Mother Mary of Jesus, Foundress of a convent in Toulouse, said that she esteemed her lot as a Religious very much, and principally for two reasons. The first, that Religious, through the Vow of Obedience, belong entirely to God; and the second, that they have the privilege of dwelling always with Jesus Christ in the Blessed Sacrament.

In the houses of Religious, Jesus Christ dwells for their sake in the church, so that they can find Him at all hours. Persons of the world can scarcely go to visit Him during the day, and in many places, only in the morning. But Religious find Him in the Tabernacle as often as they wish, in the morning, in the afternoon, and during the night. There they may continually entertain themselves with Our Lord, and there Jesus Christ rejoices to converse familiarly with His beloved servants, whom, for this end, He has called out of Egypt, that He may be their Companion during this life, hidden under the veil of the

Most Holy Sacrament, and in the next, unveiled in Paradise. "O solitude," it may be said of every Religious house, "in which God familiarly speaks and converses with His friends!"

Behold me in Thy Presence, O my Jesus! -- hidden in the Sacrament, thou art the self-same Jesus Who for me didst sacrifice Thyself on the Cross. Thou art He Who loves me so much, and Who hast therefore confined Thyself in this prison of love. Amongst so many who have offended Thee less than I, and who have loved Thee better than I, Thou hast chosen me, in Thy goodness, to keep Thee company in this house, where, having drawn me from the midst of the world, Thou hast destined me always to live united with Thee, and afterwards to have me nigh to Thee to praise and to love Thee in Thy eternal kingdom. O Lord, I thank Thee. How have I deserved this happy lot? I have chosen to be an abject in the house of my God, then dwell in the tabernacles of sinners (Ps. lxxxiii. 11). Happy, indeed, am I, O my Jesus, to have left the world; and it is my great desire to perform the vilest office in Thy house rather than dwell in the proudest royal palaces of men.

II.

Souls that love Jesus Christ much know not how to wish for any other paradise on this earth than to be in the presence of their Lord, who dwells in this Sacrament for the love of those who seek and visit Him.

Her conversation hath no bitterness, nor her company any tediousness (Wis. viii. 16). He who does not love Jesus Christ finds tediousness in His company. But those who on this earth have given all their love to Jesus Christ find in the Blessed Sacrament their treasure, their rest, their paradise, and therefore the great desire of their hearts is, as often as they can, to visit their God in this Sacrament, to pay their court to Him, offering Him their affections and laying at the foot of the altar their sorrows, their desire of loving Him, of seeing Him face to face, and, in the meantime, of pleasing Him in all things.

Receive me, then, O Lord, to stay with Thee all my life long; do not drive me away, as I deserve. Be pleased to allow that, among the many good Religious who serve Thee in this house, I, though a miserable sinner, may serve Thee also. Many years already have I lived far from Thee. But now that Thou hast enlightened me to know the vanity of the world, and my own foolishness, I will not depart any more from Thy feet, O my Jesus! Thy presence shall animate me to fight when I am tempted. The nearness of Thy abode shall remind me of the obligation I am under to love Thee, and always to have recourse to

Thee in my combats against hell. I will always keep near to Thee, that I may unite myself to Thee, and attach myself closer to Thee. I love Thee, O my God, hidden in this Sacrament. Thou, for the love of me, remains always on this altar. I, for the love of Thee, will remain in Thy presence as much as I shall be able. There enclosed Thou always loves me, and here enclosed I will always love Thee. Always then, O my Jesus, my Love, my All, shall we remain together -- in time in this House, and during eternity, in Paradise. This is my hope; so may it be. Most holy Mary, obtain for me a greater love for the Most Holy Sacrament.

Spiritual Reading

ENCOURAGEMENT TO NOVICES TO PERSEVERE IN THEIR VOCATION

There are two graces clearly distinct one from the other -- the grace of Vocation and the grace of Perseverance in one's Vocation. Many who have received a Vocation from God have afterwards, through their own fault, rendered themselves unworthy to receive the grace of Perseverance. He is not crowned except he strives lawfully (2 Tim. ii. 5). No one will receive the grace of Perseverance and the crown which God has prepared for him, who does not do what in him lies to fight and conquer his enemies: Hold fast that which thou hast, that no man takes thy crown (Apoc. iii. 11). My dear young friend, you who, by so special a favor, have been called by Our Lord to follow Him, hear how He exhorts and encourages you: "Be careful, My son, to preserve the grace which you have received from Me, and tremble lest you should lose it and another gain the crown which is prepared for you."

He who enters a Novitiate enters into the service of the King of Heaven, who tries the fidelity of those whom He accepts for His own, by crosses and temptations, and permits the devil to assail them. Because thou wert acceptable to the Lord, it was necessary that temptation should prove thee (Tob. xii. 13). And the Holy Ghost says to all who leave the world to give themselves to God: My son, when thou comes to the service of God ... prepare thy soul for temptation (Ecclus. ii. 1). So that the novice, on entering the House of God, ought to prepare himself, not for consolations, but for temptations, and for the war which the devil wages against those who give themselves wholly to God. And be well persuaded that the devil would rather tempt a novice to abandon his Vocation than a thousand seculars, especially if he enters an active Order. Yes, for the devil knows that if this novice perseveres and is faithful to God, hell will lose thousands of souls who will obtain salvation through his zeal. Hence, the enemy uses every means to win him and every device to beguile him.

The temptations by which the devil most frequently endeavors to induce novices to abandon their Vocation are the following.

I. TENDERNESS FOR PARENTS AND FRIENDS

First, he tempts them by tenderness for their parents. To resist this, it is necessary to reflect on the declaration of Jesus Christ: He who loveth father or mother more than me is not worthy of me (Matt. x. 37). And He declares that He came not to send peace, but division. I came not to send peace, but the sword; for I came to set a man at variance against his father, and the daughter against her mother (Matt. x. 34, 35). And why this great desire to separate relations from each other? Because Our Lord well knew the injury that comes from such intercourse, and that in the affairs of eternal salvation, especially where there is question of a Religious Vocation, there are no greater enemies than relations; and this Our Lord declared, saying: A man's enemies shall be of his own household (Matt. x. 36). O how many unhappy youths, through affection for their relations, have first lost their Vocations, and then, as so easily happens, their own souls. History is full of such sad instances. I will tell you of some. Father Jerome Piatti relates of a novice who was visited by a relation who said to him: "Listen to me; I only speak because I love you, and I beg you to reflect that your constitution is not fitted to undergo the labors and studies of the Religious life; by remaining in the world you can please God better, especially by giving to the poor a large share of the riches with which He has blessed you. If you persist in your undertaking you will repent of it, for, in the end, with shame, you will be obliged to quit the Community, seeing yourself made porter or cook on account of your little talent and poor health. Therefore, it is wiser to do at once that which you will be at last obliged to do." The poor young man, thus perverted, left the monastery, but many days had not elapsed before he fell into all kinds of vices; and in a quarrel with some of his rivals, he, together with the relation who had perverted him, was so severely wounded that within a short time they both died on the same day; and, what is still worse, the unfortunate novice expired without confession, of which he must have stood in so great need. We read in the Life of St. Camillus of Lellis that a young man, who was received into his Community in Naples, was persecuted by his father. At first, he resisted with courage. He had to go to Rome on business, and there, in an interview with his father, he yielded to the temptation. On dismissing him the Saint predicted that he would come to an evil end and die by the hand of justice. This was verified. The young man married, and later, in a fit of jealousy, murdered his wife and two servants. He was apprehended and brought to justice, and although his father expended his whole fortune to save the life of his unhappy son, he was beheaded in the marketplace of Naples, nine years after his departure from the monastery.

Be, therefore, most watchful, my dear brother, should the devil seek by this means to make you lose your Vocation. The Lord, Who, by an especial grace, has called you to quit the world, desires you not only to leave, but also to forget your country and your friends.

Hearken, O daughter, and see and incline thine ear, and forget thy people and thy father's house (Ps. xliv. 11). Hearken then to what God says to you and know that if you desert Him for the love of your relations, great will be your sorrow and remorse at the hour of death. You will then remember the House of God which you abandoned, and behold around your death-bed brothers and nephews in tears, who, at a time when you need spiritual help, will press you to leave them your goods, and not one will speak to you of God; they will even try to delude you, not to increase your pain by the thought of death; they will hold out vain hopes of recovery, and thus you will die without preparation. Contrast with this the joy and peace you will feel on dying in Religion, where you will have the happiness of seeing around you your brethren, whose prayers will assist you to fix your hopes in Heaven, and who, instead of deceiving you, will aid you to expire in peace and joy. Reflect also, that though it be true that your parents have loved you for many years with some tenderness, God loved you long before, and with far greater love. Your parents have loved for twenty or thirty years or more, but God has loved you from all eternity. I have loved thee with an everlasting love (Jer. xxxi. 3). Your parents have, it is true, been at some expense for your welfare and suffered on your account, but Jesus Christ shed all His Blood and gave His life for you. When, therefore, your tenderness for your parents urges you to be grateful to them and not to displease them, remember that much greater gratitude is due to God, who has done more for you and loved you more than all others. Say, then, to yourself: "Relations, if I leave you, it is for God, who merits my love more and loves me better than you." And by such words as these you will vanquish this terrible temptation of your kindred, which has caused the ruin of so many in this world and in the next.

Evening Meditation

THE LOVE THAT GOD HAS SHOWN US IN BECOMING MAN

I.

The Word was made flesh ... and delivered himself for us (Jo. i. 14. Eph. v. 2).

Let us consider the immense love which God shows us in becoming Man in order to procure us eternal life.

Our first parent, Adam, having sinned and rebelled against God, was driven out of Paradise, and condemned to everlasting death with all his descendants. But behold the Son of God, Who, seeing man thus lost, to deliver him from death offers to take upon Himself human flesh, and to die condemned as a malefactor upon the Cross. But, my Son, we may suppose the Father saying to Him, consider what a life of humiliation and suffering Thou wilt have to lead upon earth. Thou wilt have to be born in a cold cave, and to be laid in a manger for beasts. Thou wilt have to fly as an Infant into Egypt to escape from the hands of Herod. On Thy return from Egypt, thou wilt have to live in a shop as a humble servant, poor and despised. And, finally, worn out by sufferings, thou wilt have to give up Thy life upon a Cross, insulted and forsaken by all. -- Father, all this matters not, replies the Son; I am content with enduring all, provided man is saved.

O great Son of God, thou hast become Man to make Thyself loved by men; but where is the love that men bear to Thee? Thou hast given Thy Blood and Thy life to save our souls; why, then, are we so unthankful towards Thee, that, instead of loving Thee, we treat Thee with so much ingratitude and contempt? And behold, O Lord, I have been one of those who more than others have thus ill-treated Thee. But Thy Passion is my hope. Oh, for the sake of that love which induced Thee to assume human flesh and die for me on the Cross, forgive me all the offences I have committed against Thee.

I love Thee, O Incarnate Word, I love Thee, O my God!

II.

What would be said if a prince were to take compassion upon a dead worm, and were to choose to become a worm himself, and to make, as it were, a bath of his own blood, to die to restore the worm to life? But the Eternal Word has done even more than this for us; for, being God, He has chosen to become a worm like us, and to die for us, to purchase for us the life of divine grace which we had lost. When He saw that all the gifts, He had bestowed upon us could not secure to Him our love, what did He do? He became Man, and He gave Himself entirely to us: The Word was made flesh ... and delivered himself for us (Jo. i. 14. Eph. v. 2).

Man, by despising God, says St. Fulgentius, separated himself from God; but God, through His love for man, came from Heaven to seek him. And why did He come? He came in order that man might know how much God loved him, and that thus, out of gratitude at least, he might love Him in return. Even the beasts, when they show us affection, make us love them; and why, then, are we so ungrateful towards a God Who descends from Heaven to earth to make us love Him?

One day, when a priest was saying these words in Mass: Et verbum caro factum est -- And the Word was made flesh -- a man who was present neglected to make an act of reverence; upon which the devil gave him a blow, saying: "Ah, ungrateful man! if God had done as much for me as He has done for thee, I should remain continually prostrate with my face to the ground returning thanks to Him."

O Infinite Goodness, I love Thee, and I repent of all the injuries I have done Thee. Would that I could die of sorrow for them. O my Jesus, give me love. Let me not live any longer ungrateful for the affection Thou hast borne me. I am determined to love Thee always. Give me holy perseverance!

O Mary, Mother of God and my Mother, do thou obtain for me from thy Son the grace to love Him always -- even until death. Amen.

Tuesday--Fourth Week of Advent

Morning Meditation

CONSIDERATIONS ON THE RELIGIOUS STATE. XIII.

Consider that the life of a Religious resembles mostly the life of Jesus Christ.

Jesus wished to live poor on this earth as the Son and Helpmate of a mechanic, in a poor dwelling, with poor clothing and poor food, that thereby He might give His servants to understand what ought to be the life of those who wish to be His followers. O my Lord, I will leave all and will follow Thee.

I.

The Apostle says that the Eternal Father predestines to the kingdom of Heaven those only who live conformably to the life of the Incarnate Word. *Whom he foreknew, he also predestinated to be made conformable to the image of his son* (Rom. viii. 29). How happy, then, and secure of Paradise should not Religious be, seeing that God has called them to a state of life which, of all other states, is most like the life of Jesus Christ.

Jesus, on this earth, wished to live poor, the Son and Helpmate of a mechanic, in a poor dwelling, with poor clothing and poor food: *Being rich he became poor for your sake, that through his poverty you might become rich* (2 Cor. viii. 9). Moreover, He chose a most mortified life, far removed from the delights of the world, and ever full of pain and sorrow, beginning with His birth and ending with His death; hence by the Prophet He was called: *The man of sorrows* (Is. liii. 3). By this He wished to give His servants to understand what ought to be the life of those who wish to follow Him: *If any man will come after me let him deny himself, take up his cross, and follow me* (Matt. xvi. 24). Following this example, and accepting this invitation of Jesus Christ, the Saints have endeavored to despoil themselves of all earthly goods, and to take upon themselves pains and crosses, to be like their beloved Lord.

Thus, we see that St. Benedict, who, being the son of the lord of Norcia, a relative of the Emperor Justinian, and born amidst the riches and pleasures of the world, while yet a youth of only fourteen, went to live in a cavern at Subiaco, where he received only a piece of bread brought him every day as an alms by the hermit Romanus.

Ah! my Master and my Redeemer, Jesus, I am, then, of the number of those fortunate ones whom Thou hast called to follow Thee. O my Lord! I thank Thee for this. I leave all; would that I had more to leave, that I might draw near to Thee, my King and my God, Who, for the love of me, and to give me courage by Thy example, didst choose for Thyself a life so poor and so painful. Walk on, O Lord, I will follow Thee. Choose Thou for me what cross Thou wilt and help me. I will always carry it with constancy and love. I regret that in the past I have abandoned Thee, to follow my lusts and the vanities of the world; but now I am resolved to leave Thee no more. Bind me to Thy Cross, and if through weakness I sometimes resist, draw me by the sweet bonds of Thy love. Suffer it not that I ever leave Thee again.

II.

St. Francis of Assisi renounced in favor of his father the whole of his inheritance, and even his garments, and, thus poor and mortified, consecrated himself to Jesus Christ. Nor was it different with St. Francis Borgia and St. Aloysius Gonzaga, one being Duke of Gandia, the other of Castiglione. Both left all their riches, their estates, their vassals, their country, their home, their parents, and went to live a poor life in Religion.

So have done many other noblemen and princes even of royal blood. Blessed Zedmerra, daughter of the King of Ethiopia, renounced the kingdom to become a Dominican nun. Blessed Johanna of Portugal renounced the kingdom of France and England to enter Religion. In the Benedictine Order alone there are found twenty-five emperors, and seventy-five kings and queens who left the world to live poor, mortified and forgotten by the world, in a poor cloister. Ah! indeed, these and not the grandees of the world are the truly fortunate ones.

At present worldlings think these to be fools, but in the Valley of Josaphat they shall know that they themselves have been the fools; and when they see the Saints on their thrones crowned by God they shall say, lamenting and in despair: These are they whom we had sometime in derision ... we fools esteemed their life madness, and their end without honor. Behold, how they are numbered among the children of God, and their lot is among the saints! (Wis. v. 3, 4, 5).

Yes, my Jesus, I renounce all the satisfactions of the world; the only satisfaction I seek is to love Thee, and to suffer as Thou pleases. I hope thus to come one day to be united to Thee in Thy kingdom by the bond of eternal love, there to see Thee and to love Thee without fear of ever being separated from Thee. I love Thee, O my God, my All, and will always love Thee. Thou art my hope, O Most Holy Mary, thou, the most conformed to Jesus, art now the most powerful to obtain this grace. Be thou my protectress!

Spiritual Reading

ENCOURAGEMENT TO NOVICES

II. ANXIETY CONCERNING HEALTH

Another temptation with which the devil is wont to attack a novice, is too much anxiety about his health. The deceiver thus insinuates himself into the mind of the novice: "Do you not perceive that by leading such a life you will ruin your health, and then you will be no use either to the world or to God." The novice must repel this temptation by confidence in Our Lord, for He Who has given him a Vocation will also give him health to follow it. If he has entered into the House of God solely to please Him, as we suppose he has, let him console himself by saying: "I concealed nothing concerning the state of my health from my Superiors, and they received me and have not yet dismissed me; it is then the will of God that I should remain here, and if it be His will that I should suffer and even die in His House what does it signify? How many anchorets have gone to suffer for Him in forests and caverns! How many Martyrs have run with joy to give their lives for Him! If, then, it be His will that I should lose my health or my life for His love, I am content; I desire nothing else, I can desire nothing better." Thus, will the fervent Religious speak who desires to become a Saint. If a novice is not fervent during his novitiate, it is certain that he will never be so in after life.

III. THE INCONVENIENCES OF COMMUNITY LIFE.

A third temptation is the fear of not being able to undergo the inconveniences of the common life, such as scanty and ill-prepared food, a hard bed, little sleep, prohibition to go out of the house, the observance of silence, and, above all, not being allowed to follow one's own will. When the novice is assailed by this temptation, he should repeat what St. Bernard used to say to himself: "Bernard, why art thou come hither?"

He must remember that he has not come to the House of God to make himself comfortable, but to become a Saint; and how can he become a Saint? Is it by comfort and pleasure? No; but by sufferings, and by dying to his own disorderly affections and appetites. St. Teresa says, that "to expect that God will admit to His love those who are fond of their own ease, is a great mistake." And in another place: "Souls who truly love God cannot ask for repose." He, therefore, who is not firmly resolved to suffer and to bear everything for the love of God, will never become a Saint. No; he will never become a Saint, nor even enjoy true peace. And why? Do you, perhaps, imagine that true peace is to be found in the enjoyment of worldly goods or sensual pleasures, or perhaps you fancy that the highborn rich, who abound in these things, have arrived at it? They are most miserable; they are nourished upon gall. All is vanity and affliction of spirit (Eccles. i. 14). It was thus that Solomon described earthly goods, which he had fully enjoyed. When a man places his affections upon these things, the more he has the more he desires, and he is never at rest; but when he places all his happiness in God, in Him he finds perfect peace. Delight in the Lord, says David, and he will give thee the requests of thy heart (Ps. xxxiv. 4). Father Charles of Lorraine, brother to the Duke of Lorraine, became a Religious, and when alone in his poor cell he felt so great an interior peace that he danced for joy. Blessed Seraphim, a Capuchin, said that he would not give a foot length of his cord for all the wealth and dignities of the earth; and St. Teresa would often encourage others under difficulties by saying: "When a soul is resolved to suffer, the suffering ceases."

IV. DISCOURAGEMENT IN ARIDITIES

But here we must take notice of an error by which the devil tempts a novice when he feels this affliction of spirit. "Do you not see," he says to him, "that you have not found peace here? You have lost devotion, everything is wearisome -- prayer, spiritual reading, Communion, even recreation. These are signs that God does not wish you to remain in Religion." Oh, what a terrible and dangerous temptation this is for a new and inexperienced novice! To overcome it he must first consider the true nature of peace of soul whilst on earth, which is a place of trial, and therefore must be one of pain. This peace does not consist, as we have already seen, in the enjoyment of the good things of this world. It does not consist even in spiritual delights, for these do not increase our merit, or make us dearer to God. True peace is to be found only in conformity of our will to the will of God, and the peace we ought to desire is that of having our will perfectly united to the Divine will, even in our darkness and desolation. O, how dear to God is the soul that faithfully perseveres in Spiritual Reading, Meditation, Communions, and other pious exercises solely to please Him, without feeling any sensible consolation! O, the great merit of good works when performed purely for God's sake, without looking for reward here below! The Venerable Father Anthony Torres wrote to a person in spiritual desolation: "When we carry the Cross of Jesus without consolation, our soul runs, nay, flies towards perfection." When a novice is in a state of aridity he should say to God: "O Lord, if it is Thy will that I should remain in desolation and deprived of all comfort, I desire to be in that state as long as it pleases Thee; I will never leave Thee; behold me ready to endure these troubles during my whole life, and even for all eternity, if Thou wills it. For me it is enough to know that it is Thy will." It is thus a novice who really desires to love God will speak; but let him be certain that such sufferings will not last forever. By such insinuations the devil seeks to destroy his confidence, causing him to believe that his desolation will last forever, that it will bring him to despair, and that at length he will be unable to endure it. These terrible storms, however, which the enemy can raise in the soul when it is in darkness and desolation, will not endure forever. To him that overcomes, I will give a hidden manna, says Our Lord. (Apoc. ii. 17). Yes, those who pass through such tempests of aridity and desolation with patience, and overcome such temptations, shall be consoled by the Lord Himself, who will give them to taste a hidden manna -- that interior peace which, according to St. Paul, surpasses all understanding (Phil. iv. 7). This one thought -- I am doing the will of God, I am pleasing God -- gives a peace far superior to all the joys, pastimes, feastings, honors, and dignities of the world. God cannot fail in the promise He has made to those who have left all things for His love. And everyone that hath left house, or brothers, or sisters, or father, or mother, or wife, or children, or lands, for my name's sake, shall receive a hundredfold here, and shall possess life everlasting (Matt. xix. 29). He promises them Paradise in the next world and a hundred-fold in this. And what is this hundred-fold? It is the testimony of a good conscience, which immeasurably surpasses all the pleasures of this life.

Evening Meditation

JESUS HAS DONE AND SUFFERED EVERYTHING TO SAVE US.

I.

He hath loved me and delivered himself for me (Gal. ii. 20).

The Son of God being true God is infinitely happy; and yet, as St. Thomas says, He has done and suffered as much for man as if He could not be happy without him. If Jesus Christ had been obliged to earn for Himself upon this earth His Eternal Beatitude, what could He have done more than to burden Himself with all our weaknesses, and assume all our infirmities, and then end His life with a death so severe and ignominious? But no, He was innocent, He was holy, and was in Himself blessed; whatever He did and suffered was all to gain for us divine grace and Paradise, which we had lost.

Miserable is he who does not love Thee, my Jesus, and does not pass his life enamored of so much goodness.

If, therefore, my Jesus, thou hast for love of me embraced a laborious life and bitter death, I may, indeed say that Thy death is mine, Thy sufferings are mine, Thy merits are mine, Thou Thyself art mine; since for me Thou hast given Thyself up to so great sufferings. Ah, my Jesus, there is nothing that afflicts me more than the thought that once Thou wert mine, and that I have so often willingly lost Thee. Forgive me and unite me to Thyself; suffer me not in future ever to offend Thee again. I love Thee with all my heart. Thou wills to be all mine; and I will be entirely Thine.

II.

If Jesus Christ had permitted us to ask Him for the greatest proof of His love, who would have dared to propose to Him to become a Childlike one of us, to embrace all our miseries, to make Himself of all men the most poor, the most despised, the most ill-used, even to dying in torments the infamous death of the Cross, cursed and forsaken by all, even by His own Father? But that which we should not have dared even to think of, He has both thought of and done.

My beloved Redeemer, I beseech Thee to bestow upon me the graces which Thou hast merited for me by Thy death. I love Thee and am sorry for having offended Thee. Oh, take my soul into Thy hands; I will not let the devil have dominion over it anymore; I desire that it may be entirely Thine, since Thou hast bought it with Thy Blood. Thou alone loves me, and Thee alone will I love. Deliver me from the misery of living without Thy love, and then chastise me as Thou wills. O Mary, my refuge, the death of Jesus and thy intercession are my hope.

Wednesday–Fourth Week of Advent

Morning Meditation

CONSIDERATIONS ON THE RELIGIOUS STATE. XIV.

Consider the zeal that Religious ought to have for the salvation of souls.

Our Redeemer did not impose on St. Peter penance, prayers, or other things, but only that he should endeavor to save His sheep. *Simon, son of John, lovest thou me? ... Feed my sheep* (Jo. xxi. 17).

Yes, O my Lord, I will serve Thee with all my strength in this great work.

I.

He who is called to the Congregation of the Most Holy Redeemer will never be a true follower of Jesus Christ, and will never become a Saint, if he does not fulfil the end of his Vocation, and has not the spirit of the Institute, which is the salvation of souls, especially souls that are the most destitute of spiritual succor, such as the poor people in the country.

This was truly the end for which our Redeemer came down from Heaven: *The spirit of the Lord*, our Divine Master says, *hath anointed me to preach the Gospel to the poor* (Luke iv. 18). He sought no other proof of Peter's love for Him but that he should procure the salvation of souls: *Simon, son of John, lovest thou me? ... Feed my sheep* (Jo. xxi. 17). He did not impose upon him, says St. John Chrysostom, penance, prayers, or anything else, He only asked that he endeavor to save His sheep: "Christ did not say to him, give your money away, fast, weaken your body with hard work, but He said: Feed My sheep." And He declares that He would look upon every benefit conferred on the least of our neighbors as conferred on Himself. Amen, I say to you, as often you have done it unto one of these my least brethren, you have done it unto me (Matt. xxv. 40).

Every Religious ought, therefore, with the utmost care, to nourish this zeal, and this spirit of helping souls. To this end must his studies be directed; and his constant thought and his whole attention bestowed on work for souls assigned to him by his superiors. He would be wanting in this spirit, who, through the desire of attending only to himself and of leading a retired and solitary life, would not accept wholeheartedly the work imposed on him by obedience.

O my Lord Jesus Christ, how can I thank Thee enough, in that Thou hast called me to the same work Thou didst Thyself perform on earth; namely, to help in the salvation of souls by my poor labors? In what have I deserved this honor and this reward, after having offended Thee so grievously myself, and having caused others also to offend Thee? Yes, O my Lord! Thou calls me to help Thee in this great undertaking. I will serve Thee with all my strength.

II.

What greater glory can a man have than to be, as St. Paul says, a co-operator with God in this great work of the salvation of souls? He who loves the Lord ardently is not content to be alone in loving Him, he would draw all to His love, saying with David: O magnify the Lord with me, and let us extol his name together (Ps. xxxiii. 4). Hence St. Augustine exhorts all those who love God to "draw all men to His love."

A good ground of hope for his own salvation has he who, with true zeal, labors for the salvation of souls. "Have you saved a soul?" says St. Augustine, "then you have predestinated your own." The Holy Ghost promises: When thou shalt pour out thy soul to the hungry, and shalt satisfy the afflicted soul ... the Lord will fill thy soul with brightness ... and thou shalt be like a watered garden, and like a fountain of water whose waters shall not fail (Is. lviii. 10, 11). In this — namely, in procuring the salvation of others — St. Paul placed his hope of eternal salvation, when he said to his disciples of Thessalonica: For what is our hope, or joy, or crown of glory? Are not you, in the presence of our Lord Jesus Christ at his coming? (1 Thess. ii. 19).

Behold, O Jesus, I offer Thee all my labors and my blood, and even my life to obey Thee. Nor do I in this seek to gratify my own inclination, or to gain the applause and esteem of men; I desire nothing but to see Thee loved by all as Thou deserves. I prize my happy lot, and call myself fortunate, that Thou hast chosen me for this great work, in which, I now protest that I renounce all the praise of men and all self-satisfaction and seek only Thy glory. To Thee be all the honor and satisfaction, and to me only the discomfort, the blame, and the reproach. Accept, O Lord, this offering which I, a miserable sinner, who wish to love Thee and to see Thee loved by others, make of myself to Thee, and give me strength to do what I desire.

Most Holy Mary, my advocate, who loves souls so much, help me.

Spiritual Reading

ENCOURAGEMENT TO NOVICES

V. DOUBTS ABOUT THE VOCATION ITSELF

But I have not yet done. There remains a still more dangerous temptation. Those which I have hitherto described are worldly and carnal, and it is easier therefore to recognize them as coming from the devil and overcome them. It is different with temptations which conceal themselves under the appearance of devotion and a greater good; these are more terrible, and more easily mislead.

The first of these temptations, ordinarily, is to throw doubt on the Vocation itself. "Who can say," the devil suggests, "whether yours is a true Vocation, or only fancy? If you have not been really called by God, you will not receive the grace of perseverance, and after you have made the vows, you will repent and apostatize; you might have saved your soul in the world, and here it may be lost." To overcome this temptation, you must consider how one can know that his Vocation is certain. A Vocation is certain when three things concur — first, a good intention; that is to say, the desire of escaping from the dangers of the world, of better ensuring eternal salvation, or of becoming more closely united to God; secondly, when there is no positive impediment in regard to health or talent, or necessity of parents, and upon all these the novice should be perfectly at rest after he has submitted them to the judgment of his superiors sincerely and truthfully; thirdly, when he is accepted by the superiors. Now, where there is a concurrence of these three things, the novice should not doubt that he has a true Vocation.

VI. THE THOUGHT THAT ONE COULD LIVE MORE DEVOUTLY IF ONE WERE FREE

Another temptation which the evil spirit employs with those who, before entering Religion, led a spiritual life, is: "When you were in the world," he says, "you prayed more than now, you practiced more mortifications, you observed silence better, were more recollected, and gave more alms and so forth. You are not able to do all these good things now, and still less will you be when you have finished your novitiate, for your superiors will then put you to study or employ you in some office in the Community, or in other things of obedience which will divert you from these pious works." O what an illusion! If a novice heeds such a temptation it is a sign that he does not understand the great merit of obedience. He who offers all his prayers to God (and St. Mary Magdalen de Pazzi says that everything which is done in a religious community is prayer), his alms, his fasts and penances, gives to Him a part of what belongs to him, but not all; or, to speak more correctly, he gives what he possesses, but he does not give himself; whereas he who renounces his own will by a vow of obedience, gives himself entirely to God, and may say: "Lord, having consecrated my whole will to Thee, I have nothing more to give." His own will is the thing of which it is the most difficult for a man to divest himself, but it is the gift which is most acceptable to God, and which He requires of us. My son gives me thy heart (Prov. xiii. 26), that is, thy will; and therefore, Our Lord declares that obedience is more pleasing to Him than all other sacrifices. Obedience is better than sacrifices (1 Kings, xv. 22). Thus, he who gives himself to God by obedience obtains, not once only, but forever, a victory over the riches, honors, and pleasures of the world, and whatever else may stand in the way of his perfection. An obedient man shall speak of victory (Prov. xxi. 28). A man who lives in the world, no doubt, gains merit by his fasts, disciplines, prayers, and such like, but following in these his own will, he gains less than a Religious, who does all through obedience. The Religious gains more merit, and gains continually, because everything in the Community is done under obedience. Here he merits not only when he prays, or fasts, or takes the discipline, but also when he studies, or takes the fresh air, or sits at table, or makes recreation, or takes repose. St. Aloysius Gonzaga used to say, that in the vessel of religion we always advance, even when we do not ply the oar. Hence, we understand how persons who have led a spiritual life in the world have sought to submit themselves to obedience by entering some Religious Order, well knowing the greater merit of good works that are performed through obedience.

Evening Meditation

JESUS COMES TO LEAD AN AFFLICTED LIFE

I.

Having joy set before him he endured the cross (Heb. xii. 2).

In creating man in the beginning, God did not place him on earth to suffer, but put him into the paradise of pleasure (Gen. ii. 15). He put man in a place of delight in order that he might pass thence to Heaven where he would enjoy for all eternity the glory of the blessed. But by sin man unhappily made himself unworthy of his earthly Paradise and closed against himself the gates of the Heavenly Paradise, willfully condemning himself to death and to everlasting misery. But what did the Son of God do to rescue man from such a state of misery? From being blessed and most happy as He was, He chose to be afflicted and tormented. Our Redeemer could, indeed, have rescued us from the hands of our enemies without suffering. He could have come on earth and continued in His happiness, leading a life full of joys, and receiving the honor due to Him as King and Lord of all. One drop of His Blood, a single tear of His offered to God would have redeemed the world, and a countless number of worlds, on account of the Infinite dignity of His Person. But no! — having joy set before Him, He endured the Cross. He renounced all pleasures and honors and made choice on earth of a life full of toil and ignominy. "What was sufficient for Redemption," says St. John Chrysostom, "was not sufficient for love."

Yes, because this Man was born on purpose to suffer, therefore He took to Himself a body particularly adapted for suffering. As the Apostle tells us, He said to His Eternal Father as He came into this world: Sacrifice and oblation Thou wouldst not, but a body thou hast fitted to me (Heb. x. 5). Thou hast given Me a body as I requested of Thee, delicate, sensitive, and made for suffering. I gladly accept this body and offer it to Thee; because by suffering in this body all the pains which will accompany Me through life and finally cause My death upon the Cross, I shall propitiate Thee on behalf of the human race and gain for Myself the love of men.

Glory be to God in the highest (Luke ii. 14). I thank Thee, O Jesus, in the name of all mankind, but I thank Thee especially for myself, a miserable sinner. What would have become of me, what hope could I have had of pardon and salvation, if Thou, my Savior, hadst not come down from Heaven to save me? Therefore, do I praise Thee, and thank Thee, and love Thee.

II.

Behold, then, Jesus has scarcely entered this world when He begins His sacrifice by beginning to suffer. While an Infant in His Mother's womb, Jesus endures for nine months the darkness of that prison; He endures all the pain and is fully alive to all He endures. Jesus was in wisdom, not in age, a Man, while yet unborn, says St. Bernard. He comes forth from His Mother's womb; but He comes forth to fresh suffering. He chooses to be born in the depth of the winter in a cavern, where beasts find stabling, and at the hour of midnight! He is born in such poverty that He has no fire to warm Him, or clothes to screen Him from the winter's cold. "A noble pulpit is that manger!" says St. Thomas of Villanova. Oh, how well does Jesus teach us the love of suffering in the grotto of Bethlehem!

If thou wish to love Jesus Christ, learn from Him how thou must love Him. "Learn from Christ how thou must love Christ," says St. Bernard. Rejoice to suffer something for the God Who suffered so much for thee. The desire of pleasing Jesus Christ, and of showing Him the love they bore Him was what rendered the Saints hungry and thirsty, not for honors and pleasures, but for sufferings and contempt. This made the Apostle say: God forbid that I should glory save in the cross of our Lord Jesus Christ (Gal. vi. 14). And St. Teresa: "Either to suffer or to die!" And St. Mary Magdalen de Pazzi: "To suffer and not to die!" And St. John of the Cross: "O Lord, that I may suffer and be despised for Thy sake!"

O my dear Redeemer, I praise Thine infinite Mercy! I praise Thine infinite Charity! I love Thee above all things, I love Thee more than myself. I love Thee with my whole soul and I give myself all to Thee. Receive, O Sacred Infant, these acts of love. If they are cold because they come from a frozen heart, do Thou inflame this poor heart of mine, a heart that has offended Thee, but is now penitent. O most holy Mary, obtain for me the grace to live always bound to thy Son by the blessed chains of love. Pray to Him for me. This is my hope.

Thursday--Fourth Week of Advent

Morning Meditation

CONSIDERATIONS ON THE RELIGIOUS STATE. XV.

Consider how necessary are the virtues of meekness and humility for Religious.

Our Most Holy Redeemer willed to be called a Lamb that He might show us how meek and humble He Himself was, and that His disciples might learn from Him to be likewise meek and humble of heart (Matt. xi. 29). The Holy Ghost says: That which is agreeable to him is faith and meekness (Ecclus. i. 34, 35).

I.

Learn of me because I am meek and humble of heart. Meekness and humility of heart are virtues that Jesus, the Lamb of God, principally requires of Religious who profess to imitate His most holy life. He who lives as a solitary in a desert has not so much need of these virtues; but for him who lives in a community, it is impossible not to meet, now and then, with a reprimand from his superiors, or something disagreeable from his companions. In such cases, a Religious who loves not meekness will commit a thousand faults every day and live an unquiet life. He must be all sweetness with everybody -- with strangers, with companions, and with inferiors if he should ever become Superior; and if he be an inferior, he must consider that one act of meekness in bearing contempt and reproach is of greater value to him than a thousand fasts and a thousand disciplines.

St. Francis said that many make their perfection consist in exterior mortifications, and, after all, are not able to bear one injurious word. "Not understanding," he added, "how much greater gain is made by patiently bearing injuries." How many persons, as St.

Bernard remarks, are all sweetness when nothing is said or done contrary to their inclination but show their want of meekness when anything crosses them! And if one should ever be a Superior, let him believe that a single reprimand made with meekness will profit his subjects more than a thousand made with severity. "The meek are useful to themselves and to others," as St. John Chrysostom teaches. In short, as the same Saint said, the greatest sign of a virtuous soul is to see it preserve itself in meekness on occasions of contradiction. A meek heart is the delight of the Heart of God. That which is agreeable to him is faith and meekness.

O most humble Jesus, Who, for love of me didst humble Thyself, and become obedient unto the death of the Cross, how have I the courage to appear before Thee, and call myself Thy follower? I who see myself to be such a sinner and so proud that I cannot bear a single injury without resenting it. Whence comes such pride in me, who for my sins have so many times deserved to be cast forever into hell with the devils? Ah, my despised Jesus, help me and make me conformable to Thee. I will change my life.

II.

It would be well for a Religious to represent to himself in his meditations, all the contradictions that may happen to him, and arm himself against them; and then when the occasion presents itself, he ought to do violence to himself, that he may not be excited or break out in impatience. Therefore, he should refrain from speaking when his mind is disturbed, till he is certain that he has become calm again.

But to bear injuries quietly, it is above all necessary to have a great fund of humility. He who is truly humble is not only unmoved when he sees himself despised, but is even pleased, and rejoices at it in his spirit, however much the flesh may resent it; for he sees himself treated as he deserves, and made conformable to Jesus Christ, Who, worthy as He was of every honor, chose, for the love of us, to be satiated with contempt and injuries.

Brother Juniper, a disciple of St. Francis, when an injury was done to him, held up his cowl, as if expecting to receive pearls from Heaven. The Saints have ever been more desirous of injuries than worldlings are covetous of applause and honors. And of what use is a Religious who does not know how to bear contempt for God's sake? He is always proud; humble only in name, and a hypocrite whom divine grace will repulse, as the Holy Ghost says: God resists the proud, but to the humble he giveth grace (1 Peter v. 5).

O Jesus, for love of me Thou hast borne so much contempt; I, for love of Thee, will bear every injury. Thou, O my Redeemer, hast made contempt honorable, indeed, and desirable since Thou hast embraced it with so much love during Thy own life. God forbid that I should glory save in the cross of our Lord Jesus Christ (Gal. vi. 14). O my most humble Mistress, Mary, Mother of God, thou who was in all, and especially in suffering, the most conformed to thy, Son, obtain for me the grace to bear in peace all the injuries which henceforward may be offered to me. Amen.

Spiritual Reading

ENCOURAGEMENT TO NOVICES

VII. THE THOUGHT THAT ONE COULD BE MORE USEFUL TO ONE'S NEIGHBOURS IN THE WORLD THAN IN RELIGION

There is a temptation yet more dangerous, namely, the devil represents to a novice that he can be of more use in the world than in Religion. "You are come," he says, "into this Community, where there are so many others striving to assist souls, but you could do far better by remaining in your own country, which has such need of Apostolic laborers to help souls." A man who feels this temptation must remember that the greatest good which we can possibly do is that which God wishes of us. He has no need of anyone, and if He sees fit to send more help to your countrymen, He can do it by others. As He has called you into His House, it is there that you will find the good which He has appointed for you to do and it is this: to be perfectly obedient to your Rule and to the commands of your Superiors. If through obedience, you should remain inactive in any one place or be employed in sweeping the house or washing the dishes -- these are the best works for you.

And what good can a man do in his own country? Jesus Christ Himself when asked to preach and do good in His own country, replied: No prophet is accepted in his own country (Luke iv. 24). This is so true that people have, indeed, a great repugnance to confess great faults to a priest who is their own relative and fellow-countryman, and is constantly amongst them, and they frequently prefer to go to strangers. As regards sermons, it is often said that those of a fellow-countryman are little valued by his hearers, because he is one of themselves, and they are accustomed to his voice. If a preacher were a St. Paul he would be listened to, at first, with great effect, but when he had been heard for six months or a year he would please less and be of less profit to his hearers. Missionaries for this reason do much good in the places they visit, because they are strangers, and their voice is new to the people. It is certain that a priest belonging to a community, and, above all, a missionary, will save more souls in a single month and in a single mission, than if he had remained ten years laboring in his native place. Besides, by remaining in the same place, he can only assist those immediately around, whereas if he is engaged in missions, he will save souls in a hundred, in a thousand different places. Again, a secular is sometimes doubtful and uncertain as to which, among different good works, is most pleasing to God; a Religious in obeying his superior, is certain of the will of God. Religious are those servants who may say with confidence: We are happy O Israel; because the things that are pleasing to God are made known to us (Baruch. iv. 4).

In fine, the devil tempts those whom God has, perhaps, favored with spiritual consolations, such as the gift of tears, and sensible emotions of love, saying: "Do you not perceive that you are not called to an active life in Religion, but are intended for the contemplative, for solitude, and for union of the soul with God? You should choose some other Order or a hermitage." If the devil were to tempt me in this manner, I should answer: "As you have mentioned Vocation, I ought to follow my Vocation rather than my inclination, or your suggestions; and, as God, in the first instance, has called me to an active Order, who will assure me that the thought of leaving it is an inspiration, and not a temptation?"

I would say just the same to you, my brother. God no doubt calls some to the active, and others to the contemplative life. But, as He has called you to an active Order, you should believe that any other thought comes from the devil, who thus tries to make you lose your true Vocation. St. Philip Neri says: "that we ought not to leave a good state for a better, unless we are certain that it is the will of God; and, therefore, if you would avoid error, you should be more than morally certain that God desires you to change." But what certainty can you have, especially if your superior and your spiritual Father tell you that it is a temptation? Consider, moreover, St. Thomas teaches that though the contemplative life is more perfect than the active, yet the mixed life -- that is, one divided between prayer and action -- is the most perfect of all; for such was the life of Jesus Christ Himself. And such is the life in all well-ordered active Communities, in which many hours are each day devoted to prayer and silence; and we may say that the Religious lead an active life when abroad, but are like so many hermits at home.

Therefore, my dear brother, suffer not the enemy to lead you away by specious pretexts, and be assured that if you leave the Congregation which has accepted you, you, like so many others, will repent when it will be too late to apply a remedy; for he who has once abandoned the Religious life will find it very difficult to be received again.

Evening Meditation

THE SORROW THAT THE INGRATITUDE OF MEN HAS CAUSED JESUS

I.

He came unto his own, and his own received him not (St. John i. 11).

During the holy time of Christmas St. Francis of Assisi went about the highways and woods, weeping and sighing with inconsolable lamentations. When asked the reason he answered: "How can I help weeping when I see that Love is not loved? I see a God become as it were foolish for the love of man, and man so ungrateful to this God!" Now, if this ingratitude of men so afflicted the heart of St. Francis, let us consider how much more it must have afflicted the Heart of Jesus Christ Himself. Scarcely was He conceived in the womb of Mary than He saw the cruel ingratitude He was to receive from men. He had descended from Heaven to enkindle the fire of Divine love, and this desire alone had brought Him down to this earth, to suffer here the greatest sorrows and ignominies: I am come to cast fire on the earth; and what will I, but that it be kindled? (Luke xii. 49). And then He beheld the awful sins which men would commit after having seen so many proofs of His love. It was this, says St. Bernardine of Sienna, which made Him feel an infinite grief.

It is true, then, O my Jesus, that Thou didst descend from Heaven to make me love Thee; didst come down to embrace a life of suffering and the death of the Cross for my sake, in order that I might welcome Thee into my heart; and yet I have so often driven Thee from me and said: "Depart from me, Lord; go away from me, Lord; for I do not want Thee." O God, if Thou wert not infinite Goodness, and hadst not given Thy life to obtain my pardon, I should not have the courage to ask it of Thee. But I feel that Thou Thyself dost offer me peace: Turn ye to me, saith the Lord of hosts, and I will turn to you (Zach. i. 3). Thou, Thyself, Whom I have offended, O my Jesus, make Thyself my Intercessor: He is the propitiation for our sins (1 Jo. ii. 2). I will therefore not do Thee this fresh injury of distrusting Thy mercy. I repent with all my soul of having despised Thee, O sovereign

Good; receive me into Thy favor, for the sake of the Blood which Thou hast shed for me: Father, I am not worthy to be called Thy son (Luke xv. 21).

II.

Even amongst us it is an insufferable sorrow for one man to see himself treated with ingratitude by another; for, as the Blessed Simon of Cassia observes, ingratitude often afflicts the soul more than any pain afflicts the body: "Ingratitude often causes more bitter sorrow in the soul than pain causes in the body." What sorrow, then, must our ingratitude have caused Jesus, who was our God, when He saw that His benefits and His love would be repaid by offences and injuries? And they repaid me evil for good, and hatred for my love (Ps. cviii. 5). But even at the present day it seems as if Jesus Christ is going about complaining I am become a stranger to my brethren (Ps. lxviii. 9). For He sees that many neither love nor know Him, as if He had not done them any good, nor had suffered anything for love of them. O God, what value do so many Christians even now set upon the love of Jesus Christ? Our Blessed Redeemer once appeared to Blessed Henry Suso in the form of a pilgrim who went begging from door to door for a lodging, but everyone drove Him away with insults and injuries. How many, alas! are like those of whom Job speaks: Who said to God: Depart from us ... whereas he had filled their houses with good things (Job xxii. 17). We have hitherto joined these ungrateful wretches; but shall we continue always like them? No; for that amiable Infant does not deserve it, who came from Heaven to suffer and die for us in order that we might love Him.

No, my Redeemer and my Father, I am no longer worthy to be Thy son, having so often renounced Thy love; but Thou, by Thy merits, dost make me worthy. I thank Thee, O my Father. I thank Thee, and I love Thee. Ah, the thought alone of the patience with which Thou hast borne with me for so many years, and of the favors Thou hast conferred upon me after the many injuries that I have done Thee, ought to make me live constantly on fire with Thy love. Come, then, my Jesus, for I will not drive Thee away anymore, come and dwell in my poor heart. I love Thee and will always love Thee; but do Thou inflame my heart more and more by the remembrance of the love Thou hast borne me. O Mary, my Queen and my Mother, help me, pray to Jesus for me; make me live during the remainder of my life, grateful to that God Who has loved me so much, even though I have so greatly offended Him.

Friday--Fourth Week of Advent

Morning Meditation

JESUS WISHES TO BE LOVED.

A child is born to us and a son is given to us (Is. ix. 6).

Behold the end for which the Son of God willed to be born an Infant -- to give Himself to us from His Childhood, and thus draw to Himself our love. Thus, He wished to be born because He wished to be loved.

I.

God conferred so many blessings on men in order to draw them to love Him; but these ungrateful men not only did not love Him, but they would not even acknowledge Him as their Lord. Only in one corner of the earth, in Judea, was He recognized as God by His chosen people; and by them He was more feared than loved. He, however, who wished to be more loved than feared by us, became Man like unto us, chose a poor, suffering obscure life, and a painful and ignominious death. And why? To draw our hearts to Himself. If Jesus Christ had not redeemed us, He would have been no less great or less happy; but He determined to procure our salvation at the cost of so many labors and sufferings, as if His happiness depended on ours. He might have redeemed us without suffering; but no -- He willed to free us from eternal death by His own death; and though He was able to save us in a thousand ways, He chose the most humiliating and painful way of dying through pure suffering on the Cross, to purchase the love of us, ungrateful worms of the earth. And what, indeed, was the cause of His miserable Birth and His most sorrowful death, if not the love He had for us?

Ah, my Jesus, may Thy love for me destroy in me all earthly affections, and consume me in the fire which Thou didst come to kindle on the earth. I curse a thousand times those shameful passions which cost Thee so much pain. I repent, my dear Redeemer, with all my heart, of all the offences I have committed against Thee. For the future I will rather die than offend Thee; and I wish to do all that I can to please Thee. I love Thee, my only Good, my Love, my All.

II.

Drop down dew, O ye heavens, from above, and let the clouds rain the just (Is. xlv. 8). Send forth the Lamb, the Ruler of the earth (Is. xvi. 1).

Thus did the holy Prophets desire for so many years the coming of the Savior. The same Prophet Isaias said: Oh, that thou wouldst rend the heavens, and wouldst come down: the mountains would melt away at thy presence ... the waters would burn with fire (Is. lxiv. 1, 2). Lord, he said, when men shall see that Thou didst come on earth out of love for them, the mountains shall be made smooth, that is, men in serving Thee will conquer all the difficulties that at first appeared to them insuperable obstacles. The waters shall burn with fire, and the coldest hearts will feel themselves burning with Thy love, at the sight of Thee made Man; and how well has this been verified in many happy souls! -- in St. Teresa, in St. Philip Neri, St. Francis Xavier, who even in this life were consumed by this holy fire. But how many such are there? Alas! but too few.

Ah, my Jesus, amongst these few I wish also to be. How many years ought I not already to be burning in hell, separated from Thee, hating, and cursing Thee forever! But no, Thou hast borne with me with so much patience, that Thou might see me burn, not with that unhappy flame, but with the blessed fire of Thy love; for this end Thou hast given me so many illuminations, and hast so often wounded my heart while I was far from Thee; finally, Thou hast done so much that Thou hast forced me to love Thee by Thy sweet attractions. Behold, I am now Thine. I will be Thine always and altogether. It remains for Thee to make me faithful, and this I confidently hope from Thy goodness. O my God! who could ever have the heart to leave Thee again and to live even a moment without Thy love? I love Thee with all my heart, but this is too little. My Jesus, hear me, give me more love, more love, more love. O Mary, pray to God for me.

Spiritual Reading

ENCOURAGEMENT TO NOVICES

VIII. ON THE MEANS OF PERSEVERING IN THE RELIGIOUS STATE

1. The first means for persevering in the Religious State is to avoid willful faults. Let each one be persuaded that the devil tempts him to commit faults, not so much that he may do evil, as that he may lose his Vocation, for by deliberate faults he begins to lose his fervor in prayer, at Communion, and all the spiritual exercises. The Lord then justly withholds His especial graces, according to that of St. Paul: He who sows sparingly, shall reap sparingly (2 Cor. ix. 6). And this the more certainly if his defect be pride, for God resists the proud, and over these the devil acquires great power. So that whilst on the one hand, the tepidity of the novice increases, on the other, the Divine light diminishes; and thus, it will not be difficult for the enemy to succeed in making him give up his Vocation.

2. Another means is to blow up the mine; that is, to reveal the temptation to the Superior. St. Philip Neri said, "that a temptation made known, is a temptation half conquered." As an abscess, if unopened, becomes gangrened, so a temptation concealed brings on our own ruin. Experience shows that those who hide such temptations in their own bosoms, allow themselves to be brought into a position where they know not whether they should take the right or the left (that is, to doubt which way they ought to take, the right or the left), and generally lose their Vocation. It is necessary, therefore, to make one great effort, and discover all to the Superior. God will be so pleased by this act of humility, and by the violence the novice does to his feelings, that He will instantly enlighten his darkness and dissipate his doubts.

3. The third means is Prayer, that is, recourse to God, that He may give you the grace of Perseverance, a grace which, according to St. Augustine, can only be obtained by prayer. But let that novice who has received from God the gift of Vocation, and is tempted to abandon it, take care when he prays to Our Lord, not to say: "Lord, show me what I ought to do; enlighten me" -- because God has already given him light by calling him to His holy House, and if he only asks for this grace, the devil, who can easily change himself into an angel of light, may deceive him and make him believe that the thought of leaving Religion is an effect of divine light. His prayer should rather be: "O Lord, thou hast given me a Vocation, give me also strength to persevere in it." A certain young man was called by God to the Religious state, and his Vocation being approved by his director, after many trials he joined a Religious Community. His parents did all in their power against him and

succeeded in prevailing upon him to go to another place, that he might more thoroughly examine his Vocation; unfortunately, instead of returning to the Community, he went home, satisfying his parents by this step, but displeasing God. When I asked him how it happened that he committed such an error, he replied, that he had prayed to God in these words: Speak, Lord, for thy servant heareth (1 Kings iii. 9). And afterwards he adopted the resolution of returning to his family. I said to him: "O my son, you were mistaken in your prayer. Your Vocation was certain, being confirmed by so many evident signs; you should not have said: Loquere, Domine, for God had already spoken, but: Confirma hoc, Deus, quod operatus es in me (Ps. lxvii. 26). (Give me, O Lord, strength to execute Thy will, which Thou hast made known to me). You omitted to do this, and, therefore, you lost your Vocation." Let the misfortune of this young man serve as an admonition to others. Again, let not the novice endeavor to tranquilize his mind by the light of his own reason in such times of temptation, for they are indeed seasons of darkness and confusion; let him simply offer himself anew to God, saying: "O my God, I give myself to Thee, I will never leave Thee, help me lest I become unfaithful to Thee." By repeating these words whenever the temptation returns, and, as I have already said, by making his state known to his Superior, he will certainly be victorious. He should recommend himself particularly at such times, to Mary, the Mother of Perseverance.

A novice once suffered himself to yield to a temptation of this kind, and was on the point of quitting the monastery, but, passing before an image of the Mother of God, he stopped and knelt down to repeat an Ave Maria, when he suddenly found himself fixed to the spot and unable to rise; upon which he repented, and made a vow of perseverance. He was immediately freed, and rising, went to ask pardon of the Master of novices, and continued firm in his Vocation.

Finally, I entreat you, my brother, whenever you are tempted concerning your Vocation, to reflect on these two points. First, that the grace of Vocation which God has given you, He has not given to many of your companions, some, perhaps, more deserving than you: He hath not done in like manner to every nation (Ps. clvii. 19). Therefore, you should fear to be so ungrateful as to turn your back upon Him, for by so doing you would greatly endanger your eternal salvation. And rest assured that you will not have peace, but will be tormented, even to your dying day, with remorse because of your infidelity.

Secondly, if the temptation should present itself to your mind, that if you remain in Religion you will fall into despair and repent of it, and have to render an account to God for it, or things like those we have already spoken of; call to your thoughts the hour of death: you will not then regret that you followed your Vocation, but you will be filled with peace and contentment, instead of the anguish and remorse which would have followed on your having abandoned it. Keep this thought before your mind, and you will not lose your Vocation; you will enjoy in life, and at death, that peace, and hereafter that crown of glory, which God has prepared for His faithful servants.

An Act of Oblation and Prayer which the Novice should make frequently to obtain from God the Grace of Perseverance in his Vocation.

My God, how can I ever thank Thee enough for having called me so lovingly to Thy family? How have I merited this grace after having committed so many offences against Thee? How many of my companions are left in the world amidst so many dangers of losing their souls, and in occasions of sin! and I am admitted to Thy House, and to the company of so many of Thy dear servants, and to so great an abundance of all things necessary for my sanctification! I hope one day O Lord, to testify my gratitude to Thee in Heaven, by singing eternally Thy mercies to me. Meanwhile I am all Thine, and desire to be so forever. I will remain faithful and will never leave Thee, even had I to lay down my life, nay, a thousand lives, for Thy sake. I here dedicate myself to Thy will without reserve. Do with me whatever Thou pleases. Let me live desolate, infirm, despised, if such be Thy pleasure. It is enough that I obey and please Thee. I desire only the grace to love Thee with all my strength, and to remain faithful to Thee till death. Most Holy Mary, my dear Mother, it is you who have obtained from God the so great graces which I have received, pardon of my sins, my Religious Vocation, and the strength to follow it; accomplish your work and obtain for me Perseverance unto death. This is my hope: so may it be!

SOME ADVICE TO A NOVICE UPON THE MEANS BY WHICH HE MAY PRESERVE HIS FERVOUR

When reproved or accused, never excuse yourself, and love cordially in God the person who accuses or reproves you. Love to be made little of in whatever manner it may be, whether in employment, or dress, or cell, or food, etc. Do not give your opinion unless you are asked.

Mortify yourself in all things, according to prudence and obedience, in eating, in sleeping, in hearing, seeing, etc.

Observe modesty when alone, as well as in the presence of others. Lay not your hand upon any person, nor look steadfastly in his face; keep your eyes continually cast down, especially in the church, at table, during recreation, and when abroad. Observe silence, except when there is need to speak for the glory of God, or for your own or your neighbor's benefit. Be careful particularly during the time of recreation, not to raise your voice too loud. Avoid disputing or talking about your birth, talents, or riches; about eating, hunting, sports, war, or on the means of acquiring honors, riches, and such secular subjects, but endeavor to introduce pious conversation upon the vanity of honors, riches and pleasures of the world, on the love we owe to Jesus and Mary, on the happiness of the Saints, and on the means of advancing in perfection.

If you commit a fault, immediately humble yourself, make an act of contrition, and then rest in peace.

Desire nothing but what God wills.

Seek not consolations; and, in aridity, say to God with entire humility and resignation: "O Lord, I do not deserve consolations; I am content to remain in this state all my life."

Frequently raise your mind to God by means of ejaculations, such as the following:

My God, I desire nothing but Thee,
Show me Thy will and I will accomplish it.
Do with me what Thou wilt.
I desire, O God, whatever Thou willest.
My Jesus, I love Thee, I love Thee.
I renounce all; Thou alone are sufficient for me.
My God and my all.
Jesus our love, and Mary our hope.
O good Jesus, mayst Thou be ever praised.
My life was Thy death, Thy death is my life.

Evening Meditation

THE LOVE OF GOD MANIFESTED TO MEN BY THE BIRTH OF JESUS.

I.

> The grace of God our Savior hath appeared to all men instructing us that ... we should live ... godly in this world, looking at the blessed hope and coming of the glory of the great God and our Savior Jesus Christ (Titus ii. 11).

Consider that by the grace that is said to have appeared is meant the tender love of Jesus Christ towards men -- a love we have not merited, and which, therefore, is called a "grace." This love was, however, always the same in God, but did not always appear. It was at first promised in many prophecies and foreshadowed by many figures; but at the Birth of the Redeemer this Divine love appeared and manifested itself by the Eternal Word showing Himself to man as an Infant, lying on straw, crying and shivering with cold; beginning thus to make satisfaction for us for the penalties we have deserved, and so making known to us the affection which He bore us, by giving up His life for us: In this we have known the charity of God, because he hath laid down his life for us (1 Jo. iii. 16). Therefore, the love of our God appeared to all men.

But why is it, then, that all men have not known it, and that even to this day so many are ignorant of it? This is the reason: The light is come into the world, and men loved darkness rather than the light (Jo. iii. 19). They have not known Him, and they do not know Him, because they do not wish to know Him, loving the darkness of sin rather than the light of grace.

O my holy Infant! now I see Thee, poor, afflicted, and forsaken; but I know that one day Thou wilt come to judge me, seated on a throne of splendor, and attended by the angels. Forgive me, I implore Thee, before Thou hast to judge me. Then Thou wilt have to act as a just Judge; but now Thou art my Redeemer, and the Father of mercy. I have been of those ungrateful ones who have not known Thee, because I did not choose to know Thee, and therefore, instead of being inclined to love Thee by the consideration of the love Thou hast borne me, I only thought of satisfying my own desires, despising Thy grace and Thy love. But into Thy sacred hands I commend my soul, which I have so long neglected; do Thou save it: Into thy hands I commend my spirit; thou hast redeemed me, O Lord, the God of truth (Ps. xxx. 6).

II.

But let us endeavor not to be of the number of those unhappy souls who are ignorant and ungrateful. If in times past we have shut our eyes to the light, thinking little of the love of

Jesus Christ, let us try, during the days that remain to us in this life, to have ever before our eyes the sufferings and death of our Redeemer, in order to love Him Who has loved us so much: Looking for the blessed hope and the coming of the glory of the great God and our Savior Jesus Christ. Thus, may we justly expect, according to the divine promises, that Paradise which Jesus Christ has acquired for us by His Blood. At His first coming Jesus appeared as an Infant, poor and humble, and showed Himself on earth born in a stable, covered with miserable rags, and lying on straw; but at His second coming He will appear as Judge on a throne of majesty: We shall see the Son of Man coming in the clouds with great power and majesty (Matt. xxiv. 30). Blessed then will he be who shall have loved Him, and miserable those who shall not have loved Him.

In Thee do I place all my hopes, knowing that, to ransom me from hell, Thou hast given Thy Blood and Thy life: Thou hast redeemed me, O Lord, the God of truth. Thou didst not condemn me to death when I was living in sin, but hast waited for me with infinite patience, in order that, coming to myself, I might repent of having offended Thee, and might begin to love Thee, and that thus Thou might be able to forgive and save me. Yes, my Jesus, I will please Thee. I repent, above every other evil, of all the offences I have committed against Thee; I repent and love Thee above all things. Do Thou save me in Thy mercy, and let it be my salvation to love Thee always in this life and in eternity. My dearest Mother Mary, recommend me to thy Son. Do thou represent to Him that I am thy servant, and that I have placed all my hope in thee. He hears thee and refuses thee nothing.

www.ingramcontent.com/pod-product-compliance
Lightning Source LLC
Chambersburg PA
CBHW050252010526
44107CB00003B/286